THE GENTILE COMES TO UTAH: A STUDY IN RELIGIOUS AND SOCIAL CONFLICT

(1862–1890)

This dissertation was conducted under the direction of Richard J. Purcell, Ph.D., Head of the Department of History of the Catholic University as Major Professor, and was approved by Dr. Leo F. Stock and the Rev. Dr. Joseph B. Code, as readers.

THE

GENTILE COMES TO UTAH

A Study in Religious and Social Conflict

(1862-1890)

A DISSERTATION

*Submitted to the Faculty of the Graduate School of Arts and Sciences
of the Catholic University of America in Partial Fulfillment
of the Requirements for the Degree of*

DOCTOR OF PHILOSOPHY

by

ROBERT JOSEPH DWYER

PRIEST OF THE DIOCESE OF SALT LAKE

WESTERN EPICS
254 South Main Street
Salt Lake City, Utah 84101

Revised 2nd Edition

1971

Western Epics

LITHOGRAPHED IN U.S.A. BY

PUBLISHERS PRESS
SALT LAKE CITY, UTAH

PREFACE

IN UTAH, center of Mormonism and substitute Zion of the followers of the Prophet Joseph Smith, the non-Mormons have always been known as the "Gentiles." The paramount interest in the fortunes of the Church of Jesus Christ of Latter Day Saints has overshadowed the story of the minority group, even to the extent of denying it that modest emphasis which it justly deserves. The purpose of this study is not to deprive Mormonism of its undoubted claim to the center of the local historical stage, but rather to complete the setting by calling attention to the role played by that portion of the population of Utah which constituted the opposition to the dominant Church. The territorial history of Utah is emphatically one of social and religious conflict. By the very nature of its teachings, Mormonism awakened antagonism. The hegira to the barren valleys of Utah merely afforded the sect an opportunity to consolidate its forces against the threat of national disapproval. Had it proved possible for the Mormon leaders to "build a wall around Zion," the subsequent train of events which led to the disavowal of polygamy and theocratic government might have furnished different reading. But the Gentile could not be excluded. Indeed the record shows that a few non-Mormons entered the Valley of the Great Salt Lake in company with the pioneers and during the first decade of Brigham Young's supremacy (1847–1857), were suffered to remain as merchants and traders.

The Utah War (1857–1859), though often described in terms that suggest a Mormon victory, actually resulted in the confirmation of federal authority in the Territory. Albert Sidney Johnston and his army decamped as the impending struggle between North and South became more menacing, but federal concern for the policing of the Territory resulted in the establishment, in 1862, of a more permanent military force with headquarters in Salt Lake City. The advent of Colonel Patrick Edward Connor and his California Volunteers, in the early autumn of that year, marks the beginning of a long-drawn battle between the Mormon majority and the Gentile minority for the political and economic control of the region. Into that struggle was injected, not unnaturally, a religious debate of unmitigated bitterness. As the years went on, the Mormons, while maintaining numerical supremacy, found themselves being driven along toward political and economic defeat. The Utah Gentiles, regarding themselves as the custodians of national religious and political morality, and in control of the most profitable sources of local wealth, made unceasing efforts to secure congressional legislation that would ultimately disfranchise the entire Mormon body. To achieve this end, they organized a distinctive political party, strenuously opposed the granting of statehood to Utah, and enlisted the active support of a majority of the federal officials appointed to executive and judicial posts in the Territory. The Gentile lobby and press, the Protestant missions, as well as the glaring fact of polygamy, all contributed to arouse the American conscience. As the 1880's wore away, the Mormon leaders were forced to reconsider their position. With polygamists disfranchised and the Gentiles gaining the upper hand politically, the times were out of joint. The Manifesto of 1890, by which the Church disavowed the further practice of plural marriage, whether conscientious compromise or not, ended one phase of the conflict.

This study of the Gentile in Utah, published in 1941 as a doctral dissertation submitted to Graduate School of Arts and Letters, the Catholic University of America, was the first fairly comprehensive work in the specific field undertaken up to that time. Subsequently, in 1960, Professor Norman E. Furniss, of the Department of History, Colorado State University, wrote a detailed study of the earlier period of Mormon-Gentile relations, *The Mormon Conflict*, 1850-1859 (Yale University Press). Inevitably, there is some overlapping, but substantially these studies complement one another.

The present work has been long out of print. That it should be re-published, when it is generally conceded that there is nothing quite so dead as a thirty-year-old doctoral dissertation, is simply due to the fact that thus far it has not been superseded. Inasmuch as the cost of such re-publication precludes much in the way of textural emendation, it has been thought better to issue it substantially in its original form, with some addenda and corrigenda.

The writer has been long removed from the scenes of his native

Utah, where he grew up very cheerfully as a Gentile, hardly con-
scious of "the old, unhappy, far-off things, and battles long ago."
For the help and encouragement he received during his formative
years from teachers, counsellors, and fellow students, Mormon and
Gentile alike, he is forever grateful. For the special interest of
Professor David Miller, Department of History, Univesity of Utah,
Mr. Sam Weller, Zion's Book Store, Salt Lake City, and Mr. George
Egan, the Kearns Corporation, who conceived the project of re-
issuing this study and overcame the writer's understandable re-
luctance to take up Clio's gauge once more, a particular word of
thanks is due.

Archbishop Robert Joseph Dwyer
Portland, Oregon, August 1, 1971

To the Memory of the Most Reverend
Duane Garrison Hunt, D.D., 1884-1960

Bishop of Salt Lake City
A Gentile Without Guile
Friend, Counsellor, Father

CONTENTS

CHAPTER I

COLONEL CONNOR ENTERS ZION

FOR THE Reverend John Anderson, of the First Presbyterian Society of San Francisco, and chaplain of the Third California Volunteers, the march to Great Salt Lake City, October, 1862, was an exhilarating experience. Besides, it made good copy for the San Francisco *Bulletin,* to which he faithfully reported. With a flair for journalism, he was well aware that anything relating to the Mormon "empire" of Utah would entice thousands of eager readers. If Colonel Connor's command was not to see action in the main theatre of war raging between the North and the South, but to be shunted off to the comparatively mild business of protecting the Overland Route from Indian depredations, then why not heighten the interest by lending an ear to rumors that Connor had also been instructed to keep an eye on the Mormons?[1] The Utah campaign of 1857—some called it "Buchanan's Blunder"— was fresh in memory.[2] The gallant Albert Sidney Johnston, who had since left his post as commander of the Department of the Pacific for service with the Confederacy, had not distinguished himself in that affair. It was reported, indeed, that Brigham Young had been too clever for him, or that the noted busybody from Philadelphia, Colonel Thomas Kane, had spiked Johnston's

---

[1] Pursuant to requisition made on Governor John G. Downey of California by the Secretary of War, July 24, 1861, Colonel Patrick Edward Connor, a Mexican War veteran residing in Stockton, California, was placed in charge of the Third California Infantry, and detailed for service in protecting the Overland route. Not until July 5, 1862, were orders issued by General George Wright, commanding officer of the Department of the Pacific, for the movement of the "Utah Column." For details of the march and activities of the Volunteers, see Fred B. Rogers, *Soldiers of the Overland* (San Francisco, 1938), pp. 14–54.

[2] For a recent account of the Utah War, see Leland Hargrave Creer, *Utah and the Nation* (University of Washington Publications in the Social Sciences, VII, Seattle, Washington, 1929), pp. 115–160.

1

guns by arranging an unofficial compromise between the administration and the Mormons. As a result, Johnston had frittered
away the better part of 1859 at Camp Floyd, fifty miles from the
Mormon capital, west of the Jordan River, and had merely fat-
tened the purses of Mormon farmers who fed his several thousand
useless men. Would Colonel Connor, Anderson wondered, repeat
the same tactical mistake? "The Commander of the district has
a fashion of keeping his own counsel," he reported to his readers,
"and what he has determined upon will not be discovered until the
order to halt is given—if then." [3]

The column spent the night of October 16 at Camp Floyd—
rechristened Fort Crittenden. In the morning, Connor addressed
the seven hundred and fifty men in his command, enjoining strict-
est discipline for the remainder of the march. No pilfering would
be countenanced, for,

> . . . we were coming among a people whose customs
> were different from ours, but whom every man of the
> command must treat with the same courtesy and justice
> that he would show to his own people; that he, the Colo-
> nel, would not suffer a few bad men to plunge the Gov-
> ernment into a war and sacrifice the lives of good
> men. . . . [4]

Clearly, he intended to lead his army into the holy city of the Latter-Day Saints.

As the sun rose on the morning of October 18, Anderson could
discern ". . . the white specks which constitute the residences of
the modern apostles," twenty-five miles away, across "the narrow
stream called Jordan, which empties the waters of Lake Utah into
Great Salt lake." Camp gossip was rife during the day:

> When information reached the city, as it did last
> night, that Colonel Connor would not purchase the build-
> ings erected by Johnston's command in 1858, at what was
> then Camp Floyd . . . and that he designed to occupy
> some locality within striking distance of the heart of Mor-

---

[3] *San Francisco Bulletin,* October 30, 1862.
[4] Edward W. Tullidge, *History of Salt Lake City* (Salt Lake City, 1886),
p. 277, quoting the *San Francisco Bulletin.* The quotations immediately following are from the same source, pp. 277–279.

mondom, the most intense excitement is said to have prevailed. The Chief of the Danites—better known perhaps
as the Destroying Angels, whose duty it is, if report be
true, to place parties odious to the leaders of the Church
where they can never tell tales, is represented as riding
through the streets offering to bet $500 that we could and
should not cross the river Jordan. . . .

Cautiously, Anderson checked his pen: "How much truth there
may be in these advices, or how much the real state of affairs in
Salt Lake is exaggerated, I know not." While the sequel would
indicate that there had been some slight exaggeration, yet, it was
worth adding that "Colonel Connor sent word today to the above
mentioned chief of the Danites that he would 'cross the river Jordan if hell yawned below him.' " The correspondent of the *Bulletin* had not heard of the "bloody shirt," but he proceeded to wave
it with commendable vigor:

> This command . . . is disposed to treat the Mormons
> with true courtesy and strictest justice . . . ; but the mo-
> ment they become traitors the river Jordan will become
> as acceptable to us as the river Potomac, for we shall be
> fighting for the same precise principle—the flag and na-
> tional existence—as are our eastern brethren. . . .

At two o'clock on the following day, the army made the cross-
ing and found "not a solitary individual on the eastern shore . . .
a magnificent place for a fight, too, with a good sized bluff upon
the eastern side from which splendid execution might have been
done." Half disappointed, the chaplain took up the thread of his
description. Into the city they marched, receiving "not a cheer,
not a jeer" from the inhabitants lining the wide streets. No Danites were in evidence, but his critical eye saw at once that the only
American flag was that displayed on the territorial governor's mansion, before which they drew up in military array. From his car-
riage, that official welcomed them in a speech which suggested that
he was of two minds about the presence of the Volunteers in his
jurisdiction. For the benefit of the apprehensive populace, he told
the soldiers that anyone "who supposed that the Government had
sent you here that mischief might come out of it, knows not the
spirit of our Government." As for himself, "I have known noth-

ing of the disposition that has been made of you; and for the
truth of this assertion, I appeal to your commander, and to every
individual with whom I have had communication on the subject."
It was not the martial, defiant speech the soldiers had anticipated.
Colonel Connor, who, as later events showed, was never loath to
condemn the Mormons, publicly or privately, must have listened
with disgust. Then the march was resumed to the foothill bench,
to the east of the city, where Connor, during his reconnoitre of the
previous month, had selected a site overlooking the valley, with
an adequate water supply from the mountain canyons. That evening, Camp Douglas was established. For better or for worse, a
new phase in the history of Utah had begun.

The presence of a military force in Utah, though its avowed
purpose had nothing to do with the Mormons or Mormonism,
served to accentuate the social and religious conflicts between the
members of the dominant sect and the scattered non-Mormons,
called, in local parlance, Gentiles. From the first days of Mormon
immigration into the valley of the Great Salt Lake there had persisted a Gentile element, chiefly engaged in trade, and for the most
part, living in reasonably amicable relations with the Saints, as,
indeed, it was to their advantage as traders to do. The members
of this group—probably a few hundred at most throughout the
Territory—do not seem to have taken the initiative in the events
leading up to the Utah War of 1857, if the federal officers be ex-
cepted, nor in the framing of the Anti-Polygamy Act which had
been passed by Congress in July, 1862. Feeling had run high during the spring of 1859, when Judge Cradlebaugh, backed by the
troops at Camp Floyd, had instituted proceedings against the alleged perpetrators of the Mountain Meadow Massacre of 1857.[5]
But in the opinion of District Attorney Alexander Wilson (whom
Cradlebaugh accused of being a creature of the Mormons) the
fomenters of this discord were an alien coterie, including "the
Judge, Army officers, Sutlers, contractors, and all their hangers
on, and other desperate creatures, who desire that the military
force shall reign triumphant, and that the Mormon leaders may

---

[5] Creer, op. cit., pp. 218–223. These trials, as well as the history of the
Utah War, should be re-studied in the light of available documents deposited
in The National Archives, Washington, D. C.

be brought within their clutches."[6]   Confident that Utah affairs would benefit by the removal of the troops, Governor Alfred Cumming, the first Gentile to receive that appointment, had remonstrated with Brigadier General Johnston: "I am satisfied that the presence of the military force in this vicinity is unnecessary, and for this and other reasons I desire to impress upon you the propriety of the immediate disposition of the troops."[7]

For that matter, the view that Buchanan had sent Johnston's army to Utah less as a means of intimidating the refractory Mormons than as part of a plan to distract the attention of the country from the "impending conflict," would appear to be not without support.   It explains, certainly, the hesitancy and inefficiency of that campaign, the readiness with which the administration accepted a settlement, which left things practically where they were before the invasion, and the summary manner in which the United States forces were withdrawn in 1860, despite the enormous financial losses involved in disposing of the military stores collected in the Territory.[8]   For two years, Washington forgot Utah.

Now, in 1862, things were different.   Separatism in Utah, rumors of which must have found their way to official ears, and which were borne out in the public statements of the religious leaders of the Mormon people, could be ignored no longer.[9]   Utah's

---

[6] Wilson to Attorney General Jeremiah Black, April 8, 1859, National Archives (hereafter N. A.), Attorney General's MSS, Utah File (hereafter A. G. MSS, Utah).

[7] Cumming to Johnston, March 20, 1859 (N. A., A. G. MSS, Utah).

[8] Creer, *op. cit.*, pp. 126–127.

[9] Franklin D. Daines, "Separatism in Utah, 1847–1870," in *Annual Report of the American Historical Association for the Year 1917* (Washington, D. C., 1920), pp. 333–343.   In April, 1861, Heber C. Kimball, of the first presidency of the Church, said in a public discourse: "We shall never secede from the Constitution of the United States.   We shall not stop on the way of progress, but we shall make preparations for future events.   The South will secede from the North, and the North will secede from us, and God will make this people free as fast as we are able to bear it.   They send their poor miserable creatures to rule us.   Why, it would be upon the same principle that this church and authority should send some poor cuss to rule me and my family in my own house. . . .   But let me tell you the yoke is now off our neck, and it is on theirs, and the bow key is in.   The day is not far distant when you will see us as free as the air we breathe. . . .   President Young is

plea for admission as a state was refused (July, 1862). Whether the Mormons might have cast their lot with the Confederacy, or whether they might have used a victory of that cause as a signal for the assertion of their own ill-suppressed desire for independence, are, of course, academic questions. Lincoln's administration chose to take no chances; hence, Camp Douglas was established under color of protection for the Overland Trail. Concomitantly therewith, there came a recrudescence of the Mormon-Gentile quarrel. A permanent army near Salt Lake City gave body to the Gentile group and lent courage to its criticism of the peculiarities of the Saints.

The city which Colonel Patrick Edward Connor surveyed, from the eminence of his new post, was by all counts unique in the land. Though the only community of any size on the Overland Route between the Missouri and the Pacific Coast, it presented the appearance of a straggling village rather than of a city. Its ten-acre square blocks were intersected by streets of generous width, liable to become muddy sloughs in rainy weather. Trees, planted assiduously by the pioneers during the fifteen years of the city's life, were reaching their maturity, softening the harshness of the landscape. Pleasing gardens surrounded many of the plain adobe dwellings. There were few imposing buildings to be seen other than the "Old Tabernacle," completed in 1851 as a center for Mormon religious services and for numerous civic gatherings, and the Salt Lake Theatre, opened the preceding March. Nevertheless, as an oasis in the arid inter-mountain country, the city elicited fervent praise from visitors.[10] The cultivated farm lands of the surrounding and neighboring valleys bespoke the industry and ingenuity of the inhabitants, and the far-flung settlements of the Ter-

---

our leader and has been ever since the death of Joseph the Prophet. He can govern this people with his hands in his pockets, and they are not governed one whit by the men that are sent here. . . . We are going to be ruled by our Father in heaven, and the agents he sends out and appoints for us, from this day henceforth and forever." *Journal of Discourses*, IX, 9 ff. (quoted in Daines, *loc. cit.*, p. 342, where further references and quotations may be found).

[10] Numerous references might be given; the western travel literature of the period paid marked attention to the "City of the Saints," as Sir Richard Burton, the English traveller, dubbed it in his book of that name (London, 1862).

ritory paid tribute to the colonizing genius of their leader. Salt Lake City deserved its fame as the Mormon Capital.

All but a handful of its twelve thousand citizens were members of the faith. A few Gentile merchants maintained their "emporiums" along East Temple Street. Local representatives of the telegraph, and of the express companies doing business with the Northwest, California, and the mining regions of Idaho and Montana, swelled the non-Mormon group.[11] The city was strategically located, and the Yankee trader and the Hebrew merchant were willing to put up with the presence of Mormonism for the sake of gain.[12] Deserters from both sides in the national struggle were finding their way to the fastnesses of Utah.[18] Doubtless, too, the immigrant tide to California left stray individuals in Salt Lake, some of whom "joined the Church," while others remained steadfast in opposition. The governor was Stephen S. Harding, from Indiana. On his arrival, in the previous July, he had participated in the annual celebration of the coming of the first company of pioneers into the valley in 1847; holding out the olive branch, he had declared that no act of his, as governor, would ever violate the spirit of the Constitution in its guarantee of religious freedom.[14]

[11] The transcontinental telegraph line had been completed to Salt Lake City on October 17, 1861, congratulatory messages being sent to President Lincoln and J. H. Wade, head of the Pacific Telegraph Company, by Acting Governor Frank Fuller and Brigham Young. (Orson F. Whitney, *History of Utah,* Salt Lake City, 1893, II, 30–31). Ben Holladay made his headquarters in Salt Lake City, where he identified himself with the pro-Mormon Gentiles. Alexander Majors established residence there about 1869.

[12] The presence of a comparatively large number of Jewish merchants is borne out by the fact that the open letter to Brigham Young, December 20, 1866, was signed by twenty-three Salt Lake firms, many of which bore unmistakably Jewish names. (*Daily Union Vedette,* December 20, 1866.) A. P. Richardson, correspondent of the *New York Tribune* noted (*Vedette,* August 17, 1865) that, "Among the leading merchants were a number of Abrahamic descent, for it is one of the anomalies of this anomalous community that all the Jews are Gentiles."

[18] Fred J. Kiesel, native of Bordenburg, Germany, relates that after his arrival in the United States in 1857, he peddled goods in Tennessee, and in 1861 was compelled to serve as a teamster in the Confederate army. He came to Utah in 1863 "to get away from the war." ("Utah Biographical Sketches," Bancroft MSS 188-, p. 52.)

[14] Orson F. Whitney, *History of Utah* (Salt Lake City, 1893), II, 71–73: "If I know my own heart, I come amongst you a messenger of peace and

The chief justice was John F. Kinney, of Iowa. Though in the days before the Utah War, as associate justice, Kinney had agitated for military suppression of the separatist movement, he had returned in 1861 filled with benevolence for his erstwhile enemies.[15] With him on the federal bench were Justices Thomas J. Drake, of Michigan, and Charles B. Waite, of Illinois, both ardent Mormon baiters. Of such disparate elements was the Gentile group made up.

Monitory of the new spirit engendered by the presence of the California Volunteers was the address of Governor Harding to the territorial legislative assembly, which convened in Salt Lake City December 8, 1862:

> I am sorry to say that since my sojourn amongst you, I have heard no sentiments, either publicly or privately expressed, that would lead me to believe that much sympathy is felt . . . by your people in favor of the Gov-

good will. I have no wrongs . . . to complain of, and no religious prejudices to overcome. [Applause]

". . . If the right of conscience of the minority depended upon the will of the majority, then, in a government like ours, that same minority in a future day might control the conscience of the majority of today, and thus . . . would it be in the power of either . . . to impose a despotism upon the conscience of its adversary only equaled by the 'Index Expurgatoris' [*sic*], against which the Protestant world so justly complained. . . ."

[15] Evidence of Kinney's earlier activity, not heretofore published, is revealed in a letter from Kinney to Attorney General Black (Washington, D. C., March 20, 1857, N. A., A. G. MSS, Utah):

". . . 1st, The Mormons are inimical to the Government of the U. S. and to all its officers who are not of their peculiar faith. This was manifested in their attempt last fall to incite the Indians to the murder of Gen'l Burr, . . . Dr. Garland Hunt and their party who were on an official visit South, and by the brutal attack made upon Deputy Surveyor Troskolawski last August. . . . It was also repeatedly manifested by their pulpit orations during my residence there in language like the following, to wit: 'That they would cut the throats of all the Gentiles, throw their heads into Salt Lake, and use their bodies for manure.' This remark was made by Bishop Woolley in the presence of Brigham Young to about three thousand people; similar remarks from Governor Young and his corrupt associates are common. . . ."

Kinney complained further of interference in the courts; suggested Mormon complicity in the Gunnison massacre and in the murder of other "gentiles or dissatisfied Mormons"; and pleaded for the dispatch of a regiment to Utah.

See also *Report of Hon. William P. Dole, United States Commissioner of Indian Affairs* (Cong. Pub. Doc., 1863), p. 212.

ernment of the United States, now struggling for its very
existence "in the valley and shadow. . . ."

  It would be disingenuous if I were not to advert to a
question . . . of vast importance to you as a people . . .
polygamy, or if you please, plural wives. In approaching
this delicate subject, I desire to do so in no offensive manner or unkind spirit. . . . Anomalies in the moral order
cannot long exist in a state of mere abeyance; they must
from the very nature of things become aggressive, or they
will soon disappear from the force of conflicting ideas.
. . . The conflict is irrepressible.

To the attention of the assembly the governor recalled the fact that
Congress had enacted a statute prohibiting polygamy in the territories, and annulling certain acts of the legislative assembly of
Utah. He noted that sentiment in the Territory challenged the
constitutionality of that act, and that "it is recommended by those
in high authority that no regard whatever should be paid to the
same." Against such "dangerous and disloyal counsel" he warned
them. Freedom in the exercise of religion, went on the embold-
ened governor, was not without its just and reasonable limits.
Otherwise, "then in the midst of the nineteenth century, human
victims may be sacrificed as an atonement for sin, and 'widows may
be burned alive on the funeral pile.' " [16]

  Harding's manner was not calculated to temper the sharpness
of his words.[17] The assembly, wholly Mormon, heard him in silence. Of the twenty bills passed during the session, the governor
vetoed fourteen,[18] while the legislators retaliated by "neglecting"
to make the regular appropriation for the conduct of the district
courts, in a manner reminiscent of colonial Massachusetts. This
called forth a letter from Justice Waite to Attorney General Bates:

---

[16] *New York Tribune,* January 7, 1863. Since the assembly refused to
have this attack upon Mormonism printed, Harding sent copies to California
and New York papers. (Harding to Seward, February 3, 1863, N. A., State
Department MSS, Utah Territory, II, 571–572.)

[17] "The *manner* of the delivery of the message was worse than the matter,
and probably no Legislature ever felt itself more humiliated and insulted. It
was painful to observe the Legislators, as they sat quiet and immovable, hearing their faith contemned. It was interpreted as an open and gratuitous insult on the part of the Executive." T. B. H. Stenhouse, *Rocky Mountain
Saints* (New York, 1873), p. 573.

[18] Whitney, *op. cit.,* II, 88.

There being no general Criminal Code enacted by Congress, nearly all the ordinary crimes, including murder, come under the head of territorial business. But the Territorial Legislature, although they assign the Judges to their respective Districts and appoint times and places for holding Courts for Territorial Business, refuse to make any appropriation to pay the expenses of those courts; and all claims of that kind are rejected at the Treasury Department at Washington.

This winter the Legislators have adjourned without making any such appropriation, and the bills rendered for such services, have been generally rejected by the Legislature, especially if due to Gentiles.

The bearing of these facts upon my judicial duties is easily seen.

I have been assigned to the Second Judicial District, in which the famous Mountain Meadow Massacre occurred. This was an act of such atrocity, that no lapse of time, certainly not 5 or 6 years merely, should shield the perpetrators from punishment. The murder of over a hundred persons in cold blood, without any provocation, and for purposes of plunder only, is a circumstance that may well attract attention even in the midst of a desolating war.

It may be asked, would juries indict and punish the perpetrators? It is hard to say. A reaction has been going on in the public mind of that section of the country, but whether sufficient to effectuate the ends of justice, cannot be known until the attempt is made.

I respectfully call your attention to the question whether the organic Act will not admit of such construction as to authorize the expense of punishing for such high crimes to be paid from the Treasury, and if not, whether a criminal code, applicable to the territories, under some circumstances, should not be passed by Congress.[19]

There is evidence to show that the introduction of a bill by Senator O. H. Browning, of Illinois, December 11, 1862, designed to hamper Mormon control of territorial affairs by making the United States marshal responsible for the empaneling of juries, in place of the territorial marshal, confiding to the governor complete authority over the militia, known still as the Nauvoo Legion,

---

[19] C. B. Waite to Hon. Edward Bates, January 28, 1863 (N. A., A. G. MSS, Utah).

and limiting the jurisdiction of the probate courts to their proper
spheres, was approved, if not instigated, by Harding and his judicial allies.[20]

Apprehensive of the reaction to his methods, Harding wrote
to Secretary Seward, February 3, 1863:

> I do not desire to create any unnecessary alarm, still,
> I deem it my duty to say to the President, that political
> matters in Utah are far from being quiet. There is that
> peculiar element of disloyalty and religious fanaticism,
> which would at the first opportunity develope itself, and
> specially if it was believed that the Federal Government
> was powerless to inflict punishment. No individual, out-
> side of this Territory, can form a true opinion of the
> state of society here. If it could be generally known, how
> a blasphemous pretender and imposter, has wrought, by
> a cunning almost supernatural, on the superstition of an
> ignorant, credulous, and dependent people . . . the in-
> dignation would be universal. . . . Every trick, ever
> known to the most adroit jugler [*sic*] and pretender, is
> known and exercised by him. . . . There is no mistak-
> ing his ultimate object. He is aiming, if not at universal
> empire in this continent, at least, in this Territory. . . .
> Brigham Young today wields a revenue by no means in-
> significant. . . . He is procuring arms and heavy ordi-
> nance, [*sic*] how and wherefore I am unable to say. . . .
> He is at this time manufacturing shells and solid shot,
> cartridges, and a new weapon, partly a battle-ax, partly a
> lance, for what purpose may be readily imagined. I have
> been able, through *secret service* to learn that his arsnel
> [*sic*] is full of new and efficient small arms. . . . That
> this man intends to strike, if the oppertunity [*sic*] shall

---

[20] Whitney, *op. cit.*, II, 90. At the Mormon mass meeting, March 3, 1863,
Albert Carrington read the following extract from a letter received from
Washington:

"On the 11th of December last, Senator Browning introduced a bill in the
Senate which was referred to the Committee on the Judiciary. This bill was
prepared at Great Salt Lake City, and its enactment by Congress recommended by Governor Harding and Judges Waite and Drake. . . ."

Whitney says that Delegate Hooper confirmed this in a letter written late
in January: "The bill has been presented and referred back. There does not
appear to have been any action on it. . . . The bill was drawn up at Salt
Lake and attached with eyelets. Also attached was as follows: 'The bill
should be passed.' Signed, S. S. Harding, Governor; Waite and Drake, Associate Justices."

present itself favorable, is certain. . . . To find a traitor
at heart, you have only, with fewest exceptions, *to find a
Mormon.*

Turning to the theme of perennial interest, Harding continued:

There is no doubt but that Brigham Young is almost
every week adding to his Harem, the unprotected and
demented victims of his villainy. He admits that his
"quarters" are full, and that his wives' names are scarcely
remembered by him, which are scattered throughout the
settlements, yet when he sees a pretty face, some young
girl first blooming into womanhood, he informs her, or
generally her parents, that in order to make her salvation
sure in this and the world to come, he feels it to be his
duty to have her *sealed* unto him. . . .[21]

If not a wholly accurate picture of the state of things in Utah, it
was at least an illustration of the governor's state of mind. As for
himself, he went on, no cajolery had induced him to swerve from
the course of rectitude. No threat had made him for a moment
think of deserting his post. Yet ". . . I am certain, that if it was
not for the presence of Colonel Connor's Command, it would be
unsafe for me to remain." A particular grievance was the assembly's refusal to print his address.

A brisk engagement between the California Volunteers and
marauding Shoshone and Bannock Indians, in which the latter
were practically annihilated, took place on January 28–29, 1863,
in the northern part of the Territory, not far from the present site
of Preston, Idaho, on the Bear River.[22] For the time being, the
Overland was no longer menaced in Connor's district. But relations between the soldiery and the Saints were not improved. Hard
upon their arrival in Utah, Young had appointed a committee to
handle trade with the troops, fixing commodity prices, and enjoined
upon the rest of his followers strict non-intercourse with the men.[23]
Connor, in turn, saw fit to demand of the Mormon factors the oath
of allegiance to the country, whereupon the Mormon leader de-

---

[21] Harding to Seward, February 3, 1863 (N. A., A. G. MSS, Utah).

[22] Rogers, *op. cit.,* pp. 67–77.

[23] *Journal History of the Church* (Office of the Historian of the Church
of Jesus Christ of Latter Day Saints), October 26, 1862.

clared that the location of the military at Camp Douglas was a standing insult to his people.[24]

Early in March, the Mormons took action. Calling a mass meeting on the 3rd, their spokesmen publicly denounced Governor Harding and Justices Waite and Drake. The Church organ editorialized:

> For some time back, it has been very evident that the labors of Governor Harding and the Associate Justices were hostile to the interests of the people of Utah, and that the Governor particularly was straining every nerve to create difficulties. So absurd and ridiculous have of late been his Excellency's everlasting speeches that it has often been a matter of doubt whether he was perfectly responsible for his actions. . . . He unceasingly refers to his early acquaintance with the prophet Joseph and considers himself entitled to the gratitude of the community for the preservation of the first proofsheet of the title page of the Book of Mormon. . . . We have hoped for a reformation; but we have hoped in vain, and what had only been known for a long time to the few had at length become so palpable to the whole community that self-preservation forced . . . the action we have now to report.[25]

Harding's message, re-read to the people, was booed and hissed. The statement that the federal officials had endeavored to influence congressional legislation limiting the territorial self-government was received with loud indignation. A resolution calling upon the offenders to resign was drawn up, and a committee named to wait on them.[26] To Washington the following petition was dispatched:

---

[24] *Ibid.*, October 30, 1862.

[25] *Deseret News* (Salt Lake City), March 4, 1863.

[26] Whitney, *op. cit.*, II, 88–96. The committee reported, March 5, 1863:

"Governor Harding received us cordially, but, upon being informed of the purport of our visit, both himself and Judge Drake, who was in the Governor's office, emphatically refused to comply with the wishes of the people, notwithstanding the Governor had repeatedly stated that he would leave whenever he learned that his acts and course were not agreeable to the people.

"Upon being informed that, if he was not satisfied that the action of the mass meeting expressed the feelings of the people, he could have the expression of the whole Territory, he replied: 'I am aware of that, but that would make no difference.'

To His Excellency Abraham Lincoln, President of the United States:

Sir, We, your petitioners, citizens of the Territory of Utah, respectfully represent that:

Whereas, from the most reliable information in our possession, we are satisfied that His Excellency Stephen S. Harding, Governor, Charles B. Waite and Thomas J. Drake, Associate Justices, are strenuously endeavoring to create mischief and stir up strife between the people of the Territory of Utah and the Troops at Camp Douglas (situated within the limits of Great Salt Lake City) and, of far graver import in our Nation's present difficulties, between the people of the aforesaid Territory and the Government of the United States.

Therefore, we respectfully petition your Excellency to forthwith remove the aforesaid persons from the offices they now hold, and to appoint to their places men who will attend to the duties of their offices, honor their appointments, and regard the rights of all, attending to their own affairs and leaving alone the affairs of others; and in all their conduct demeaning themselves as honorable citizens and officers worthy of commendation by yourself, our government and all good men, and for the aforesaid removal and appointments your petitioners will most respectfully continue to pray.

Great Salt Lake City, Territory
of Utah, March 3, 1863.[27]

Writing to Attorney General Bates, some days later, Drake gave his version of the meeting, flavoring it with his own anti-Mormon bias:

"Your committee called at the residence of Judge Waite, who, being absent at the time, has since informed us, by letter, that he also refuses to comply with the wishes of the people." *Ibid.,* p. 96.

Cf. Mrs. C. V. Waite, *The Mormon Prophet* (Cambridge, 1866), pp. 97–99, quoting Justice Drake: "Go back to Brigham Young, your master—that embodiment of sin and shame and disgust—and tell him that I neither fear him, nor love him, nor hate him—that I utterly despise him. Tell him, whose tools and tricksters you are, that I did not come here by his permission, and that I will not go away at his desire or by his directions. . . . I have not entered a Mormon's house since I came here; your wives and daughters have not been disturbed by me. . . ." "We have our opinions," remarked one of the committeemen. . . . "Yes," replied Drake, " 'thieves and murderers can have opinions.' "

[27] *Ibid.,* II, 95–96.

Inflammatory addresses to the rabble were made by Young and his Priests and counsellors. Resolutions were adopted by these uncivilized representatives of mankind requesting (which here means directing) Gov. Harding, Judge Waite and myself to resign our offices and leave the Territory. . . . These proceedings were tumultuous, and many threats of violence were made in case the Governor and Judges did not comply. . . . What will befall us for refusing, we know not. . . .

Warlike preparations were being made by the Mormons, he went on, and hundreds of armed men constantly were standing guard within the stone wall surrounding Young's house.[28]

Fear that the next step of the federal officials would be an attempt to arrest Brigham Young, and that they would employ the Volunteers to effect this, led to these measures. Stenhouse writes:

On the inside of the high walls surrounding Brigham's premises, scaffolding was hastily erected in order to enable the militia to fire down upon the passing volunteers. The houses on the route which occupied a commanding position where an attack could be made on the troops were taken possession of, the small cannon was brought forth, and the brethren prepared to protect the Prophet.[29]

In the prevalent excitement, Connor wired to the department adjutant at San Francisco, March 8: "Mormons hard at work making cartridges; guard of 300 at Brigham's nightly; don't understand what he is about; suppose he fears I will arrest him. I am quite safe."[30] On the following day, word was circulated through the city that Connor was on his way to serve the warrant. At once, two thousand citizens gathered around the Bee-Hive House, the President's official residence. Worried Gentiles of the city wired the government that unless quick action was taken to remove the troops and the obnoxious officials, ensuing difficulties might result in the destruction of the mail and telegraph lines.[31]

---

[28] Drake to Bates, March 14, 1863 (N. A., A. G. MSS, Utah).

[29] Stenhouse, *op. cit.,* p. 604.

[30] *War of the Rebellion,* L, Pt. II, 342.

[31] *Millenial Star,* May 9, 1863. Possibly Ben Holladay led in this move. Cf. *Report of Major General M. B. Hazen,* February 7, 1867 (House Misc. Doc. No. 75, 2nd Session, 39th Congress).

However, counsels of prudence prevailed; Connor and his men failed to appear,[32] and in the evening, a writ issued by Chief Justice Kinney was served, and Young surrendered to United States Marshal Isaac Gibbs.[33]   Giving bail at $2000, he was released, and within a few weeks left the city.[34]

The immediate crisis past, Harding was quick to decry the whole business as nothing more than a shrewd trick to evade actual arrest and an honest trial.   Stating this conviction, he wrote to Seward:

> . . . I have been informed by good authority, and I have not one doubt as to the truth of the statements, that the whole thing was a devised scheme, to blind the President and to have him believe, that any military force here, for the purpose of enforcing the laws, was unnecessary and uncalled for.   The *Arrest* was made under the following circumstances.   It was reported in the city that a writ had been issued by Judge Waite . . . against Brigham Young for the violation of the statute against polygamy, and that Colonel Connor had agreed to see that the writ was served.   Immediately upon the facts being known, or rather the report receiving currency, the signal flag was hoisted over the Bee-Hive House and some thousand persons assembled with all kinds of defensive weapons to guard and shield their chief. . . . Brigham became very much alarmed and *sent* for Judge Kinney to help him out of his difficulty.   The Judge appeared *in the office of the former,* the whole matter was adroitly arranged, the paper made out, and the bond for his appearance entered into by the defendant. . . . It furnished something on which the false telegraph dispatch was made, the object of which was to make capital for Brig-

---

[32] Stenhouse, *op. cit.,* p. 607, writes: "General Connor never had orders to arrest Brigham Young, or he would have done so—or tried."   William Alexander Linn, *The Story of the Mormons* (New York, 1902), p. 549, on the contrary states that Connor, hearing of Young's arrest before he reached the city, retraced his steps.   *Cf.* Hubert Howe Bancroft, *History of Utah, 1540–1886,* (San Francisco, 1889), pp. 613–614.

[33] Colonel E. J. Steptoe, who had been offered the governorship of Utah in 1854 by President Pierce, but had declined in favor of Brigham Young, was in Salt Lake City at this time.   In the *Overland Monthly* (San Francisco, December, 1896), he takes credit for having arranged the "mock" arrest of the Mormon leader.

[34] Whitney, *op. cit.,* II, 97–98.

ham Young. Mark what followed—the April term of the
United States District Court commenced—and the Grand
Jury, after a session of two weeks ignored the whole
matter, and Judge Kinney discharged, on motion, the accused. . . . But in this connection it is worthy of note
that the same grand inquest, made *presentments* against
Camp Douglas and against the Governor of the Territory
as *Public Nuisances.* I have no doubt but the last *presentment* . . . was connived at and encouraged by the
Court. . . . I am as much in an enemies country as the
President would be, were he in Richmond or Charles-
ton. . . .[35]

Advising Connor to act with "firmness and decision" in seizing
arms and munitions intended to be used against the authority of
the United States, General Halleck ordered reinforcements to be
sent to Utah.[36] Requisition was made upon the acting-governor
of Nevada to furnish volunteers, while others were enlisted in
California. Companies from Nevada reached the Territory during
the following November; those from the coast came in the spring
of 1864 and occupied a position in Ruby Valley, to the west of
Salt Lake City.[37] On March 29 came the news that Connor had
been brevetted a brigadier-general.[38]

Less fortunate was the lot of several of the other federal officials. Apparently wishing to avoid further conflict in a country
already sufficiently distracted, Lincoln ordered the transfer of
Governor Harding to the chief justiceship of Colorado Territory,
and removed from office Secretary Fuller and Chief Justice Kin-

---

[35] Harding to Seward, April 12, 1863 (N. A., A. G. MSS, Utah).

The civic authorities complained that Camp Douglas encroached on the
municipal boundaries. But Mayor Smoot, exercising judgment, did nothing
to procure abatement of the "nuisance."

Harding was censured, not indicted, by the grand jury: "Therefore, we
present his 'Excellency' Stephen S. Harding, governor of Utah, as we would
an unsafe bridge over a dangerous stream—jeopardizing the lives of all who
pass over it—or as we would a pestiferous cesspool in our district breeding
disease and death." Bancroft, *op. cit.,* p. 620.

The immediate cause for this presentment was Harding's action in re-
leasing the persons of certain Morrisites, held in custody under orders from
Justice Kinney. See chap. IV, pp. 107 ff.

[36] March 19, 1863. *War of the Rebellion,* L, Pt. II, 358.

[37] Rogers, *op. cit.,* p. 81.

[38] Bancroft, *op. cit.,* p. 613.

ney.[89] Realizing, it would seem, that the election of a well-disposed
Gentile as territorial delegate would create a favorable impression
at Washington, the Mormons chose Kinney for that office, August
3, 1863.[40] In disgust because his court docket contained not a
single case, Waite resigned in 1864, and went to Idaho Territory,
where his wife shortly completed her book, *The Mormon Prophet,*[41]
one of the first of the long line of anti-Mormon writings coming
from the pens of Utah Gentiles. Harding was succeeded by James
Duane Doty, superintendent of Indian Affairs for the Territory,
a mildly inactive soul. John Titus of Pennsylvania was named
chief justice, and Solomon McCurdy, of Missouri, replaced Waite.

During the early autumn of 1863 an event occurred of the
greatest importance in the subsequent course of affairs in Utah,
bearing directly upon the relations between the Mormons and the
Gentiles. The discovery of the mineral wealth of the Territory
served in time to give permanence to a larger and more active non-
Mormon group than had hitherto made its home there. The suspicion that Utah's mountains held treasures of precious metal could
hardly have escaped the Mormons themselves, since the West as
a whole was interested in little else. Boutwell writes:

> The need of food supplies led the pioneers to take up
> agriculture first. The same need, it is said, caused the of-
> ficers of the Mormon Church to discourage prospecting.
> . . . No doubt, however, this policy was followed partly
> to prevent the influx of Gentiles, which would surely fol-
> low the discovery of gold. It is certain, at any rate, and
> the fact is significant, that not until the dusty valley had
> been developed by fifteen years of painful effort into the
> productive fields and orchards of the Mormon farmers

[89] *Ibid.,* p. 621.

[40] Kinney served until August 3, 1865, when Hooper was re-elected. Whitney, *op. cit.,* II, 138.

[41] Mrs. C. V. Waite, *The Mormon Prophet and His Harem: or, An
Authentic History of Brigham Young, His Numerous Wives and Children*
(Cambridge, Mass., 1866).

The *Daily Union Vedette,* July 13, 1866, thus reviewed the book: "Mrs.
Waite came to Utah at a time when the lines of society between the Mormons and the Gentiles were not so closely drawn as at the present, which
enabled her to obtain an insight into the inner life of the Mormon people
that cannot be attained by anyone outside of the "church" at this period when
the Saints are so jealous of Gentile influence."

were the ore-bearing deposits investigated to any extent, and then not by the Mormons.[42]

Whatever the actual circumstances of the discovery of argentiferous ore in what is now Bingham Canyon, twenty-five miles southwest of Salt Lake City, may have been,[43] there can be little doubt that General Connor was the moving spirit behind the development of the industry. As a Californian, mining was in his blood; as well, he saw in this a means of solving the vexed Mormon question, according to his lights, by inviting a flood of Gentiles into the region.

On September 17, 1863, the first mining claims were legally recorded in the name of the West Mountain Mining Company, the shareholders of which were principally officers of the Volunteers. Bishop Archibald Gardiner, in charge of the Mormon settlement on the Jordan nearest the point of discovery—a man, evidently, who did not see eye to eye with the authorities of his Church—was elected recorder. The laws adopted were framed by Connor himself.[44] A month later (October 23), he wrote to departmental headquarters to inform his superiors of these developments.

> The results so far have exceeded my most sanguine expectations. Already reliable reports reach me of the discovery of rich gold, silver and copper mines in almost every direction. . . . If I be not mistaken in these anticipations, I have no reason to doubt that the Mormon question will at an early date be finally settled by peaceable means, without the increased expenditure of a dollar by Government, or, still more important, without the loss of a single soldier in conflict.[45]

In the first issue of the *Union Vedette*, November 14, 1863, he published the following circular:

---

[42] John Mason Boutwell, *Geology and Ore Deposits of the Park City District, Utah* (Washington, D. C., 1912), p. 17.

[43] For a discussion, see Robert Wallace, "Early History of Lead Smelting in the West," in *Ax-I-Dent-Ax* (Salt Lake City), XIV, No. 5, 1929.

[44] A facsimile of the first claim filed is in *Salt Lake City Chamber of Commerce Mining Booklet* (Salt Lake City, 1929), n. p. See also Wallace, *loc. cit.*, p. 2.

[45] *War of the Rebellion*, L, Pt. II, 656–657.

> The General commanding the District has the strong-
> est evidence that the mountains and canons in the Terri-
> tory of Utah abound in rich veins of gold, silver, copper
> and other minerals, and for the purpose of opening up the
> country to a new, hardy, and industrious population,
> deems it imperative that prospecting for minerals should
> not only be untrammeled and unrestricted, but fostered
> by every proper means. In order that such discoveries
> may be early and reliably made, the General announces
> that miners and prospecting parties will receive the full-
> est protection from the military forces in this District.

Even enlisted men were to be allowed to share in the game,
"when such course shall not interfere with the due and proper
performance of their military duties." Connor probably knew
that with California Volunteers on his hands, discipline could
only be maintained at the price of concessions.

During the spring and summer of 1864 mining location went
on apace. The Wasatch Mountain District, to the east of the
city, was roughly prospected, and while its greatest mineral deposits were not revealed until later years, Connor is credited with
unearthing the first silver ore in Little Cottonwood Canyon, not
far from the site of the future Emma mine, of fabulous and un-
savoury reputation.[46] To the westward, in Tooele valley, the recently arrived California companies, finding ore, laid out the village of Stockton, the first Gentile community in the Territory.[47]
Inadequacy of the fuel supply, however, made smelting practically
impossible for some years, and the prohibitive costs of transportation served to retard Utah's mining projects until the completion
of the railroad in 1869.[48]

Characteristically, the early days of discovery were filled with
enthusiasm. Writing of the appearance of Stockton, October,
1864, the editor of the *Vedette* painted a glowing picture:

> Stockton is emphatically a "live town," and presents
> a striking contrast to the surrounding Saintly settlements.

---

[46] W. C. Higgins, "Alta, Utah, Past and Present," in *Salt Lake Mining
Review*, August 30, 1907. (n. p.) The Emma mine, it will be recalled, was
the bonanza which involved General Robert Schenck, United States Minister
to the Court of St. James' during the Grant administration, in difficulties.

[47] Rogers, *op. cit.*, pp. 114–117.

[48] Wallace, *loc. cit.*, p. 6. See also Edgar M. Ledyard, "Early Mining and
Smelting South of Salt Lake City," in *Ax-I-Dent-Ax*, XVI, No. 5, May, 1931.

All is bustle, thrift, energy and activity. . . . The handsome adobe dwellings go up like magic—thrifty housewives are setting their domiciles in order—teams come and go from the mountains to the town and from the town to the furnaces. . . .[49]

From the fact that even during its "boom" period, in the early seventies, Stockton's population was only three hundred, some exaggeration may be suspected.[50]

News of the potential riches of Utah circulated throughout the nation. Thus, the *St. Louis Democrat* (December 20, 1863) took issue with its contemporary (or in the current phrase, its cotemporary) the *Republican,* for suggesting that Connor's circular implied "conflict going on between the Mormons and General Connor. . . . The order amounts merely to an invitation and promise of protection." The *Vedette* warmly seconded this defense, hailing the "inevitable progress" in store for the Territory:

The leaders of the Church, too, see it, and whether it is agreeable to them or not; whether it agrees with their previous ideas of exclusiveness in shutting out the Gentile world from their Saintly domination, they are too shrewd not to recognize and profit by inevitable fate staring them in the face, and accept their fate—the happy fate—which progress presents to them as a people. But rumors neither vague nor infrequent reach this city, that some of the inhabitants of the remote parts of the Territory, indulge in threats against persons desirous of prospecting for mines, and declare that mining shall not be carried on in their vicinity. But we indulge the hope that these threats do not emanate from the heads of the Church, but are the result of the long continued teaching of the Mormon leaders inculcating exclusiveness and opposition to Gentile influences. . . .[51]

In publishing a second circular, March 1, 1864, General Connor referred to the many inquiries he had received from outside the Territory as to the conditions obtaining there and the guarantees of protection that were offered. As part of the public domain,

[49] *Union Vedette,* October 20, 1864.

[50] Edgar M. Ledyard, "Early Mining and Smelting South of Salt Lake City," in *Ax-I-Dent-Ax,* XVI, No. 5, May, 1931, p. 3.

[51] Quoted from *Daily Union Vedette,* February 10, 1864.

he insisted, the nation looked forward to the early development
of Utah:

> In giving assurance of entire protection to all who
> may come hither to prospect for mines, the undersigned
> wishes, at this time, most earnestly and yet firmly, to warn
> all, whether permanent residents or not . . . that should
> violence be offered . . . to miners in the pursuit of their
> lawful occupation, the offender or offenders . . . will be
> tried as public enemies, and punished to the utmost extent
> of martial law.[52]

Both as a means of advertising his mining interests and as an
organ to render articulate the Gentile viewpoint, Connor founded,
in the fall of 1863, a weekly paper under the title *The Union
Vedette,* published first at Camp Douglas. Its salutatory, November
20, gave the key-note of its policy: "To every rightly constituted mind it has been a source of regret that the relations between the mass of the people and the military in Utah, have not
been either of a cordial or amicable nature." The editor pledged
his efforts to correct the mistaken notion that the government, as
represented by the soldiery, was bent on persecution. But where
the onus lay was plain,

> . . . the appeals of ambitious, crafty, designing men,
> to wean the people from the Government, that their own
> ends might be subserved—who constantly vilify and abuse
> the officers of the best Government with which this or any
> other people was ever blessed—it will be our duty to ex-
> pose. . . .[53]

The rather obvious humor of Artemus Ward, who found in polygamy a fertile field for exploitation, served as good space-filler
for the *Vedette,* and as time went on, the editor yielded more readily to the temptation to unleash his sarcasm:

> We understand there is a commotion in the counsels
> of polygamy, caused by the unheard of temerity of the
> Vedette. The Pasha of Deseret and his satraps are writh-

---

[52] *Ibid.,* March 2, 1864.

[53] For an account of the *Vedette,* see J. Cecil Alter, *Early Utah Journalism*
(Salt Lake City, 1938), pp. 361–375. File in the Salt Lake Public Library.

ing under its inflictions much like a coil of vipers handled with hot tongs. . . . We advise these gentlemen to reserve their fortitude, for, as yet, we have not commenced their torture. . . . We take up the gauntlet they have cast down, and, henceforth, mean to pursue them with a retribution as remorseless as fate. We devote ourselves to the pastime, not with reluctance, but with keen relish. . . .[54]

There was good fun, of a sort, in Mormon baiting. The only drawback was that the Church organ, *The Deseret News,* chose the very reasonable course of ignoring the *Vedette's* existence. Thus the editor complains

. . . that up to the present time the organs of the Church potentate in Salt Lake have thought fit to affect contempt of this journal, and have received its attacks upon evils inhereing [*sic*] in the system they advocate in perfect silence. . . . These moles will learn some day, perhaps, . . . that the prophet's power is waning in exact proportion as ours advances. . . .[55]

On January 5, 1864, the *Vedette* came forth as the first daily newspaper in the Territory.[56] With little expectation of local financial support, it could afford to taunt the opposition:

Understand then, once for all, ye of the rabid persuasion, that you spite us not; suit yourselves in withdrawing your support. . . . We can afford to publish until all our objects shall have been accomplished. . . . We are above patronage and independent of every consideration, but the consciousness of pursuing faithfully a just and noble cause.[57]

Editorial offices were moved to the city (June 6, 1865), and a travelling solicitor was employed to drum up subscriptions through the Pacific States and the surrounding territories. Publication

---

[54] *Daily Union Vedette,* January 10, 1865.

[55] *Ibid.,* June 6, 1865.

[56] Alter, *op. cit.,* pp. 362–364.

[57] *Vedette,* June 11, 1864. Alter, *op. cit.,* p. 365, suggests that this may imply that the United States government, through the War Department, was financing the paper.

continued until the fall of 1867, when, after a hard struggle, especially after the mustering out of the Volunteers during the previous summer, it gave up the ghost.[58]

While the infiltration of Gentiles into Utah did not gain real momentum until the end of the decade, the continued presence of the troops and their activities, so distasteful to the Mormon majority, remained a constant source of irritation. No further effort was made to attach the person of Brigham Young, but minor passages between the soldiers and the inhabitants were inevitable. Delegate Kinney, early in 1864, made a written appeal to the War Department for the withdrawal of the Volunteers, as their purpose of securing the Overland Route had been fulfilled and no further reason dictated their presence on the scene.[59] The *Vedette* seized upon this morsel of news, proclaiming that the work of the Volunteers had "only just begun"; that their business was to perpetuate peace in the Territory—and to guarantee that "there should be no more Humboldt murders or Mountain Meadow massacres." The question could be reduced to this: "If the people of Utah *are* loyal, the presence of loyal troops is no cause of offense. . . . If the people . . . are disloyal, there is need for troops here. . . ."[60] Nevertheless, Connor saw fit to make public a warning to his men to "refrain on all occasions from interference in any shape with the rights of person, property or liberty of the inhabitants of Utah."

> Relying on the intelligence of the mass of the people,
> to counteract the evil influences and unpatriotic counsels

---

[58] Alter, *op. cit.*, p. 375.

[59] *Vedette,* January 24, 1864, attacked Kinney in the following manner: "From the proceedings of Congress on the 16th of December, we extract the following little piece of buncombe:

" 'Mr. Kinney, delegate from Utah, offered a resolution *which was not agreed to,* asking that the Committee on Military Affairs be instructed to inquire into the causes which have led to the stationing of a large standing army among the peaceful and loyal people of Utah.'

". . . Like all new converts to either political or semi-religious faith, the delegate proceeds to show his devotion by the most extraordinary and radical course. . . . Perhaps there is no man in this Territory, and certainly none in Congress, who knows as much about the reasons which induced the sending of 'a large standing army' to Utah, as does this same inquiring delegate. . . ."

[60] *Ibid.,* February 3, 1864.

of evil-disposed and ambitious men, anxious to retain their hold on power and place, the soldiers of this command are directed to abstain from retaliating in kind, for the real or fancied injuries received at the hands of some of the people. It is hardly deemed necessary to repeat to you, that with the private relations, domestic practices, methods of belief or religion, you have naught to do. . . . However contrary these may seem to us, whose history, habits, education and daily walk, have instilled totally different and repugnant ideas, it is not our province to reform by violent measures, but to protect all, so long as they violate not the Constitution and the laws of the country. . . .[61]

The Nauvoo Legion, commanded by Lieutenant General Daniel S. Wells, had long been eyed with mistrust by the Californians. Under the organic act of 1850, the governor of the Territory was made commander-in-chief of the militia, but there seems to have been general disregard of this provision after the removal of Young. The spring muster of 1864, as the *Vedette* claimed to have ascertained, was called without consultation with Governor Doty. Was this simply another attempt on the part of the Theocracy to frighten prospectors from the region? the editor queried. If so ". . . we warn militia Captains and tinselled Generalissimos not to trifle with so delicate a question." [62] This impression would seem to have impelled Connor, July 9, 1864, to appoint Captain Charles Hempstead, editor of the *Vedette,* as provost marshal of Salt Lake City and to detail a cavalry company as provost guard.[63] The company was quartered in a building opposite the Tabernacle. News of the move caused President Young to rush home from a visitation of the southern settlements and to order the entrance to the Temple square to be blocked; [64] which smacks strongly of play-acting on that worthy's part. General Connor reported action to headquarters:

As set forth in former communications, my policy in this Territory has been to invite hither a large Gentile and loyal population, sufficient by peaceful means and through

---

[61] *Ibid.,* April 26, 1864.
[62] *Vedette,* May 20, 1864.
[63] Rogers (*op. cit.,* pp. 135–138) has a good account of the incident.
[64] *Journal History of the Church,* July 12, 1864.

the ballot box to overwhelm the Mormons by mere force
of numbers, and thus wrest from the Church—disloyal
and traitorous to the core—the absolute and tyrannical
control of temporal and civil affairs. . . . I have bent
every energy and means of which I was possessed . . .
towards the discovery and development of the mining resources. . . . These exertions have, in a remarkably
short period, been productive of the happiest results.
. . . Mines of undoubted richness have been discovered
. . . and the number of miners in the Territory are stead-
ily and rapidly increasing. With them, and to supply
their wants, merchants and traders are flocking into Great
Salt Lake City, which, by its activity, increased number
of Gentile stores and workshops, and the appearance of
its thronged and busy streets, presents a most remarkable
contrast to the Salt Lake of one year ago. . . .

This, again, was stretching the truth, for even a year later, the
Gentile population did not exceed three hundred souls. He continued:

This policy on my part, if not at first understood, is
now fully appreciated in its startling effect, by Brigham
Young and his coterie. His every effort having proved
unequal to the task of checking the transformation . . .
he and his Apostles have grown desperate. . . . It is un-
questionably his desire to provoke me into some act
savouring of persecution. . . . Hence he and his chief
men make their tabernacles and places of worship re-
sound each Sabbath with the most outrageous abuse of all
that pertains to the Government and the Union . . .
hence the persistent attempt to depreciate the national
currency and institute a "gold basis" in preference to
"Lincoln skins," as treasury notes are denominated in
Sabbath-day harangues.

Hence, he claimed, the establishment of a provost guard had been
a plain necessity:

I am fully satisfied that nothing but the firmness and
determination with which their demonstrations were met
. . . prevented a collision, and the least appearance of
vacillation on my part would surely have precipitated a
conflict. . . . Deeply as Brigham Young hates our Government . . . he will pause ere he inaugurates a strife,

so long as the military forces in the Territory are sufficiently numerous to hold him and his deluded followers
in check. . . .[65]

Major General Irwin McDowell had replaced Wright as commander of the Pacific area, which may explain the repetitious nature of Connor's letter. The latter's appeal for instructions was
soon answered. By special courier came a message strongly insisting that the present was no time for a Mormon war, regard-
less of what the provocation might be. Advantage could easily be
taken of such further disturbances by powers unfriendly to the
Union, with probably fatal consequences.

> Under the circumstances, it is the course of true pa-
> triotism for you not to embark on any hostilities. It is
> infinitely better that you should avoid contact with them.
> . . . This will undoubtedly tax your forebearance and
> your prudence to the utmost, but the general trusts it will
> not do so in vain.[66]

Later, orders came to withdraw the provost guard, but Connor,
probably to save his face, succeeded in having these changed to
permit maintaining part of a company in the city as a police patrol
for the troops off duty.[67] Conflict had again been staved off.

Withal, how close bitter opposition was to friendly feeling, engendered by the ultimate victory of the Union forces, found
demonstration in the spring of 1865. Lincoln's second inaugural

---

[65] *War of the Rebellion*, L, Pt. I, 893.

[66] *Ibid.*, pp. 909–910.

[67] *Ibid.*, pp. 913–923. An echo of the bitter feeling of that summer is
heard in the *Vedette*, August 20, 1864:
"The management of the Salt Lake Theater, with a pettiness of spite,
and a bigotry as unjustifiable in itself as it is discourteous to a large and respectable body of men, having adopted the rule not to admit soldiers of the
United States to their performances, we trust that no soldier will so far
lower his dignity as to even apply for admission. . . . When it comes to
this, that a man is debarred from a place of public entertainment . . . on the
mere fact that he wears the uniform of his country's service, it is high time
that loyal men, whether soldier, Jew, Gentile, or Mormon, should resent the
uncalled for insult and withhold their patronage until the rule shall be
rescinded." *Cf.* General J. F. Rusling, *Report . . . on Affairs in Utah and
the Territories for the Year Ending June 30, 1867* (Washington, D. C.,
1867), 36pp.

inspired Utahans, both Mormon and Gentile, to unite in a celebration on March 4. Leaders of the Saints, territorial officials and judges, the Nauvoo Legion and the Volunteers, marched and countermarched through the city, and listened to addresses by Chief Justice Titus and Captain W. H. Hooper, who was soon to be elected to Congress. In the evening the city council entertained the military staff at an "elegant repast," where the officers heartily responded to Captain Hempstead's toast to Mayor Smoot and the civic authorities, and the latter joined as noisily in a tribute to General Connor.[68] A few days later, the camp commander, on the eve of his departure to direct operations against Indians harassing the Overland in Wyoming and Colorado, was the honored guest at another civic banquet, where the gallant general presented his arm to the mayor's senior wife.[69] And when the news of Lincoln's assassination was telegraphed to the city, Elder Amasa Lyman, one of the Mormon leaders, and the Congregationalist minister, the Reverend Norman McLeod, were selected as the orators at the commemorative services held in the Tabernacle.[70]

[68] *Vedette,* March 6, 1865.

[69] *Journal History,* March 7 and 9, 1865. The expenses of the banquet amounted to $1000, if this account is to be believed.

[70] *Vedette,* April 21, 1865.

CHAPTER II

THE GOLDEN SPIKE IS DRIVEN HOME

IT WAS during the summer of 1865 that the handsome speaker of the House of Representatives, Schuyler Colfax, accompanied by Samuel Bowles of the *Springfield Republican,* Albert D. Richardson of the *New York Tribune,* and Lieutenant Governor William Bross of Illinois, editor of the *Chicago Tribune,* arrived in Salt Lake en route to the coast.[1] The incident is worthy of notice simply because the subsequent editorializing of the journalists and Colfax's inflammatory speeches on the Mormon question, as well as his influence over Grant, did much to call Utah to the attention of the nation and to encourage the more rabid Gentiles in their course of opposition to all things Mormon. Hospitably received, as Bowles and Richardson acknowledged in their book, *Across the Continent,* their visit climaxed with an interview with the Lion of the Lord (June 17). Young himself broached the leading question: What did the government propose to do with his people now that slavery was conquered? He had not forgotten the bracketing of polygamy with slavery as the "twin relic of barbarism" in the Republican platform of 1856. Colfax suggested that the Church herself supply the remedy, by way of a counter revelation on the subject. Admission of Utah as a state, warned the speaker, must wait upon the solution of this difficulty.[2]

In an article dated Great Salt Lake City, June 14, 1865, Bowles wrote:

> . . . The hospitality of Utah is not confined to the Mormons. The Gentiles or non-Mormons are becoming

---

[1] *Cf.* Samuel Bowles, *Across the Continent* (Springfield, Massachusetts, 1866) ; *Idem, Our New West* (Hartford, 1869) ; A. D. Richardson, *Beyond the Mississippi* (Hartford, 1867). Also, Whitney, *op. cit.,* II, 121–136, where an extensive account of the visit, which attracted much local interest, is found.

[2] Whitney, *op. cit.,* pp. 132–133; *Deseret News,* June 20, 1865.

29

numerous and influential here, and, citizens and soldiers, comprise many families of culture and influence. . . . Some of the more intelligent of the disgusted and repentant Mormons swell the circle. They have organized a literary association, established a large and growing Sunday School, largely made up of the children of Mormon parents, have weekly religious services, led by the chaplain of Camp Douglas, conduct an able and prosperous daily paper . . . and in every way are developing an organized and effective opposition to the dominant power here. These people, united, earnest and enthusiastic as minorities always are, claim a share in entertaining Mr. Colfax. . . . They are not ashamed to show us their ladies, as the Mormons generally seem to be. . . .[3]

On December 1, 1864, the Young Men's Literary Institute, the first social organization in the city purely Gentile in its membership, was formed. Few of its records survive, but it proved a nucleus of anti-Mormon activity and served to increase the self-consciousness of the Gentile group.[4]

The voice of Protestant evangelism had been but faintly heard in Utah before the middle sixties. Chaplain Anderson, of the Volunteers, had been presented with a chapel tent by the First Presbyterian Society of San Francisco, before the departure of the troops for Utah. Set up at Camp Douglas, this must have been the first non-Mormon religious "edifice" in the Territory.[5] Anderson, however, remained but a short time, for he served in the Wilderness Campaign in the capacity of superintendent of transportation.[6] Then, on January 18, 1865, the *Vedette* announced the

---

[3] *Vedette,* August 17, 1865. Justice Solomon McCurdy, who had been appointed associate justice of Utah, April 21, 1864, was much exercised by subsequent articles by Samuel Bowles appearing in the Springfield *Republican,* reflecting, as he conceived, on the federal officials in the Territory. Writing to Attorney General Speed, August 20, 1865, he complained that Bowles had intimated that "two-thirds of the Federal Officers in the Territory are Polliggamists; and others have no testimony against it." As for himself, McCurdy declared that he had his family with him, and was "a Henry Clay Whig and a Presbyterian . . . but I am not here as a missionary." (N. A., A. G. MSS, Utah).

[4] *Ibid.,* December 3, 1864. Daft's hall on Main Street was the place of meeting until the construction of Independence Hall.

[5] San Francisco *Bulletin,* September 23, 1862.

[6] Transactions, Kansas State Historical Society, VII, 178, 186, 187.

advent of the Reverend Norman McLeod, a Congregationalist
minister:

> For a long time perhaps the greatest want seriously
> felt by residents and sojourners in this vicinity, has been
> that we have had, in all this wide Territory, no minister
> of the Gospel to preach the Word of the Living God.

Something better than Temple harangues was now to be provided
for the famished Gentiles. The members of the Young Men's
Literary Association proffered McLeod the use of their hall for
the following Sunday.[7]

McLeod, as the event proved, was a violent polemist and a
bitter anti-Mormon. The Saints, he was soon heard to declare,
would find it impossible to rebuild the wall around their new
Jerusalem, for a new day had dawned and McLeod, evidently, was
not adverse to fancy himself as the morning star.[8] Much was
made of the fact that his lectures attracted furtive Mormons, and
the vials of editorial wrath were poured out upon the "human
Coyotes"—reputed spies of the Church—who came to the services,
". . . not to hear the Reverend gentleman, who preaches civilized
Christianity there, but . . . to note how many of Brigham's vas-
sals went there, under cover of darkness, to listen to the word of
God." [9] Soon the Gentile paper (practically the only source of
information available for such matters) was boasting for McLeod's
Sunday school an enrollment of one hundred and fifty children,
while decrying the insidious efforts of "those officious creatures,

---

"John A. Anderson spoke of . . . his work as correspondent of the San
Francisco *Bulletin* . . . of his own enlistment as a soldier of the Lord and of
the U. S. as a chaplain of Colonel Patrick Conner's [*sic*] 3d California regiment, and the march across the terrible Humboldt desert to Salt Lake and
Camp Douglas." He was president of the Kansas State Agricultural College
from 1873 to 1878. Rogers, *op. cit.,* p. 261, has disclosed these facts.

[7] *Vedette,* January 18, 1865. *The Utah Gazetteer and Directory for 1884,*
edited and compiled by Robert W. Sloan (Salt Lake City, 1884), p. 208, gives
January 1, 1864, as the date of McLeod's arrival, obviously an error. It also
states that he came under the direction of the American Home Missionary
Society of the Congregational Church, having previously filled a pastorate in
Denver.

[8] *Ibid.,* January 30, 1865.

[9] *Ibid.,* May 16, 1865.

called 'teachers' among the Saints," to win the youngsters back to more orthodox schools.[10]

Though the missionary responded to the civic invitation to speak at the exercises commemorative of Lincoln's death, his grievance was not thereby assuaged. Picturing himself as the intended victim of a murderous assault designed to cut short his apostolic career, and vaguely laying it at the feet of the Mormon authorities,[11] he lectured during the late summer of that year in California and Nevada with the object of raising funds for the building of a chapel in Salt Lake City.[12] Within a year of his arrival, Independence Hall, as it was named, was dedicated in the presence of the governor and his staff. A committee drew up the following resolution:

> . . . The progress made in Utah during the past year in the establishment of a Christian Church on a firm and enduring basis, evidenced by the fact that a commodious church building has been erected, in which each Sabbath the word of God is taught and expounded, a large and intelligent congregation gathered, and a Sabbath School now numbering two hundred scholars established, is a

---

[10] *Ibid.*, July 18, 1865. The Utah Gazetteer (1884), speaks of two schools, one at Camp Douglas, the other in the city, and a total enrollment of 250 pupils.

[11] The *Vedette*, August 21, 1865, prints a letter from McLeod, dated August 18, describing the alleged attack. While confined to his bed, stones were hurled at him through the open door of his house, "with such violence as to warrant the conclusion that the outrage was the act of an athletic arm and assassin's heart. . . ." The editor added, "We don't think assassination is the wisest policy for the Saints to pursue just now, for we tell them that every drop of innocent blood they shed will cry from the ground for speedy vengeance, and not in vain. . . ."

The *Vedette* of August 17, 1865, quotes from the New York *Tribune,* an account by A. P. Richardson of the attendance of the Colfax party at services at Independence Hall. "He [McLeod] is a Congregationalist; but all the anti-Mormons worship at his church. The congregation was small, but one of unusual intelligence, embracing citizens, officers from Camp Douglas, and 20 or 30 ladies. The Gentile population of this city, exclusive of the soldiers, number from 200 to 300. . . ."

[12] *Ibid.*, August 17, 1865. "The 'gentile' congregation not being numerous nor well able to do any more than they have done already—that is, bought a $3000 lot and put their names down for additional encouragement. . . ." The building, a plain, unlovely structure, was torn down in 1889.

source of just pride in the past, and a harbinger of bright promise in the future.[13]

From January to March, 1866, McLeod lectured weekly on the evils of polygamy. The faithful *Vedette* waxed eloquent. In spite of all that their leaders could do or say, inquiring Mormons ". . . flock by hundreds to hear the arguments of Mr. McLeod, and as he hurls his thunderbolts, in the choicest and most classic strains . . . their eyes flash with a new light which betokens that the reign of fanaticism and untruth is o'er." [14]   But by mid-March, the evangelist had left the city, possibly feeling that he had overshot his bolt. In Washington, he appeared before the House Committee on Territories.[15]   Thereafter, occasional reports reveal his continued activity as a lecturer on the Mormon problem in various eastern cities. A year later the *Vedette,* bemoaning the decline in attendance at the Sunday school, yearned for the spacious days of his evangelism, and rebuked the woeful lack of interest in Utah's difficulties on the part of the nation at large.

> While the Pecksniffs . . . expend millions annually in sending missionary warming pans to the Indies, . . . while the sorrows of Booriboola Gah touch the tender sympathies of the great English and American Mission Societies, no one seems to think that out in Utah is a wider and more important field for missionary labor than in all the world beside.[16]

Irish soldiers of the Volunteers had formed the John C. Egan Centre of the Fenian Brotherhood at Camp Douglas during 1864, and later maintained club rooms in the city.[17]   The Masonic fraternity was organized in the city early in 1866. A number of the officers of the post appear to have held membership in California lodges.[18]   The *Vedette* of February 7 comments:

---

[13] *Ibid.,* January 24, 1866.

[14] *Ibid.,* March 13, 1866.

[15] *Ibid.,* March 19, 1866.

[16] *Ibid.,* March 5, 1867.

[17] *Ibid.,* December 31, 1864; April 25, 1865, *et passim. Cf. ibid.,* January 21, 1866: "Sarsfield Circle, Fenian Brotherhood, will hold their regular meeting every Wednesday evening, at Fenian Hall, corner of State Road and Telegraph St., Salt Lake City. (upstairs)."

[18] Rogers, *op. cit.,* p. 77. A Masonic hall was one of the first buildings erected in Stockton, Utah, in 1864.

> One of the most cheering signs of the civilization of
> the times, in Utah, was the imposing procession and the
> interesting exercises, on the occasion of the organization
> of Mt. Moriah Lodge, U. D. F. and A. M., in this city on
> Monday afternoon. . . . At two o'clock, P.M., the Mem-
> bers, numbering between fifty and sixty, from among the
> civil and military citizens (gentiles) marched in full
> Masonic regalia from the lodge room to Independence
> Hall . . . headed by the splendid military band.

During the following decades, Masonry was to play an important role in the territorial drama. Lodges were established
wherever feasible and Mormons were rigidly excluded from fellowship. How much the past history of Mormonism, with its own
interesting Masonic affiliations at Nauvoo, had to do with this
attitude, may only be conjectured.[19]

Catholic beginnings in Utah, as presently known (1971), excluding the era of exploration prior to the Mormon settlement
date back to the summer of 1859, when a German Capuchin friar,
Father Bonaventure Keller, en route from California, paused to
minister to the Catholic soldiers of Camp Floyd for a period of
two or three months. Five years elapsed before the Reverend
Joseph Raverdy, a priest of the Diocese of Santa Fe working in
the Denver area, came to offer Mass in the old post chapel at
Camp Douglas on September 25, 1864. The Vedette noted that:

> A large number of Catholics belonging to the com-
> mand were present, and the occasion was one of interest
> to persons not of that Church—inasmuch as it is probably
> the first time that mass has been celebrated within this
> Territory, unless by some missionary among the Indians
> previous to the settlement . . . by the Whites.[20]

---

[19] *Cf.* Samuel H. Goodwin, *Mormonism and Masonry* (Salt Lake City,
1924), and *Additional Studies in Mormonism and Masonry* (Salt Lake City,
1932). An attempted refutation is found in Elmer Cecil McGavin, *Mormonism and Masonry* (Salt Lake City, 1935).

[20] It is possible that Father Keller was the first priest to offer Mass on
Utah soil. The Franciscan Fathers, Atanasio Dominguez and Silvestre
Escalante, who explored the region in 1776-1777, make no mention of saying
Mass after leaving the New Mexico settlements, nor does Father Pierre-Jean
de Smet, who claims to have visited the Great Salt Lake valley in 1840,
refer to the Mass. That fascinating diarist, John Wolcott Phelps, who was
pronouncedly anti-Catholic, writes of a priest conducting a funeral service
at Camp Floyd. Cf. the unpublished manuscript, New York Public Library,
under date of June 10, 1859, and *passim*. Monsignor Jerome Stoffel has
identified this priest as Father Bonaventure Keller (Cf. Utah Historical
Quarterly, Vol. 36, No. 1, pp. 42-62).

[21] *Vedette*, October 1, 1864.

The priest remained until Thursday as a guest of General Connor before pushing on to Virginia City, Montana.[21]

On June 4, 1866, Edward Kelly, priest of the Vicariate of Marysville, California, and pastor of Austin, Nevada, celebrated the first Mass in Salt Lake City, where he gathered his flock in Independence Hall.[22] He visited the mining camps at Stockton and Rush Valley before his return to Austin toward the end of the month.[23] Apparently, he was favorably impressed with the prospects of religion in the Salt Lake area, for he was back in September, intending to make the city his permanent headquarters. The *Vedette* recorded that:

> The Catholic services at Independence Hall last Sunday was [*sic*] well attended. . . . The Rev. Father announced that he had come to Salt Lake City for the purpose of permanently establishing a Catholic Church, and we learn that yesterday our business men subscribed a handsome sum to further the undertaking.[24]

Again, "The Rev. Father requests us to return his sincere thanks to the Gentile community of Salt Lake for the liberality they have manifested towards him and his laudable undertaking." [25] During the autumn, Father Kelly purchased property on which stood an adobe dwelling, which he proceeded to remodel with a view toward making it a convent for sisters whom he hoped to bring in as teachers. To raise funds, he announced a series of lectures on "Divine Revelation, Its Possibility, Necessity and Characteristics." Conceivably, the subject was chosen in answer to the Mormon claims in regard to their revelations.[26] But on December 6 came sad news:

> Rev. Father Kelly requests us to announce that by a letter from his Bishop O'Connell of Marysville, California, dated San Francisco, 24th November, he . . . is informed that the Archbishop of Baltimore, Maryland, has transferred the spiritual jurisdiction of the Catholic Church over the Catholics of this Territory from the said

[22] *Ibid.*, June 1, 1866, announcing the time and place of the services: "He will lecture on 'Transubstantiation,' or the 'Real Presence of Christ in the Holy Eucharist.'" Mass was also said at Camp Douglas.

[23] *Ibid.*, June 25, 1866.

[24] *Ibid.*, September 11, 1866.

[25] *Ibid.*, September 12, 1866.

[26] *Ibid.*, November 20, 1866.

> Bishop O'Connell . . . to a bishop who will soon send a
> clergyman to reside permanently in this city. As Father
> Kelly is directed to return to Austin . . . he will soon
> furnish us with a published statement of the funds which
> he has received and expended since his arrival amongst
> us. The Rev. Father intended to establish, at an early
> day . . . a school which would be conducted by sisters.
> . . . In order to have a place of residence prepared for
> these teachers, Father Kelly enlarged the dwelling house
> which was on the property. . . .[27]

The statement was duly published, showing receipts and expenditures totalling nearly three thousand dollars.[28] He remained over Christmas, singing High Mass with "musical accompaniment by the ladies and gentlemen of the city," and left soon thereafter.[29]

With the erection of the Vicariate of Colorado, in 1868, Utah Territory was detached from Marysville and placed under the jurisdiction of the Right Reverend Joseph Projectus Machebeuf,

---

[27] *Ibid.*, December 6, 1866.

[28] *Vedette,* December 8, 1866. A debt of $253.18, owed to Mr. McGrath, contractor, remained. Kelly arranged that McGrath was to occupy the dwelling until rents balanced the debt.

[29] *Ibid.*, December 21, 28, 1866: "During his short sojourn in our midst he had by his urbanity of manners and kind, Christian conduct, won for himself many friends personally, as well as making a deep impression on the minds of many, of not only the sincerity of his mission on earth, but that as an able and eloquent exponent of the true principle of his faith, he will even be a valuable and useful member of the community in which it is his lot to be stationed." May 27, 1867: "By private letter received in this city from Father Kelly, dated Marysville, Cal., May 16th, we learn that the new Catholic bishop for Utah and Colorado will be in this city soon. It is not known publicly yet, who the dignitary is; nor is it yet known where he will locate his see; but it will be undoubtedly at Denver or this city. This new diocise [sic] was created at the Baltimore Council last October." On August 7, 1867, the *Vedette* quoted the Gold Hill, Nevada, *News* of July 26: "It is said that Father Kelley of Marysville, Cal., is to be bishop of Montana; either he or a Catholic clergyman that is now officiating in this State." September 11, 1867: "Catholics, take notice: By private letters from Father Croake of San Francisco, received here, we learn that before long now, a bishop, probably of Nevada and Utah as one diocese, will be in Salt Lake. The Catholic Church cannot supply the demand on it from other points in the United States at the present time; of course Utah has been neglected in this respect, as it has by all other denominations, except the Episcopalian."

who had established his see at Denver.[30] The acute shortage of
priests at his disposal prevented that missionary prelate from supplying the needs of the handful of Catholics in Mormondom for
some time, but in November of that year he himself undertook the
first episcopal visitation of that portion of his Vicariate. At Camp
Douglas he was cordially received by General Connor, and during
the week he remained there he prepared a group of the soldiers for
Confirmation. Machebeuf's biographer described the visit:

> From the Fort he visited Salt Lake and sought out the
> few Catholic families there. He also met Brigham
> Young and other dignitaries of the Mormon church, as
> well as many of the prominent citizens, of all of whom he
> afterwards spoke very favorably. . . .
> At Salt Lake he found ground for a church with a
> house on it, but as yet there was no church building. The
> house was occupied by a Catholic family named Carroll,
> who, with three other families, constituted the settled
> Catholic population. . . . On three days of the following
> week he said mass at the house of a Mr. Marshall for the
> benefit of his little flock, and for the edification of a num-
> ber of Mormon ladies whom curiosity or some other
> motive brought to witness the services. He also baptized
> three children in the family of a Mr. Sloan, and one in
> another family, and he had two marriages on the feast of
> the Immaculate Conception.[31]

A year later, he sent Father Bourion, a native of France who
had volunteered for the Colorado missions, to Salt Lake City as
pastor.[32] However, as the Bishop wrote his sister: "Father
Bourion, whom I sent among the Mormons, could not get a living
there and has returned." [33] In the spring of 1871, Machebeuf appointed the Reverend James V. Foley as parish priest of Utah.
Foley remained only a few months, since Utah was transferred to
the jurisdiction of the Archbishop of San Francisco soon after his

---

[30] W. J. Howlett, *Life of the Right Reverend Joseph Projectus Machebeuf*
(Pueblo, Colorado, 1908), pp. 337–353; Donald C. Shearer, *Pontificia Ameri-
cana* (Washington, D. C., 1933), pp. 336–337.

[31] Howlett, *op. cit.*, pp. 350–351.

[32] *Ibid.*, p. 363.

[33] *Ibid.*, p. 365.

arrival.[34] These successive changes, as well as the lack of a permanent resident clergy, undoubtedly retarded Catholic growth during the sixties, and there are indications of rather numerous defections from the Faith.[35]

It was the Protestant Episcopal Church that first set up a definitive organization for the Gentile evangelization of Utah. On October 5, 1866, the House of Bishops, meeting in New York City, elected Daniel Sylvester Tuttle, the youthful pastor of Zion Church, Morris, New York, as missionary bishop of the Territories of Montana, Idaho, and Utah.[36] Awaiting consecration, Tuttle secured the services of four clergymen, friends of his, two of whom he dispatched to Utah in the spring. From Warren Hussey, banker and leading Episcopalian of Salt Lake City, Tuttle received a letter strongly urging a moderate course in regard to the Mormons:

> I am quite intimate with Prest. Young and have frequently heard him express himself concerning the churches coming here; and I am very sure they will meet a hearty welcome from him, *under certain circumstances.*
> . . . In a conversation had with Prest. Young since receipt of your letter he has only reiterated former statements, and assured me no minister, nor any one else, who w'd come here and mind their own business, need have the slightest fear of being disturbed by the Mormons.
> There are very few communicants here, some ½ Doz. or so to my knowledge. Other Gentiles who are not communicants, would be very glad indeed to see a church established here, and are willing to aid in supporting a minister, provided he is the right kind of a man. . . . There is no other church in operation here now but the Mormons. The Catholics will be here during the spring

---

[34] *Daily Tribune,* May 30, 1871: "Departure—Rev. J. V. Foley, the Catholic Priest who has been in this city for several months past, starts for Denver, his proper station, as we understand, tomorrow."

[35] This statement is based on the frequency with which the writer found Irish names in connection with Masonic activities, early Protestant organizations, etc. It is, of course, open to exception, but generally speaking, the unchurched miner, Catholic or Protestant, soon drifted into indifference.

[36] Daniel Sylvester Tuttle, *Reminiscences of a Missionary Bishop* (New York, 1906), p. 22. At the time of his appointment, Tuttle was twenty-nine years of age. He was consecrated in Trinity Church, New York City, January 26, 1867.

or summer, and probably the Methodists; and the first here will get most support.

. . . Prest. Young and the Mormon Church are in my opinion, the worst lied about, if I may use the expression, of any people living. Parties here who are at enmity with them, and others who desire large government contracts, are exceedingly anxious to bring about if possible a collision between them and our government, in hopes of bringing on another Mormon War. No abuse seems too low to heap upon them by these friends of Christianity; no story too big to tell and publish to the world. The Mormons would be very different people from any I saw to *like* such treatment. . . .

Prest. Young said to me he did not expect anything of this abuse and detraction from an Episcopal bishop. "They are men of education and better sense; they are gentlemen, and any gentleman is welcome here, no matter what his creed" were about his words.

The supporters of your church here will be Gentile business men generally,—men who are daily mingling in business and socially, with the Mormons and their leaders, and who are determined to live here in peace and harmony and do justice to all; and they are utterly and absolutely unwilling to give money and support to any minister who will come here and get himself and friends into trouble.[37]

The two advance missionaries, George W. Foote and T. W. Haskins, reached Salt Lake City early in May, inaugurated services in Independence Hall, and organized a Church Association for the purpose of raising funds for a school.[38] On July 4 the *Vedette* greeted the arrival of the bishop and the two other missioners as "the kind of an 'army of occupation' we want." The following day Tuttle wrote to his wife:

The Gentiles here are not at all united socially or religiously. There may be said to be three classes of them. First, the intense anti-Mormons, who say we are "knuckling under" to the Mormons in our present course. Second, the moderate, indifferent people, without great prejudice, and without great energy. Third, those who are disposed to apologize for the Mormons, and to think that in some things they are grossly misrepresented. Of

[37] Date March 13, 1867. Quoted, Tuttle, *op. cit.,* pp. 58–60.
[38] *Vedette,* May 6, 22, 1867.

this last class is Mr. Hussey, with whom many of the first class will not join in helping us on. Still, with steady work and good lives, we hope gradually to mold these classes, or what there is religious in them, into one.[39]

The Mormons had dwelt in Utah for twenty years, the Bishop reminded her;

> There are, therefore, young men and young women here who have never seen aught of the outside world, who have never witnessed Christian worship of any kind whatever, who have been taught (and from specimens here they may well believe) that all Gentiles are a cheating, blasphemous, licentious set of men. . . . Meanwhile, let it be said, there seems to be less profanity, rowdyism, rampant and noisy wickedness among the young Mormons than among the youth of any other town or city where I've been. Drunkenness is a crime almost unknown among them. They exceed the Methodists in their expressions of equality and affection. . . .[40]

Before setting out on a visitation of his vast diocese, Tuttle paid a courtesy call on Brigham Young. He was cordially received, though he noted, with some chagrin, that he was not invited to repeat the visit.

> He is so powerful a man in everything here, and so unscrupulous a man, I fear, in most things, that my policy will be to have as little as possible to do with him. With his keen sightedness he must know, that . . . by our services and our school, we are putting our clutches to his very throat.[41]

With support guaranteed by eastern benefactors, an Episcopal school, St. Mark's, was opened on July 1, with an enrollment of sixteen pupils, which was speedily increased.[42] The fact that the

---

[39] Tuttle, *op. cit.*, pp. 107–108.

[40] *Ibid.*, p. 110.

[41] *Ibid.*, pp. 111–114.

[42] *Ibid.*, p. 109. James Bonwick wrote: I was agreeably surprised to drop in upon an Episcopal Protestant school. It had been newly established for the families of coming Gentiles. The building was a small, but neat, wooden one. The master was thoroughly up to his work. He had procured suitable desks and appliances, but deeply regretted the very low condition of his

"public schools" were frankly controlled by the Mormon Church, and that tuition was charged by them, told in favor of private schools for many years. The closing years of the decade showed a slight increase in the membership of his flock; hence, Bishop Tuttle fixed upon Salt Lake as his see,[43] and plans were drawn up for a suitable cathedral, the elder Upjohn being employed as architect (1869).

Notices of occasional services held by itinerant Methodist or Presbyterian missionaries are to be found before the seventies, but no resident ministers were appointed prior to 1869 and no churches were built by these denominations, which later were to figure so prominently in the attempted evangelization of Utah.[44]

Thus, as the decade wore away, the emergence of a conscious Gentile group foreshadowed the fierce conflict of the ensuing years. Politically, after the transfer of Governor Harding, federal officials, probably reflecting the general policy of President Johnson's administration, pursued a more quiet and less obtrusive course. Governor Doty, succeeding Harding, held office until his death, June 13, 1865, when the public obsequies decreed by the civic authorities gave token of the satisfaction of the Mormon majority with his rule.[45] No less acceptable was the attitude of Governor

---

scholars." He then goes on to describe the filth and incompetence of a typical Mormon school. *Mormons and the Silver Mines* (London, 1872), p. 217 ff.

[43] *Ibid.*, pp. 243–250.

[44] *Vedette,* October 22, 1866. Tuttle, *op. cit.,* p. 111, recounting his visit with President Young: "When we came back from Mr. Young's Mr. S. [Stenhouse] again met us. 'Did the president ask you to preach in the tabernacle,' he asked. 'No,' I replied. 'Strange,' he said, 'he must have been absent-minded; he is always very liberal and invites all to preach for him.' Then he went on rambling, telling of a Bishop Jaynes and a Bishop Simpson (Methodists) who had been here."

[45] Whitney, *op. cit.,* II, 136–137. On December 20, 1864, Doty wrote to Isaac Newton, Commissioner of Territories, enclosing a *Deseret News* clipping praising his administration, which he requested be handed to President Lincoln. "I desire him to see it, that he may know that I do not provoke difficulties with this people. . . ." (N. A., State Department, Utah Territorial Papers, Vol. II). Apparently, however, even Doty was disturbed by local conditions. He wrote to Seward, January 30, 1865, reporting that he had sent Amos Reed, territorial secretary, to Washington, without first obtaining permission, ". . . as that would involve the loss of too much time and perhaps result in bringing his business too prominently before the so-called Au-

Charles Durkee, a native of Vermont, who had represented his adopted state, Wisconsin, both as congressman and senator.[46] Coming to Utah broken in health, he sedulously avoided difficulties, remarking, it is said, that "I was sent out to do nothing." He remained in office until December 21, 1869, a thorn in the side of the aggressive anti-Mormons, who denounced what they considered his craven spirit.[47]

So far as the United States district courts were concerned, the statute on polygamy remained inoperative. As District Attorney Charles Hempstead wrote to Attorney General James Speed, June 1, 1866, enclosing his oath of office:

> . . . . it is proper for me to inform you, that it would be worse than useless to attempt to enforce the Act of Congress, relative to Polygamy, until material modifica-

thorities here." Reed's exact business is not stated. Thus, when Governor Doty died, Reed, who normally would have acted *ad interim,* was absent. Colonel O. H. Irish, Superintendent of Indian Affairs, assumed authority, as Doty had directed. On the afternoon of Doty's funeral, June 15, two Mormon leaders of the assembly, George A. Smith and John Taylor, the former president of the legislative council, called at the mansion house, expecting that Smith would take office, as next in rank. Irish refused to relinquish the post. (Irish to Hon. William P. Dole, Commissioner of Indian Affairs, June 15, 1865, N. A., State Department, Utah Territorial Papers, Vol. II) ; Brigham H. Roberts, *A Comprehensive History of the Church of Jesus Christ of Latter-day Saints* (Salt Lake City, 1930) V, 179–180, quotes the "History of Brigham Young" (MS) 1865, pp. 419–421, to the effect that a group of Mormons petitioned President Johnson for the appointment of Colonel Irish as territorial governor.

[46] Edward H. Anderson, "Territorial Governors of Utah—Charles Durkee, Sixth Governor," in *Improvement Era,* IV, No. 4, February, 1901, 241–246.

[47] *Cf. Vedette,* November 4, 1865. Durkee is excoriated for accepting an invitation to review the Nauvoo Legion, at which he appeared without staff, and took "second place to Brigham Young." Durkee's message to the assembly at the 15th Session, 1865–66, includes this paragraph: "An examination of the Territorial laws now in force in this Territory relative to the organization of the militia has satisfied me that such laws are insufficient to comply with the requirements of the organic act. No staff is provided for the executive, nor are reports upon the points above indicated made to him for his information and guidance. . . ." *Governor's Message to the Legislative Assembly of the Territory of Utah, Fifteenth Annual Session, 1865-6* (Salt Lake City, 1865), p. 6. Copy in N. A., State Department, Utah, II, 626.

tions shall have been made in the laws relative to Courts,
Juries, Marshals, etc., in the Territory.

Hempstead's only consolation was that Justice Charles Wilson, who
had recently taken up his duties, had been able to make some
progress in restricting the jurisdiction of the territorial probate
courts.

> At the last term of the District Court, Wilson de-
> cided that the Probate Courts had no civil or criminal
> jurisdiction. . . . He has also, on quo warranto, ousted
> the Territorial Marshal, and substituted in his place the
> United States Marshal. . . .
> Your Excellency will at once observe that these two
> decisions are vital objects to be reached by the Legisla-
> tion, known as the Cullom Bill, and are terrible, if not
> fatal blows at Mormon rule and Mormon power in Utah.
> Judge Wilson has done all this with so quiet a man-
> ner, without street discussion, and without direct or harsh
> reflections on Mormonism, when giving his judicial opin-
> ions, that as yet, although greatly affected by his legal
> conclusions, they have not charged him with any unpar-
> tiality or unfairness on the Bench. . . .[48]

Even earlier, Associate Justice Drake, holding court at Provo,
had refused to recognize the competence of the probate courts to
issue naturalization papers. Further, Hempstead himself had denied petitions for naturalization coming from those practicing polygamy, either before or after the Act of 1862.[49]

The Cullom bill, introduced by Congressman Shelby M. Cullom
of Illinois, in 1869, was designed to subject Utah to something like
complete federal control. It failed to pass the Senate. As a result,
the legal situation continued in statu quo, in spite of the rulings of
the judiciary. In large measure, the irregularities in jurisdiction
thus noted were endemic in the early period for most of the territories. In Utah, they were prolonged by special antagonisms between the people and the federal government.

The *Vedette* kept up a running fire of criticism directed against
the territorial assembly, particularly in regard to its efforts to

---

[48] Hempstead to Speed, June 1, 1866 (N. A., A. G. MSS, Utah).
[49] *Vedette*, April 28, 1866.

secure statehood for Utah. Thus, following the submission of a plea, in January, 1866, it addressed the Mormon lawmakers:

> What has been the burden of your discourse, in Tabernacle and Ward meeting houses, but the vilest abuse of the troops, and of the Gentiles, and the most insolent treason against the Government? Did you not, with the malignity of incarnate fiends, exult in the losses sustained by the Union and Confederate armies? . . . In a document which is an insult to the sole executive authority in this Territory, Governor Durkee, you complain that Congress has not responded to your memorial for admission to the Union.

Other territories, continued the oracle, lately had been received into the sisterhood of states, but "At the bar of the Union . . . they appeared, not drabbled and prostituted, deformed with the evidence of crime, and too loathsome for a union with liberty, but in all their virgin purity." [50]

Since Utah's failure to achieve statehood in 1861, a solemn comedy of electing a full state ticket, governor, legislature, and the rest, had been regularly acted out. This extra-legal legislature being identical in personnel with the territorial assembly, the former would meet with "Governor" Young, immediately after the annual session, listen to his message, ordinarily a much more interesting document than that declaimed by the federal official, and then ratify their own enactments as members of the territorial body.[51] Even Governor Doty seems to have been irritated by this harmless irregularity, for in a letter to Secretary Seward he described it as a "fourth government." [52] For the *Vedette*, the whole procedure

---

[50] *Ibid.*, January 25, 1866.

[51] Daines, "Separatism," *loc. cit.*, p. 341.

[52] Doty to Seward, January 28, 1865 (N. A., State Department, Utah, II, 617). "In addition, the same party [Mormon Church,] in 1861, formed an Independent government for the 'State of Deseret,' whose boundaries include Utah and portions of Idaho and Arizona. This form of government is preserved by annual elections of all the State officers; the Legislature being composed of the same men who are elected to the Territorial Legislature, and who, by a Resolution, reenact the same laws for the 'State' which have been enacted for the Territory of Utah.

"For the information of the Department I herewith transmit a copy of a paper containing the proceedings of the Governor and Legislature of this

was a "disgusting farce" reeking with disloyalty and treason.[53]

Anxiously awaiting positive action by Congress in regard to polygamy, the Gentile organ wearied not in its denunciations of the "crime." In imaginative flight, it predicted the disastrous results of continued Mormon resistance. "Strong raiding forces, sent north and south, would carry devastation through these valleys, sweeping them with the besom of destruction." [54] When the assembly, January, 1867, drew up a memorial to Congress asking the repeal of the Act of 1862, the editor, anticipating federal interposition, described it as "A bold flank movement," savouring "decidedly of irony and sarcasm." [55] Such an item as the charge of Chief Justice Titus to the grand jury of the third district, April 1, 1867, was a welcome tid-bit:

> It was the most bold, argumentative, and impressive vindication of the Anti-Polygamy Law of Congress that has ever emanated from the lips of any living man. Judge Titus commenced from the creation of the first man and woman in the Garden of Eden; he travelled down the long vistas of ages, and at every step added new proofs against that system; he traced with a masterly hand the origin of this assumed form of religion, depicting the downfall and ruin of every country that had adopted it, and drew a vivid picture of the present state of those countries where it is now tolerated. . . . The Judge . . . warned . . . of the fearful retribution that must ensue, sooner or later. He commented on the leniency of our Government in its forbearance, and disclaimed that he was actuated by a spirit of censure or of prejudice. . . .[56]

Whatever the pith of his eloquence or the value of his anthropology, Judge Titus was wasting his breath. No grand jury in Utah Territory, in 1867, would indict for violation of the statute.

Hopelessly outnumbered though they were, the non-Mormons launched a political campaign that year. Captain William H.

---

embryo State at a session held in this city on the 23d of this month, by which it will be perceived this *fourth* government is now fully inaugurated."

[53] *Vedette,* January 25, 1866.

[54] *Ibid.,* March 5, 1866.

[55] *Ibid.,* January 14, 1867.

[56] *Ibid.,* April 2, 1867.

Hooper, candidate of the Mormon Church party for delegate to Congress, stood for re-election in February. Inspired by the zeal of a young attorney from Ohio, Robert N. Baskin, who had joined the Gentile ranks, the opposition determined to enter the contest.

> After business hours, certain Gentile business men of Salt Lake City were in the habit of meeting at the office of Abel Gilbert, a merchant, and a gentleman of infinite wit and social qualities. At these meetings the state of affairs in Utah was often discussed and condemned. At one of these meetings, in 1867, at which William McGroarty, several other men, . . . and myself were present . . . I stated that if we intended to stay in the Territory we should organize and oppose the political control of the priesthood. As my suggestions were approved by all the other persons present, I moved that we begin by nominating Mr. McGroarty . . . in opposition to Captain Hooper. . . . McGroarty stroked his long beard and said "Barkis is willing." [57]

A convention was called, and met in Independence Hall, on January 29, with General Connor in the chair. The "caucus" nominee was ratified by acclamation, and McGroarty responded with a vigorous oration. As the election day drew near, the "regular" candidate scouted the suggestion that there was anything farcical in the venture. "Mr. McGrorty [*sic*] positively denies that he has any intention of withdrawing from the canvass. . . . The friends of the candidate do not expect an overwhelming majority, but do believe he will be their representative in the next Congress." [58] McGroarty polled exactly 105 votes.[59] The *Vedette,* chagrined, would have the last word:

> We have seen the course pursued by the Nullifiers of the South . . . , we have visited the polls in the Sixth Ward in New York . . . , we have been a constant spectator of all the elections in San Francisco from 1849 to 1861 . . . , but we have never yet witnessed an election where all the requirements of law, all the observance of custom, all adherence to rule and usage were so openly

---

[57] Robert N. Baskin, *Reminiscences of Early Utah* (Salt Lake City, 1914), p. 23.

[58] *Vedette,* January 30, February 2, 1867.

[59] Baskin, *op. cit.,* p. 23.

and flagrantly violated as was that of yesterday. . . .
While we are willing to admit that the day passed quietly
off without a fight . . . yet to one who is familiar with
the usual safeguards ever thrown around the ballot-box,
in every other part of the country, it was indeed a strange
sight.[60]

The editor failed to make his charges more specific. Mc-
Groarty carried the contest to Washington, on the grounds that
the Mormons were not qualified voters,—thus inaugurating a procedure to be followed time and again in the succeeding years. But
the House refused to be convinced, and Hooper took his seat.[61]

It sounds like *opera bouffe*. Actually there was a dead earnest-
ness on the part of many of these early Gentiles in their efforts to
destroy polygamy and what they described as "priestly domination." For a man like Baskin it was to be a life-long struggle, un-
softened even in retrospect. He and his fellows were politically-
minded. They laid, in 1867, the foundations of their party—the
Liberal, as it was later termed—unique in the period, as it sought to
combine non-Mormons whether normally Republicans or Democrats into a cohort to defeat the Mormon power.

If the governors were faineants, the courts unable to move, and
political action premature, life in the Territory continued to display
unmitigated antagonism. On April 2, 1866, occurred the murder
of Newton Brassfield, a Gentile who had recently moved to Utah
from Nevada. Brassfield, it seems, had had the temerity to marry
the polygamous wife of a Mormon elder during the latter's absence
on a foreign mission. His murder was promptly ascribed to the
Church by the friends of the victim.[62] News of this and of other

---

[60] *Vedette*, February 5, 1867.

[61] *House Miscellaneous Documents, 40th Congress, Second Session, No.
135; House Report No. 79*, pp. 6–40. Cf. Charles B. Waite, *Argument before
the Committee on Elections, House of Representatives, March 25–27, 1868,
in the Case of William McGroarty v. William H. Hooper* (n. p., 1868),
32 pp.

[62] *Vedette*, April 4, 1866. "It would be useless to deny the fact that in
the opinion of the Gentile community of this city, the killing of Mr. Brassfield was a deliberately planned scheme, concocted and advised by men high
in authority in the Mormon Church. It is a reminder of the days that were,
and a foretaste of what will be again, 'when the troops are removed.' The
community is struck dumb by the appalling audacity of the affair." Justice

alleged Mormon atrocities drew from General Sherman, in command of the Department of the Missouri, the following message to President Young:

> Sir: A telegram comes to me from four responsible officers that four men styled "Gentiles" have been murdered by the Mormons, and that there is apprehension of further danger from this class. By Gentiles I understand American citizens not of your religious belief. I am bound to give protection to all citizens, regardless of religious faith and shall do so. These murderers must be punished, and if your people resort to measures of intimidation they must cease. . . . I know little or nothing of the causes of local trouble in Utah, but it is well for you to know that our country is now full of tried and experienced soldiers who would be pleased at a fair opportunity to avenge any wrongs you may commit against any of our citizens, even in that remote region. I will soon have regular troops in Utah and on the road leading there, when I hope to receive reports on which to base accurate opinions; and I send you this message, not as a threat, but as a caution that a sensible man should heed.[63]

Though Young was prompt to reply that the suggested charges were untrue and that Gentiles were perfectly safe in Utah,[64] troops of the regular army were dispatched to Camp Douglas to replace the California Volunteers, who were mustered out of service in July, 1866,[65] and Connor was brevetted Major General. This move, however, was not wholly displeasing to the Mormon leader, who wrote, August 11, to his sons, Brigham, Jr., and John W. Young, in Liverpool:

McCurdy, a few days before the murder, had granted to Brassfield custody of his wife's children by her polygamous union.

Following the incident, on April 8, McCurdy telegraphed General Connor, then in New York City: "I married O. N. Brassfield to a Mormon woman on the 28th ultimo. Brassfield was assassinated on the night of the 3rd instant. I have been denounced and threatened publicly. Government officials have telegraphed the Secretary of War to retain troops here until others are sent to relieve them. Call on Secretary of War to learn his conclusions. I feel unsafe in person and property without protection." *Vedette,* January 25, 1867.

[63] *Missouri Republican* (St. Louis), May 14, 1866.

[64] Stenhouse, *Rocky Mountain Saints,* p. 616.

[65] *Vedette,* July 20, 1866.

We have but few troops here at present, and they are regulars. Connor is out of the service, and is here now as plain "Pat," engaged in mining business, which, as Government pap has been withdrawn, will very likely, if he pursues it diligently, break him up financially. Col. Smith (commanding officer at the Fort) still continues friendly. We have had quite an influx of lawyers into the city of late. Like the birds of prey they snuff the carcass from afar. Business is poor where they have been; but they imagine that with the land claims and other business the enemies of truth promise them here they will reap an abundant harvest. Armies have not been found to operate well in breaking us up, but it is now hoped that vexatious law-suits, and setting up and enforcing claims for our land, may do it. . . .[66]

It would be interesting to know if Young, in referring to these land squabbles, specifically had in mind the case of Dr. King Robinson, who had come to Utah as an assistant surgeon of the Volunteers, settled in Salt Lake City, and married an apostate Mormon. As an active supporter of McLeod, he had assisted in the conduct of the Sunday School, obnoxious to the Church as a snare to entice young Mormons from their allegiance. His principal contention, however, was with the civic authorities. Robinson laid claim to property near the city containing natural sulphur springs, with the object, seemingly, of building a health resort. He was summarily ejected and his improvements, such as they were, confiscated. Suit in the district court, presided over by Justice Titus, failed to vindicate his claim. In October, moreover, the city moved the abatement of an amusement hall of which Robinson was a partial owner. Exasperated, the physician-realtor loudly proclaimed his determination to secure justice. But on the night of October 22, responding to a supposed professional call, he was murdered on one of the main streets of the city.[67] The Gentiles were convinced that the deed was perpetrated by direct command of the ecclesiastical power, a conviction strengthened by subsequent less serious outrages against other Gentile "squatters."[68] The inquest,

---

[66] *Millennial Star*, XXVIII, September 22, 1866.

[67] Linn, *op. cit.*, pp. 554–556; Whitney, *op. cit.*, II, 151–164.

[68] *Vedette*, October 24, 1866. "It would be sheerest hypocrisy to attempt to disguise that this outrage has not merely cast a gloom, but a thrill of horror and a deep, outspoken feeling of distrust and insecurity among the

held intermittently until November 6, was unsuccessful in furnishing grounds for indictment, though the prosecutor felt justified in
accusing the city police of dilatory action, with the broad suggestion that they were shielding the guilty parties.   The opposing
counsel, on the other hand, declared that the jury, dominantly Gentile, would refuse to entertain the consideration of any alleged
accomplices in the case who were not Mormons.[69]

Reflecting the perturbed Gentile view, General W. B. Hazen,
who was in the city during the episode, reported to Congressman
John Bidwell of California, member of the House Committee on
Territories in regard to this and other other atrocities:

> There is no doubt of their murder from Mormon
> Church influences, although I do not believe by direct
> command.   Principles are taught in their churches which
> would lead to such murders.   I have earnestly to recom-
> mend that a list be made of the Mormon leaders, accord-
> ing to their importance, excepting Brigham Young, and
> that the President of the United States require the com-
> manding officer at Camp Douglas to arrest and send
> to the States' prison at Jefferson City, Missouri, begin-
> ning at the head of the list, man for man hereafter killed
> as these men were, to be held until the real perpetrators
> . . . be given up.   I believe Young, for the present, nec-
> essary for us there.[70]

---

entire so-called Gentile part of the community.   When such a man as Dr.
Robinson, who is believed to have had no personal enemy in the country,
can be coldly and murderously waylaid and shot down by a band of assassins,
what citizen can avoid the feeling that his turn may come next?

". . . Will the Government stand idle until our streets run with blood?"

[69] Text in Stenhouse, *op. cit.*, appendix I, and in Whitney, *op. cit.*,
pp. 154–162.   It seems that John B. Weller, former governor of California,
who led the investigation, was actuated by a determination to fix the crime
on the Mormons as a body.   His presentation, if correctly reported, makes
strange reading.

[70] *House Misc. Doc., 75, 39th Cong. 2nd Sess.*, p. 4.   Concerning Connor's
actions in Utah, Hazen reported: "General Connor, who commanded there
during the war, I think, treated Mormonism too harshly, due probably to
his zeal as a Catholic; yet he exercised a strong influence against Mormonism,
and was a true man in the interests of the government, and any clamor or
charges made against him for corruption there, I believe to have had their
origin with Mormon leaders . . . to counteract his influence."   The *Vedette*,
April 8, 1867, scouted the idea that Connor acted as a "zealot or a sectarian
bigot."

The report stressed the demoralizing effect Mormonism was exercising on the Gentiles. Earlier in the autumn, indeed, many of the wealthier non-Mormons had taken advantage of the departure of Buckmaster and Alexander's train starting for the Missouri, to send their wives and daughters home for the season, to "a purer atmosphere where the sacred name of woman is honored and reverenced as it deserves and where she is not compelled to hear the base propositions of lecherous, grey-haired sinners, for their Saintly delectation and her debasement." [71]

The Robinson murder, whatever its inspiration, was coincidental with a renewed effort on the part of the Mormon leaders to preach the policy of non-intercourse with the Gentile. In later years the complaint would be made that the Saints had pre-empted all the available farming land, to the evident disadvantage of the non-Mormon settler; in the sixties, however, that phase was of minor interest. The economics of the quarrel centered around the Gentile merchant and miner. Non-intercourse, if rigidly enforced, spelled ruin for the traders along East Temple Street in Salt Lake and at whatever other points in the Territory they had established themselves. That the Mormon authorities at this time could no longer command complete and unquestioning obedience to "counsel" is evidenced by the fact that the majority of the Gentile merchants survived the storm; but the immediate effects, the curtailment of their trade and the reduction of their margin of profit, caused loud complaints. Finally, a group of these merchants in the capital city drew up a remonstrance to the heads of the Church:

> Gentlemen: As you are instructing your people of Utah, through your bishops and missionaries, not to trade or do any business with the Gentile merchants, thereby intimidating and coercing the community to purchase only of such merchants as belong to your faith or persuasion; therefore, in anticipation of such a crisis being successfully brought about by your teachings, the undersigned, Gentile merchants of Great Salt Lake City, respectfully desire to make you the following propositions, believing it to be your earnest desire for all to leave the country that do not belong to your creed or faith, namely:
> On the fulfillment of the conditions herein named,

---

[71] *Vedette,* September 24, 1866.

first—the payment of our outstanding accounts owing by
members of your Church.

Secondly—All of our goods, merchandise, chattels,
houses, improvements, etc., to be taken at a cash valuation, and we to make a deduction of 25% from total
amount.

To the fulfillment of the above, we hold ourselves
ready, at any time, to enter into negotiations, and on final
arrangements being made and terms of sale complied
with, we shall freely leave the Territory.[72]

It is a little difficult to believe that the note was meant to be
taken seriously, but at all events, it gave Brigham Young the opportunity, which he promptly seized, for a crushing reply:

Gentlemen: Your communication of December 20th,
addressed to the "leaders of the Mormon Church," was
received by me last evening. In reply, I have to say that
we will not obligate ourselves to collect your outstanding
debts, nor buy your goods, merchandise, and other articles, that you express yourselves willing to sell. If you
could make such sales as you propose, you would make
more money than any merchants have ever done in this
country, and we, as merchants, would like to find pur-
chasers upon the same basis. Your withdrawal from the
Territory is not a matter about which we feel any anxiety; so far as we are concerned you are at liberty to stay
or go as you please. . . . What we are doing . . . we
are willing that all the world should know. In the first
place, we wish you to distinctly understand that we have
not sought to ostracize any man or body of men because
of their not being of our faith. The wealth that has been
accumulated in this Territory from the earliest years of
our settlement by men who were not connected with us
religiously, and the success which has attended their business operations, prove this. . . .

There is a class, however, who are doing business in
the Territory, who, for years, have been the avowed enemies of this community. They have . . . put into circulation the foulest slanders. . . . Missionaries of evil,
there have been no arts too base, no stratagems too vile
for them to use to bring about their nefarious ends. . . .
They have donated liberally to sustain a corrupt and venal
press, which has given publicity to the most atrocious
libels concerning the old citizens. . . .

[72] *Vedette*, December 21, 1866. The letter was dated December 20.

What claims can such persons have upon the patronage of the community? . . . Have we not the right to
trade at whatever store we please? Or does the Constitution of the United States bind us to enter the stores of
our deadliest enemies, and purchase of them? . . .
I have much more to say upon this subject.[73]

The Lion of the Lord did not confine himself to rhetoric.
Rather, he turned his attention to the development of a plan of
co-operative buying and selling among the Saints, which, had it
been inaugurated at an earlier date, might well have insured
Mormon exclusiveness for years to come. In 1868, the day was
too far spent; too many of his own people had already adopted a
veneer of sophistication. The transcontinental railroad was
within sight of completion. With Utah linked to civilization, both
east and west, mining would dominate local economy, and mining
was in the hands of the Gentiles. The handful of "outsiders"
would become a force to be reckoned with seriously; the temper of
the times would change, for better or for worse. The co-operative
enterprise, preached by the Mormon Church organ, the *Deseret
News,* during the autumn of 1868, and suggested in a general way
by Young at the October Conference in Salt Lake City, was clearly
designed as a last stand against the Gentile peril.[74]

On October 16, a paper organization was formed with Young
as president, and a subscription office was opened.[75] Immediately
the plan encountered opposition, not merely from the excluded
Gentile merchants, but from Mormons themselves whose business
had prospered under the policy of non-intercourse. Nevertheless,
inspired by the success of a co-operative set up in Provo, second city
of the Territory, Zion's Co-operative Mercantile Institution

---

[73] *Salt Lake Daily Telegraph,* December 21, 1866. On December 29,
1866, the *Vedette* noted developments: "At the Tabernacle last Sunday
Brigham Young re-enunciated from the stand his determination that the
Mormons should not only keep aloof from unsaintly associations, but must
withdraw their patronage from the Gentiles. This doctrine . . . is taught
through the press and enforced from the pulpit. Nor . . . is it confined
to this city—where Gentiles most do congregate—but from one end of the
Territory to the other has the fiat gone forth, and bishops, elders, deacons,
and teachers . . . are engaged in the work of proscription."

[74] Daines, "Separatism," *loc. cit.,* pp. 342–343.

[75] "Zion's Cooperative Mercantile Institution" (Bancroft MS), p. 1.

opened its doors on March 1, 1869. Theoretically, every member of the Church was entitled to become a stockholder, with shares selling at $100 par.[76] In actual practice, however, the subscription list was never widespread, and in later years the project degenerated into a typical joint-stock corporation, nominally under Church control. At the beginning, however, the institution, with its branches in the larger Mormon communities of Utah and Idaho, enlisted a degree of loyal support and infectious enthusiasm.[77] But for the advent of the railroad, the Gentile tradesmen of necessity would have been forced to sell out at any sacrifice and leave. As for the disgruntled Mormon business men, a small number, prominent among whom were the Walker brothers, early commission agents, left the Church. According to the manuscript account preserved in the Bancroft collection:

> . . . Walker Bros. had refused to pay tithings before, but were willing to donate such amounts as we saw fit to the poor. We refused to recognize the rights of the Church to colect [sic] tithings from anybody.

[76] Ibid., p. 2.

[77] "Utah Biographical Sketches" (Bancroft MS), 188–, p. 52. "Account of Fred T. Kiesel, of Ogden."

"I worked for Gilbert and Sons for four years in Soda Springs, Idaho and opened the first store in Wellsville, Cache County, Utah, 1864. Gilbert and Sons were under a cloud with the Church authorities, and I opened it in my own name. . . . The co-op store then started and I was driven out again. Apostle Rich produced a letter from Brigham Young telling people that I was an enemy to them and a pupil of Gilbert and Sons.

"It was the despotism of Brigham Young that nearly drove all the Gentile firms out of the Territory, or broke them up in business. That was the case until 1871 when the mining commenced, and of course it was the salvation of us out here."

In the same account, Kiesel lays the murder of one of his clerks to Mormon influence. "They said the Indians did it, but it was inside a settlement. I would have trusted myself with the Indians in those days quicker than with the Mormons."

"Account of Frederick H. Auerbach, of Salt Lake City," p. 9.

"Our business gradually increased until 1868, when the institution known as Zion's Co-operative Mercantile Institution was started, which for a time seemed to threaten our existence here as merchants, and had it not been for the discovery of minerals here, and the steady development of the mining industry it would certainly have proved unprofitable for us to stay here in this Territory. . . . We have abstained from interference in the political status . . . having come here as merchants and not as missionaries."

About this time the Co-ops were started, Brigham and other church dignitaries saw an opportunity to cast us out by these means and went so far as to embody it in their sermons and to run down all Gentile merchants and Walker Bros. in particular. Cutting down the sales from $50,000 to $5,000 per month and putting secret police in front of store to frighten the Mormon trade away from us and intimidate them. . . . We then determined for self-preservation to retail at such figures as the Co-op wholesaled so as to make the dollar overcome the power of church influence. We offered together with other merchants to take 5 cents on the cost of $1.00 Real Estate . . . and leave the Territory . . . which was flatly refused thinking perhaps they would be able to crush us.[78]

Others of the same group joined the "Godbeite Schism," so-called after William S. Godbe, an English convert to Mormonism who owned a large drug establishment in Salt Lake City. In 1884, at the request of H. H. Bancroft, he wrote:

Finding my business in the mercantile direction virtually closed upon me, I was compelled to seek for a new field . . . and so determined to start in mining . . . a year or two after I was excommunicated.
You see, it was said by the people there that "in ninety days," to use their terse if not elegant phraseology—they said that "in ninety days there wouldn't be a grease spot left of me," and to carry out that prediction the Zion drug store was started and I found the competition altogether too severe for me and was forced to close.[79]

But Godbe's first impulse, in 1869, was to "reform" the Church from within, rather than to break with it. Associating with himself a group that for various reasons found itself at loggerheads with the politicians of the controlling faction, including such men as Amasa Lyman, apostle of the Church, T. B. Stenhouse, editor of the pro-Mormon *Daily Telegraph,* and E. L. T. Harrison, an able publicist, he launched the "New Movement," of which advance notice was given through the columns of the *Utah Magazine,* which they founded and supported.[80] Therein, a reversal of the

---

[78] "Merchants and Miners in Utah" (Bancroft MS), 1884.

[79] "Statement of William S. Godbe, September 2, 1884" (Bancroft MS).

[80] Alter, *op. cit.,* pp. 352–362. A letter in the first issue of the *Mormon Tribune,* January 1, 1870, states:

Mormon attitude toward mining and trading was advocated, and covert criticism of Young's infallibility found expression. On October 25, 1869, the ringleaders of the movement were excommunicated.[81] As announced in the official Church organ:

> The *Utah Magazine* is a periodical that in its spirit and teachings is directly opposed to the work of God. Instead of building up Zion and uniting the people, its teachings, if carried out, would destroy Zion, divide the people asunder, and drive the Holy Priesthood from the earth. Therefore, we say to our brethren and sisters in every place, the Utah Magazine is not a periodical suitable for circulation among or perusal by them, and should not be sustained by the Latter-day Saints.[82]

As an attempt to reform the policies of the Church, the movement proved a complete failure. For a time, meetings of the schismatic "branch" were held in Independence Hall, and Godbe, something of a mystic, claimed the sanction of divine revelation for his teachings; but he found few to recognize their authenticity, and indeed, was himself much more interested in acquiring a fortune in speculative mining.[83] Some of the Godbeites eventually returned to the bosom of the Church; others identified themselves with the fortunes of the Liberal party and the Gentile cause. Out of the *Utah Magazine* emerged the *Mormon Tribune,* which, in turn, by

---

". . . Brother Godbe was not influenced to his course by the love of money. . . . In obedience to what he believed to be the will of Heaven, he has, as one of the publishers of the Utah Magazine, sunk over $10,000 in sustaining that periodical for the sole benefit of the people of this Territory."

[81] Baskin, *Reminiscences,* pp. 80–81. Whitney, *op. cit.,* II, 332–333.

"Brigham Young did his utmost to prevent mining, and I advocated the cause of mining interests in the Territory in an article which was published in a magizine [*sic*] in Salt Lake City and Brigham Young was very much incensed at its production and sent for us to appear before them and we were excommunicated. . . . Brigham Young . . . said on one occasion in public that he wanted to make a wall so thick and so high around the Territory that it would be impossible for the Gentiles to get over or through it." "Statement of William S. Godbe" (Bancroft MS), September, 1884.

See also statement by H. W. Lawrence, a member of the group, in the *Salt Lake Tribune,* January 8, 1887.

[82] *Deseret News,* October 26, 1869.

[83] Linn, *Story of the Mormons,* pp. 564–566; Stenhouse, *Rocky Mountain Saints,* p. 631.

1871, became the *Daily Tribune,* the anti-Mormon organ *par excellence* of the succeeding decades.

At Promontory Point, fifty-three miles west of Ogden, Utah, on May 10, 1869, the "golden spike" was hammered home. The transcontinental railroad linking East and West had been completed. The effect upon Gentile Utah was instantaneous. Mining, the lodestar for thousands, could now be operated profitably. The Little Cottonwood District was soon alive with activity, with shipments of ore being sent via San Francisco to the refineries at Swansea, Wales.[84] Further discoveries were in the offing, and Utah was soon to become known as one of the richest silver producing regions of the West. A sharp rise in the proportion of Gentiles to Mormons was inevitable, with the importation of Cornish and Irish mine labor and the increase in the number of men engaged in merchandising and transportation. The day longed for by the *Vedette* had come at last:

> We have before said that Utah is most deeply interested in the early completion of the Pacific Railroad. When the iron horse shall reach her metropolis, . . . it will bring her renewed prosperity and increasing wealth. But above this, the hope is confidently indulged that it will prove the potent lever to upturn the incubus which rests like a nightmare upon her highest interests. If Mormonism can withstand the assaults of intelligence, contact with the world, the friction of civilization, and the influence of daily and rapid commerce, we are content.
>
> The test of its truth and sincerity must come at an early day. . . . Its isolation, hitherto and still barring out discussion and fair play, and independence of thought and action, under the "counsel" of men whose word has more than the validity and potency of the laws of the Medes and Persians, has alone rendered possible the state of affairs now existing in Utah.[85]

The conflict, Governor Harding had remarked six years before, echoing a phrase that had done yeoman service, was irrepressible. The inauguration of President Grant, March 4, 1869, was heavy

---

[84] Wallace, "Early History of Lead Smelting in the West," *loc. cit.,* p. 7. The charge for transportation per ton from Ogden to San Francisco, on the Central Pacific, was $32.50.

[85] *Vedette,* January 22, 1867.

with significance for Utah.   With Vice-President Colfax at his
elbow and with Dr. John Philip Newman, pastor of the Metro-
politan Methodist Episcopal Church of Washington, D. C., as his
spiritual guide, the victor of Appomatox was ready to deal with
the Mormon problem according to the limited lights by which he
lived.

CHAPTER III

DANIEL IN THE LION'S DEN

IN THE spring of 1870, Salt Lake City wore the expectant air of a boom town. So it seemed, at least, to Joseph Rosborough, a Carolinian who had joined the gold rush to California twenty years before, had followed fortune to the Idaho mines in 1864, and now for the first time, gazed upon the fabled city of the Saints.

> It struck me as the liveliest mining camp I ever saw, looking at the number of wagons. There were about two miles of wagons coming in every day with ore and bullion. . . . The Emma mine and some other mines contiguous were putting out great quantities of ore. That was the great period for the Emma.[1]

It was into the development of this mine that the Walker brothers and their associates, following their difficulties with the Mormon Church, had flung their capital, convinced "that to save this Territory for all coming people it was necessary to ascertain the presence of mineral in paying quantities." Hence "starting with a quarter interest . . . for which we paid $30,000 and furnished the necessary coin and stuff to open up the mine," they began operations, built the camp of Alta, and were soon riding the wave of success:

> Notwithstanding Brigham Young's prophesy [sic] that there would be no ore come out of the mines to pay, we had at the first American celebration of the 4 July in this Territory numerous teams loaded with ore and bullion and devices such as Zion's Redeemer met with the greatest enthusiasm as they passed by Brigham Young's residence.[2]

---

[1] "Utah Biographical Sketches" (Bancroft MS, 188–), p. 17.

[2] "Merchants and Miners in Utah" (Bancroft MS, 1884). See also *Report of the Utah Commission for the year 1887* (Washington, 1887), p. 9. The Walker family sold out their interests in the mine to "New York Capi-

Bonanza ore was struck at the Emma in the fall of 1869, and within two years, the Walkers shipped ten thousand tons to Liverpool where it sold at a cash price of thirty-six pounds sterling per ton of ore.[3]

In quick succession other mines in the Little Cottonwood district began to pay rich dividends. The population of the mining camp swelled to fifteen hundred; in 1874 it was credited by the *Gazeteer [sic] of Utah* with fifteen saloons and a shooting gallery. Of religious life there was little, according to the local correspondent of the *Daily Utah Mining Journal* who wrote that, "If some minister of the Gospel, of the Methodist, Baptist, or Quaker persuasion would give us a call and speak us a piece about the sins of others, we will try to make it interesting for him."[4]

The older "West Mountain Mining District," first explored and staked by Connor and his men, quickly responded to this new life. The first claim in the Ophir region, not far from the village of Stockton, was filed August 23, 1870, by one William Tecumseh Barbee, who was further distinguished by the title of Judge. Mercur, a camp in the same area, was founded in the same year; promising strikes soon gave it the name "Johannesburg of America." Bingham Canyon, by 1872, was reputed to have produced $1,000,000 in gold. The first ore shipments from the Territory had been made from that point in 1868 by the Walkers, who had hauled it to the railhead at Uintah, Utah, shipping it from there to Baltimore. To the east of Salt Lake City ore was discovered in a mountain valley called Parley's Park. Rufus Walker staked a claim there in 1869, though the actual development of the region, still one of the richest silver-producing districts of the United States, was

talists" in the spring of 1871, the sale price being $1,500,000 (Justice C. J. Hawley to Lyman Trumbull, Department of Justice MSS, April 12, 1871). Shortly thereafter, operation became unprofitable, but the gentlemen of New York succeeded in transferring their leases to England, incidentally involving Minister Robert Schenck in the transaction. Godbe (Bancroft MS) rather quaintly remarks: "The Emma mine . . . did immensely well, although the English people were somewhat hurt by it."

[3] Robert Wallace, "Early History of Lead Smelting in the West," *Ax-I-Dent-Ax*, XIV, No. 5, May 1929, 7.

[4] J. Cecil Alter, *Early Utah Journalism* (Salt Lake City, 1938), p. 17; Edward L. Sloan, ed., *Gazeteer of Utah and Salt Lake City Directory* (Salt Lake City, 1874), p. 113; *Utah Mining Journal,* July 11, 1872.

delayed for several years because of the difficulties of road-building through the canyons.[5]

Mining operations in the southern reaches of the Territory followed within a few years. Bonanza City, later christened Silver Reef, was founded in 1875, near the Mormon settlement of St. George in the southwest corner of Utah, on the strength of claims located there by Judge Barbee.[6] To the Salt Lake *Tribune* he wrote, December 13, 1875:

> This is the most unfavorable looking country for mines that I have ever seen in my varied mining experience, but as the mines are here, what are the rock sharps going to do about it? . . . They [the Mormons] have a hard time serving the Lord in this desolate, god-forsaken looking country, and it is about time for something to turn up to take the place of sorghum and wine as a circulating medium.

For a decade, Silver Reef made mining history, then sank a ghost town into the desert sands.

Though the Gentiles controlled the mines, it was Mormon enterprise that pushed the construction of intra-state rail communications. The Utah Central, connecting the capital city with the main transcontinental line at Ogden, was completed on January 10, 1870, President Young driving the last spike as the climax of a civic celebration.[7] Subsequently, lines were extended south to

---

[5] Edgar M. Ledyard, "Early Mining and Smelting South of Salt Lake," *Ax-I-Dent-Ax*, May 1931, pp. 3 ff., 9; John Mason Boutwell, *Geology and Ore Deposits of the Park City District, Utah* (Washington, D. C., 1912), p. 19; T. J. Almy, "History of the Ontario Mine, Park City, Utah," *Transactions of the American Institute of Mining Engineers*, XVI, 35; Ovando J. Hollister, "Gold and Silver Mining in Utah," *loc. cit.*, XVI, 13. Boutwell quotes from a letter received from Rector Steen, an early miner in the Park City area, December 10, 1902: "Parley's Park . . . was a very pretty valley with several shanties scattered over it; and several springs were in the valley. . . . There was not a house near the mine when we were there. All lived in tents and brush shanties, and very few of them."

[6] Mark A. Pendleton, "Memories of Silver Reef," *Utah Historical Quarterly*, III, No. 4, 99–118.

[7] Whitney, *History of Utah*, II, 262–264. "President Young used . . . a large, elegantly chased steel mallet. . . . Engraved upon the top of the tool was the emblematic beehive, surmounted by the inscription 'Holiness to the Lord'. . . ."

Provo, with branches running up the mouth of Little Cottonwood, tapping the Alta mines, and to Bingham Canyon; west to Stockton; north to Brigham City and Corinne. At convenient junction points smelting furnaces were erected. The scientific application of chemical principles to metallurgy by a German technician, Anton Eilers, who came to Utah in 1876, made it possible to improve and increase the output.[8] By 1878, Governor Emery could report to Secretary Carl Schurz that "profitable mining is no longer an experiment here," and could point to a total annual profit to the producers of seven or eight million dollars to endorse his statement.[9]

All this spelled increase in the Gentile population. Yet, rich as the Utah mines proved, the other part of Connor's forecast, that the Mormons would quickly be outnumbered, failed to materialize. Though the Gentiles were counted by hundreds in 1869 and by thousands in 1878, Emery, in the report cited, could only write them down as constituting one-tenth of the entire population:

> It may be proper in this connection to say that agricultural pursuits here are carried on almost exclusively by Mormons, and, on the other hand, the mining enterprises of the Territory are almost entirely conducted by anti-Mormons. . . .
> Probably three-fourths of the population is foreign-born or of foreign parentage. . . . From the best information I have on the subject, nine-tenths of the people here are Mormons.[10]

Even so, their relative growth imparted to the Gentiles a feeling of strength and solidarity. Outside of the mercantile group in Salt

---

[8] Wallace, *loc. cit.*, pp. 7 ff., 12: "Nothing remains except the Mingo slag dump to suggest that Sandy, now the quiet town of homes . . . was once the greatest shipping, smelting, and sampling point in Utah. . . . But if the oldest resident could bring before our imagination the phantoms of the past, we might see the early English-owned furnaces, where all the smeltermen were Welsh and Irish."

[9] *Report of the Governor of Utah Made to the Secretary of the Interior for the Year 1878* (Washington, D. C., 1878), *passim*.

[10] *Loc. cit.*, p. 3. Governor Eli H. Murray, in the *Report* for 1880 (p. 5), remarked: "The population of Utah is far beyond that of any Territory in the history of the United States. In 1870 the population was 86,786. In 1880 it is shown to be 145,000, an increase of over 58,000 souls. The mines of the Territory, with their attendant business, have drawn, I may safely say, of this . . . increase, fifty per cent."

Lake City, reinforced, as time went on, by bankers and commercial agents, there were several communities that boasted an alert non-Mormon minority. Indeed, one town, Corinne, northwest of Ogden, gave promise of becoming the "Gentile Capital." Founded in 1869 as a railroad construction camp, hopes were entertained that it would continue as the junction point for transcontinental and state traffic. The superior location of the Mormon village of Ogden, as the event proved, countered the claims of the Gentile settlers of Corinne. For a few years, however, the town controlled freight routes to the Idaho and Montana mines. But as the decade of the seventies wore away, its doom became increasingly evident. In its brief hey-day, Corinne played a leading role in local history. A center of Protestant activity, it rejoiced in the fact that no Mormon meeting house could be found within its limits. There, on February 9, 1870, the Liberal party was formally organized. Though its population never reached a thousand, and by 1880 had declined to two hundred and seventy-two, journalism flourished and anti-Mormon editors gave free rein to their favorite pastime of ridiculing the Saints.[11]

The mining camps, naturally, were almost wholly Gentile in complexion, but the transient character of the inhabitants, as well as their isolation in the mountains, prevented them from figuring with the prominence in political controversies that their numbers warranted.

Inevitably, friction between miners and the agricultural Mormons grew more irritating as time went on. The swashbuckling, lawless life of the camps was looked upon with dour disfavor by the Church authorities, who saw therein the snares of Satan laid for their people. They agreed with Apostle George Albert Smith who warned the apostates, Godbe and Harrison, that if they per-

---

[11] Tuttle, *Reminiscences*, p. 106. "It was thought that Corinne would speedily absorb into itself all the non-Mormon population and business of the Territory. The large mercantile firms of Salt Lake, such as the Walker Brothers, opened branch houses in Corinne, in preparation for the future transfer of all their business"; Baskin, *Reminiscences*, p. 23; S. A. Kenner, *Utah As It Is* (Salt Lake City, 1904), p. 127; Alter, *op. cit.*, pp. 50–63. *Cf.* Phil Robinson, *Sinners and Saints* (Boston, 1883), pp. 269–270. Robinson visited Corinne in 1880, and found it a dismal place, "A Gentile failure on the very skirts of Mormon success."

sisted in their course, "they would bring all hell here." [12]   And, indeed, the young Mormon was in danger.   One of them later described his own reactions:

> To a boy from a quiet village, Silver Reef, with its
> brightly lighted saloons and stores and ceaseless activity,
> was a never ending delight.   Peddlers and freighters were
> constantly coming and going.   Wagons loaded with ore
> and others loaded with cord-wood were ever on the move
> to the mills where the stamps pounded the ore to powder.
> Hundreds of miners were on the trails mornings and eve-
> nings on their way to or from the mines. . . .   These
> men, Americans, Cornishmen, Irishmen, fine specimens
> of manhood, after ten hours of toil in the mines, emerged
> from their cabins dressed in the best that money could
> buy and walked the streets with the air of kings.   China-
> town, with its queer inhabitants and strange tongue, its
> unusual merchandise and Oriental coloring, was a source
> of wonder. . . .[13]

As a policy, however, non-intercourse could not be maintained after 1870.   Its preachment, once the dismay of the Gentile merchant, became rather a subject for recrimination.   Thus, the *Tribune*, May 16, 1874, reflected upon this change:

> We have the statement of a gentleman who spends
> many thousands of dollars monthly in paying the wages
> of Mormon laborers, teamsters and mechanics in one of
> our mines, that arrangements are perfected for the sub-
> stitution of Gentile labor in their stead, and that proprie-
> tors and superintendents in all the camps are determined
> to assist the Prophet in carrying out his plan of non-
> intercourse. . . .
> The non-employment of Mormon labor, and the fail-
> ure of the Gentiles to purchase from Mormon dealers for
> the next sixty days, would drive every Church merchant,
> including Zion's C. I. [Cooperative] into irretrievable
> bankruptcy. . . .   It is made a sin for a Latter-day Saint
> to trade with a Gentile; let it be deemed dishonorable in
> a Gentile to interfere with their new belief.

The shoe was on the other foot, the editor gloated, and the winning cards in the hands of the Gentiles.   The Mormons might

---

[12] *Salt Lake Tribune,* January 8, 1887 (letter from H. W. Lawrence).
[13] Pendleton, *loc. cit.,* p. 99.

still possess numerical advantage, but with the minority lay the wealth. A central theme of the Gentile publicists for a generation was the pressing need for a rectification of the balance of political power in the light of this distribution. If the mines paid the taxes, the Gentile mine-owners should have controlling voice in territorial affairs.

> We have now in this city [Salt Lake] a mixed popu-
> lation, and that influential part of it not belonging to the
> Mormon Church and owing no allegiance to its priesthood
> represent [sic] a vast bulk of the wealth of this Territory
> and the principal part of its commerce and enterprise.
> Our city authorities cannot too soon learn that hence-
> forth the public must be consulted rather than Mr.
> Young. . . . It is their duty to give to Mr. Young to
> understand that they shall in the future consult the public
> and not him, excepting in his legitimate capacity as one of
> our leading citizens. . . .[14]

Though the Mormon leaders were accused of receiving "tens of thousands of dollars in taxes and illegal license money from Gentile purses" and of battening on Gentile enterprise, "not a man of the Gentile persuasion is admitted to their legislative or municipal assemblies."

While the nub of the Utah question was polygamy, these aspects of the quarrel should not be overlooked. It is probably true to say that the bulk of Gentiles who came to Utah in the seventies were only incidentally interested in the moral issue. It was the old problem of a settled, agrarian people who found themselves pitted against an exploiting minority in control of the chief sources of wealth, a conflict duplicated in California during the days of '49 and in the Mexican Republic in more recent years. In the case under consideration it is difficult to distinguish the genuinely crusading zeal of a portion of the anti-Mormon group from the more pragmatic motives governing the majority of the same class. Mormon monopoly of the arable land, Mormon political domination, even the periodic success of Mormon co-operative ventures, were all factors making for bitterness and hatred.

In March, 1870, J. Wilson Shaffer, of Freeport, Illinois, came to Utah as the successor to Governor Durkee. During the War

---

[14] *Tribune,* August 2, 1872.

between the States Shaffer had served as chief-of-staff to General
Ben Butler at New Orleans, learning, it is conceivable, something
of the fine art of dictatorship from that distinguished exponent.
His appointment was said to have been due to intimacy with the
new secretary of war, John A. Rawlins. Whether, as legend states,
Shaffer entered upon his office with the declaration that "Never
after me, by God, shall it be said that Brigham Young is governor
of Utah" must be left for debunkers of Ethan Allen to decide.[15]
But there is no doubt that he reflected faithfully the determination
of Grant's first administration to crush disloyalty in Utah. From
Salt Lake City he wrote to Secretary of State Stuyvesant Fish
(April 1, 1870) :

> I have the honor to report that I arrived here on
> March 19th, and have delayed writing you in hopes I
> might have some information that would be of value to
> you. So far I have not, except to state the broad fact that
> the Mormons are supreme here. And unless something
> like the Cullom or the Cragin bill passes, the U. S. officers
> will be powerless. I will write you in a short time a state-
> ment of outrages perpetrated by the Mormons on the Gen-
> tiles. I am fully satisfied that this people are worse than
> their enemies ever charged. I of course speak of the lead-
> ers, but with a good strong law every trouble can be
> settled without the aid of a single soldier. I shall be as
> prudent and firm as possible in my administration of
> affairs.[16]

A week later, unburdening his soul to his friend Congressman
Cullom, he expressed his conviction that his office was "a mere
sinecure," and that of federal authority, only a "miserable skele-
ton" remained.

----

[15] Edward H. Anderson, "Territorial Governors of Utah—J. Wilson
Shaffer," *Improvement Era*, IV, No. 5, March, 1901, 321–325; Whitney, *op.
cit.*, II, 488 ff.

[16] Shaffer to Fish (N. A., State Department MSS, Utah Territorial
Papers, II, No. 679). The Cragin bill, submitted by the Chairman of the
Senate Committee on the Territories, December 13, 1867, proposed the
abolition of jury trials in polygamy cases. It was not considered until
December 21, 1869, and was then withdrawn in favor of Congressman
Shelby H. Cullom's bill. See *United States Public Documents, 41st Congress,
Senate Document 286.*

As affairs now stand, the oath which I have taken
to execute the laws is nothing more than a useless form,
a mockery, a farce. For without the enactment of a Statute containing the main features of the bill which you introduced on the subject of Utah, I am rendered powerless,
and the laws . . . may . . . be violated with impunity.
. . . It is hard to be nominally Governor of Utah, if
Brigham Young is permitted to exercise the powers of
lawgiver and autocrat of the Territory. As the leader of
the Mormon Church, he arrogates to himself power and
control of spiritual, temporal, and political affairs. In the
midst of this fair Republic is established a Theocracy, and
for twenty years has carried it on [sic] in insolent defiance
of the authority of the United States. . . . He claims to
be the infallible agent of God. . . . And, when practi-
cable, adroitly uses the forms of law in aid of his rule, but
when this cannot be done, he spurns to acknowledge the
supremacy of the Government in matters which run counter to his will, he laughs to scorn the idea of testing the
validity of the laws of Congress through the ordinary
channels of the courts, but refers the question to a court
not human, and whose decisions . . . are communicated
to him in visions and revelations.[17]

As for the assembly, Shaffer continued, it was composed of
Young's "most subservient instruments" ready always to do the
bidding of the Prophet. "The dominant party, while they constantly complain of persecution, are themselves most proscriptive
and intolerant." Murder, as witnessed by recent atrocities, has
been no stranger to their history. "It is a very significant fact that
among these numerous secret murders in no instance have the
perpetrators ever been detected and punished."

This succeeded in 1857 and since then it is the resort
on all occasions, and will continue to be so as long as a
temporizing policy is pursued. . . . But let that policy
which comports with the dignity and honor of the Nation
. . . be adopted. . . . Let no Federal officer remain here
who will not fearlessly and promptly cooperate in the assertion of his authority . . . and the conflict . . . will
soon end.

---

[17] Shaffer to Cullom, April 27, 1870 (N. A., State Department MSS,
Utah, No. 686).

If Congress fails to act, then woe betide! Like "Buchanan's imbecile efforts in 1857," Young would interpret it as a personal victory over the nation, the nation of which, "according to an accepted prophecy among the Saints, he is at no distant day to become the ruler." Application of the law, thought Shaffer, would work no real hardship upon the derelict polygamous wives. As things stood, they supported themselves while in polygamy, and once out of it, they could find suitable mates readily enough. "There is little danger, even in Utah, of having an overstock of women." Neither "knowing or in fact careing [*sic*] much whether it was in my province as Governor or not," Shaffer signed the letter. In due course, it reached the hands of Secretary Fish, who frigidly noted that it contained "interesting information." [18]

The death of his wife, early in the summer of 1870, was a blow to the governor. His own health was wretched. Yet as Shaffer wrote to President Grant July 7, he was "determined, as far as the law will support me, to clean this Augean Stable." [19] To effect that end, he caused the removal of Territorial Secretary Stephen S. Mann, who was in the good graces of the Theocracy by reason of his compliance, while acting governor, in signing a bill enfranchising women. [20]

Durkee had failed to exercise his appointive power over a number of offices reserved to the governor; these had been filled by popular election, and Shaffer moved to oust the illegal incumbents. If Congress would not pass the Cullom bill, he urged at least action that would enable the district courts to empanel their own juries. The problem of the probate courts, he informed Fish, cried out for solution. Territorial law provided for the selection of probate judges by the legislature, with confirmation by the executive.

> The Mormons would not trust the Governor to appoint, nor allow the people of their respective counties to select the Probate Judges, for the reason that it is necessary that these men should be abject tools in the hands of the head of the Church, they being clothed with almost

[18] Fish to Shaffer, May 9, 1870 (N. A., State Department, Domestic Letters, 1870, LXXXIV).

[19] Shaffer to Grant, July 7, 1870 (N. A., State Department MSS, Utah, II, No. 703).

[20] Bancroft, *Utah,* pp. 657–658.

unlimited power in their respective counties, consequently can execute any and all decrees emanating from Brigham Young. In addition . . . the Legislature have clothed them with concurrent jurisdiction with the Federal Courts.[21]

Particularly irritating was the power of the probate courts to designate polling places:

> Since the opening of the mines in the Territory, vast numbers of Gentiles (so-called) and Anti-Brighamites, have flocked into the mountains. (No orthodox Mormons are in the mines). These Judges have so arranged the voting places in all the mining counties, that miners, in order to vote, must travel from twenty to fifty miles. We are now running a Gentile candidate for Delegate to Congress, and our Territorial Central Committee have urged the Probate Judges to locate voting places to accommodate the miners, which they most positively decline to do. The result will be that not more than half the mining vote will be polled.[22]

Secretary Fish, however, was not prepared to interpose federal authority too hastily. After consultation with legal advisors of the State Department, he answered Shaffer in a way that must have caused that fiery veteran of the Butler regime in Louisiana acute annoyance:

> Some of the attributes of these courts are unusual and anomalous, but it is to be observed that in construing provisions for the self-government of an inchoate State, under our principles of administration, every intentment is to be made in favor of the powers of the local Legislature, and in restriction (if need be) of the residuary power which Congress may have retained, if it had thought proper to do so by distinct reservation or necessary implication. . . .[23]

Checkmated on this front, Shaffer cast about for other means of asserting his authority. One soon appeared. On August 16,

---

[21] Shaffer to Fish, July 22, 1870 (N. A., State Department MSS, Utah, II, No. 705).

[22] *Ibid.*, No. 706.

[23] Fish to Shaffer, August 2, 1870, *loc. cit.*, No. 709.

1870, Lieutenant-General Daniel S. Wells, commanding the Nauvoo
Legion, issued orders for a general muster of all the militia of the
Territory.   Apprized of this move, Shaffer hastened home from
California, where he was seeking relief from his physical ailments,
and published two proclamations, the first appointing Major-General Connor to command the territorial militia, the second prohibiting "all musters, drills or gatherings of militia . . . except by my
orders, or by the orders of the United States Marshal . . ." and
demanding the delivery of all military equipment to the new assistant adjutant-general, Colonel William M. Johns.[24]

Wells protested that such action would cause violation of the
congressional law calling for an annual report from territorial militias, to which Shaffer rejoined:

> I have the honor to acknowledge the receipt of your
> communication of yesterday, in which you sign yourself
> "Lieutenant-General commanding the militia of Utah Territory."   As the laws of the United States provide for but
> one Lieutenant-General, and as the incumbent of that
> office is the distinguished Philip H. Sheridan, I shall certainly be pardoned for recognizing no other.
>   In your communication you address me as "Commander-in-Chief of the militia of Utah Territory."   It is
> now twenty years since the act to organize this Territory
> was passed . . . and so far as I am informed, this is the
> first instance in which you, or any of your predecessors,
> in the pretended office which you assume to hold, have
> recognized the Governor to be, as the Organic Act makes
> him, the Commander-in-Chief.   My predecessors have
> been contemptuously ignored or boldly defied. . . .
>   . . . Mr. Wells, you know as well as I do, that the
> people of this Territory, most of whom were foreign-born
> . . . have been taught to regard certain private citizens
> here as superior in authority . . . to the Federal officials. . . .   Ever since my proclamation was issued, and
> on a public occasion, and in the presence of many thousands of his followers, Brigham Young, who claims to
> be, and is called "President," denounced the Federal officials . . . with bitter vehemence, and on a like occasion,
> about the same time, and in his (Young's) presence, one
> of his most conspicuous followers declared that Congress
> had no right whatever to pass an organic act for this Ter-

---

[24] Quoted in Whitney, op. cit., II, 497–498.   The proclamations were
issued September 15, 1870.

ritory; that such was a relic of colonial barbarism, and that not one of the Federal officials had any right to come to, or remain in, this Territory.

By the provisions of the Organic Act, the Governor is made commander-in-chief . . . and, sir, so long as I continue to hold that office, a force so important as that of the militia shall not be wielded or controlled in disregard of my authority. . . .[25]

General Wells penned an able reply, scoring several palpable hits, but to no avail.[26] The order stood, and as a result, the Nauvoo Legion was disrupted, it being a little too much to expect that Mormon volunteers would respond to commands issued by General Connor. Four days after he had written his letter to Wells, Shaffer died (October 31, 1870). Funeral services were conducted by the local Methodist minister with Masonic honors.[27]

In the meantime, an unfortunate incident served to exacerbate the popular distrust of the regular army forces stationed in Utah. During the summer of 1870 a small detachment had been sent from Camp Douglas to a site near Provo, some forty-five miles south of the capital, with the hardly veiled intention of keeping the outlying districts under closer surveillance. On the evening of September 22, a group of the enlisted men, following a wild party in a village tavern, got out of hand and committed acts of vandalism and of personal outrage upon several of the Mormon inhabitants, as they filled the air with threats against the lives of "Mountain Meadow Massacreers." [28] The *Deseret News* improved the shining hour: "So this is a sample of the moral force to be exerted over us by the troops which the government, on the recommendation of a ring of contemptible conspirators, has seen fit to station near our settlements." [29] Brigadier-General Philip R. de Trobriand, commanding at Camp Douglas, commenced a leisurely investigation, the pace of which failed to satisfy Governor Shaffer, anxious as he was to vindicate the good name of the federal government. Hence,

---

[25] Quoted in Whitney, *op. cit.*, pp. 500–501.

[26] *Ibid.*, pp. 501–503.

[27] The Reverend George M. Peirce, Methodist clergyman, began to conduct services in Salt Lake City in the spring of 1870. *World's Fair Ecclesiastical History of Utah* (Salt Lake City, 1896), p. 258.

[28] Whitney, *op. cit.*, pp. 505–519.

[29] September 24, 1870.

he wrote to de Trobriand, September 27, demanding immediate action, "If the United States soldiery cannot fulfill the high object they were sent here for, then, far better for the sake of the credit of the Nation and American justice we be let alone to ourselves." This letter Shaffer gave to the Mormon paper, probably to offset reflections on federal indifference.[30] De Trobriand, not unnaturally, resented this reflection on his course, and lost no time in informing the governor, and the world as well, through the Mormon press, that he was fully engaged in the prosecution of his duties. These, he declared, did not include the responsibility of keeping Shaffer posted "about what occurs in your Territory, when you shut deliberately your door and your ears to any common information which could disturb your sickly slumbers or interfere with your little private schemes." As for the governor's alternative, the commanding officer, who was reputed to be on excellent terms with the Mormons, was perfectly agreeable:

> That you be "left alone to yourselves" *you*, meaning of course, the people of this Territory, its Governor, its churches, its militia, its legislature, its judiciary, its municipality, etc., etc.,—would certainly be a great blessing to all, and I am happy to agree with you on that point. . . . Rest assured Sir, that in such a case we will all obey without hesitation or murmur, letting you alone to the full enjoyment of that popularity which so justly distinguishes your administration and surrounds your person in the Territory of Utah.[31]

How much of this was personal pique, how much conviction, may only be surmised. The upshot was that de Trobriand was relieved of command in October, and his place was taken by Colonel W. W. Morrow, an officer whose views on Mormonism were more acceptable to the federal coterie.[32]

---

[30] *Deseret News,* October 5, 1870.

[31] *Ibid.,* October 5, 1870.

[32] An interesting file on Camp Rawlins is preserved among the War Department papers of the National Archives. During the spring of 1871, Colonel Morrow was ordered to take command of the camp, and de Trobriand was re-assigned to Camp Douglas. This caused a storm of protest from the federal officials in Salt Lake, and General C. C. Augur, head of the Department of the Platte, wrote to Sherman, March 13, 1871, advising Morrow's retention in Salt Lake. "The Officials at Salt Lake object very

Shaffer's immediate successor was Vernon H. Vaughan, of Alabama, who had served for a short time as territorial secretary in place of Mann. Vaughan's rule was brief and unmarked by special friction.[33] On January 23, 1871, the senate confirmed the nomination of George L. Woods of Oregon. A Missourian by birth, Woods had drifted to the Northwest, where he had run a ferry in Idaho, dabbled in mining, and acquired a reputation as a politician in Oregon, of which State he held the governorship from 1866 to 1870.[34] It is an added reflection on the Grant administration that a man of such doubtful calibre should have been selected to preside over any territory, and especially over Utah where circumstances demanded probity and intelligence. Woods, though he painstakingly advertised his teaching of a Bible class in his spare moments,[35] was distinctly a carpetbagger. Yet in spite of evidence offered to show that he had acted, if not dishonestly, certainly with singular imprudence in lending his official position to the promotion of dubious mining ventures,[36] he was retained

---

seriously to de Trobriand, and if he returns to command there, I am certain of no end of trouble." Concerning Camp Rawlins, he wrote: "You are aware of the reasons which determined the establishment of a post at Provo. Since that time, however, a wonderful change has come over Utah. The opening of the mines has brought such increase to the gentile population, that it is now really the controlling element in that Territory, and from what I hear, there is no longer any necessity for a post at Provo. . . ." Governor Woods also wrote to Augur, requesting that Morrow remain, as did McKean and Strickland. McKean's letter, March 8, 1871, reads in part, ". . . Without attacking, or even naming any one, I may say that there was at least one commander of that Post [Douglas] who made himself very obnoxious, even offensive, to the friends of the Government in this City. Whether intentionally or not, he caused the disloyal leaders of this peculiar people to believe that his sympathies were with them and against us; and he gave us too much reason to think so, too." Morrow was left at Camp Douglas, but Camp Rawlins was abandoned by order of General Sheridan, July 21, 1871.

[33] Anderson, loc. cit., IV, No. 6, April, 1901, 401–402. Dean W. L. Harris numbered Mrs. Vaughan among the parishioners of St. Mary Magdalene's Church. Catholic Church in Utah (Salt Lake City, 1909), p. 284.

[34] Anderson, loc. cit., IV, No. 6, April, 1901, 402–405.

[35] Utah Mining Journal, August 3, 1872, and passim.

[36] On July 7, 1872, the Salt Lake Herald published an account of this transaction. It appears that Woods, while governor, acted as Utah manager of a "Mining Bureau" organized by one J. Berton, French vice-consul at Sacramento, California. On June 12, 1872, the London Times carried a

in office until his retirement, December 28, 1874. That he was whole-heartedly anti-Mormon was sufficient to insure for him the vocal support of the extremists in the Territory, even though an undercurrent of disgust with his methods on the part of the more temperate Gentiles was manifested from time to time. The *Tribune,* enthusiastically loyal to him, made reiterated appeals for Gentile unity, lamenting the apathy of the group as a whole.[37]

The chief interest of the years 1871–1875 centered in the determined effort of the federal officials and judiciary to enforce the Act of Congress of 1862, prohibiting polygamy in the territories. Chief Justice James B. McKean, commissioned June 17, 1870, arrived at his post in Salt Lake City shortly before the death of Governor Shaffer and became protagonist in this crusade. Born in Bennington, Vermont, McKean, son of a Methodist minister, regarded his mission to Utah in the light of a campaign to exterminate a moral evil that he considered a blight on the Christian conscience of the country. A leading Republican from the time of the organization of the party in New York State, his adopted home, he could recall the clarion call of the party platform of 1856 to root out not only slavery, but the "twin relic." Elected to Congress in 1858, he resigned in 1862, to raise the Seventy-Seventh New York Volunteers. As Colonel, he led the regiment in the Peninsular Campaign. Illness cut short his military career, and it was while he was practicing law in New York City that he received "the reward of a grateful party" in the Utah appointment.[38] Associate Justices Obed F. Strickland, of Michigan and Cyrus Hawley, of Illinois, commissioned April 5 and April 19,

---

letter written by Woods, advertising the bureau, and stating that its reports would be certified under his executive seal, an action which called forth severe criticism from the London *Investor's Guardian,* June 15, which made proper reflections on the Emma Mine case and Minister Schenck. Woods was summoned to Washington, July 5, 1872 (N. A., State Department, Domestic Letters, XCIV, 486), but apparently succeeded in allaying suspicion. Thomas Fitch, former congressman from Nevada and one of Brigham Young's attorneys, then wrote to Fish, August 8, (N. A., State Department MSS, Utah, II, No. 750) offering detailed proof of Woods' mining activities and his authorship of the letter to the *Times.*

[37] As late as January 10, 1890, chronicling the death of Woods, the *Tribune* paid tribute to his ". . . strength, courage and ability."

[38] William Alexander Linn, *Story of the Mormons* (New York, 1902), p. 567; Whitney, *op. cit.,* II, 543 ff.

for us by legislation, or if in some way we do not get help from Washington, the time is near at hand when we shall be so helpless—so powerless for good, that perhaps the only honorable thing left for us to do will be to tender to your Excellency our resignations.[42]

Attorney General Akerman, to whom the letter was referred, showed it to Territorial Delegate Hooper, from whom certainly no aid was forthcoming. Hooper wrote, March 4, 1871, "Without exception, so far as I am advised, it has been the uniform rule in all our Territories . . . that officers of the Territorial courts other than the United States Judges, were chosen by the Territory." [43] Hence, though Akerman assured McKean that he was in hearty sympathy with his course, and would do all in his power to promote needed legislation, he could take no immediate steps to remedy the financial imbroglio.[44] Whereupon the chief justice, with a grandiloquent gesture toward the gallery, dismissed the grand jury summoned for the March term in a speech which he caused to be printed:

> Gentlemen of the Grand and Petit Juries, I am not about to deliver a charge to you, but I am about to send you to your homes. . . . The reason is this: the proper officer of this court has no funds with which to pay the per diem allowance which will be properly yours. . . . I do not think it right to detain you here without compensation and at your own expense. . . . The United States Treasury promptly pays the Legislative Assembly, but the High Priesthood of the so-called "Church of Jesus Christ of Latter Day Saints" who control the Assembly . . . refuse to permit the expenses of the United States Courts to be paid, unless they are allowed to control these courts. . . . A few months since, in the presence of thousands of the people . . . one of the High Priesthood said, and I heard him say: "There is not in the Federal Constitution the dotting of an 'i,' nor the crossing of a 't,' giving to any Federal official any right to be in this Territory. Congress had no right to pass any act to organize this Territory, and the organic act is a relic of colonial barbarism. . . ."

---

[42] McKean to Grant, February 13, 1871 (N. A., D. J. MSS, Utah).
[43] Hooper to Akerman, March 4, 1871.
[44] Akerman to McKean, May 6, 1871 (Dept. Just. Letter Book H).

> . . . Gentlemen . . . I am a Federal official in Utah;
> I apologize to nobody for being here; I shall stay so long
> as I choose, or so long as the Government at Washington
> shall choose to leave me here; and I will venture the pre-
> diction, that the day is not far in the future, when the
> disloyal High Priesthood . . . shall bow to and obey the
> laws that are elsewhere respected, or else those laws will
> grind them to powder.[45]

The summer of 1871 passed uneventfully, so far as the legal
situation was concerned. The fall term of the Salt Lake district
court opened on September 18, Colonel Patrick again coming to
the rescue with the funds necessary to transact business. A grand
jury was empaneled, the Mormons among the talesmen being
"excused" by reason of their confession of faith in the doctrine
of plural wives.[46] The object of the crusading judge was clear:
to try the President of the Mormon Church. For some reason,
however, the precise charge was not based upon the statute of
1862, but upon a territorial law, passed in 1852, providing severe
penalties for the crimes of adultery and lewd and lascivious cohabitation, a law which certainly had not been framed with any
suspicion that it might be used as a weapon in the hands of enemies.[47]

On Monday, October 2, Marshal Patrick served warrant of
arrest on Brigham Young.[48] It is hardly to be doubted that even
at that late date had he wished it so, the Lion of the Lord could
have called upon his followers to strike a blow for him, rather than
suffer him to submit to this indignity. A realist, however, he
knew that advancing time and the closing frontier left little ultimate choice. Pleading illness, Young remained in his home under
the guard of a deputy. On the following day counsel for the
accused applied for bail, in view of the prisoner's inability to
answer the summons. This McKean refused to admit, but granted
extension of time for the preparation of the defense, and ordered
withdrawal of the guard. Subsequently, a group of the most

---

[45] Printed copy enclosed, McKean to Akerman, March 22, 1871 (N. A.,
D. J. MSS, Utah).

[46] Whitney, *op. cit.*, II, 586–588.

[47] *Ibid.*, pp. 589–590.

[48] *Ibid.*, p. 592.

prominent Mormons of the city were cited to answer like charges, but on appearance were admitted to bail.[49]

The case was called on Monday, October 9. The entrance of Brigham Young, the marks of illness and age upon him, was calculated to arouse the deepest indignation of his own people and the sympathy even of critics who feared his power. The callous *Tribune* acknowledged the striking impression created by his air of passive resignation:

> If there was any malice against him before, the sight of Brigham Young, at least practically acknowledging the authority of the United States to try him for the highest crimes in the law, and the respectful bearing which he put on, disarmed much of that malice.

Perhaps "there was more respect and sympathy felt . . . when he left the court-room feeble and tottering from his recent illness, having respectfully sat in the presence of his judge three-quarters of an hour after bail had been taken, than ever there was before in the minds of the same men." [50]   The defense opened with a denial of the legal competence of the grand jury, summoned in violation of the territorial law, to indict. It is of incidental interest to note that one of the leading defense attorneys was the same Major Charles Hempstead who, as Connor's adjutant, had edited the *Vedette* seven years before.[51]

McKean overruled this and other demurrers in an extraordinary opinion from the bench:

> The learned counsel for the defendant need not be assured that any motion which they may make in behalf of their client, shall be patiently heard and carefully considered. . . . But let the counsel on both sides, and the court also, keep constantly in mind the uncommon character of this case. The Supreme Court of California has well said: "Courts are bound to take notice of the

---

[49] These included Daniel H. Wells, mayor of Salt Lake City, George Q. Cannon, Apostle of the Church, and Henry W. Lawrence, a follower of Godbe. Lawrence was probably brought to court under color of impartiality.

[50] *Salt Lake Daily Tribune,* October 10, 1871.

[51] Thomas Fitch also appeared for Young. Of his nine attorneys, five were Gentile members of the Salt Lake bar. Robert N. Baskin and General George W. Maxwell were the prosecutors.

political and social condition of the country which they judicially rule." It is therefor proper to say, that while the case at bar is called "The People versus Brigham Young," its other and real title is, "Federal Authority versus Polygamic Theocracy." . . . A system is on trial in the person of Brigham Young.[52]

The defendant entered a plea of not guilty, and continuation was granted for further preparation.

In the meantime, Washington was watching these proceedings with a paternal eye.[53] The selection of a prosecuting attorney was of major concern. One prominent Utah Gentile, turning down the proposition, wrote to Akerman:

> The responsibility for the U. S. Attorney for Utah, just as *this* time, is much greater than that of any other Territory or State in the Republic.
> The sympathy of the great mass of the people here is *with* the parties to be prosecuted. Ninety thousand ignorant and fanatical people have been moulded into a Theocracy inimical to, and in direct conflict with, the Government and laws of the United States and of Christian civilization. . . . Hence, the Prosecuting Attorney should know all law, Religion, and politics. All History, Mythology, Logic, Rhetoric, and the human heart, and should have a grace of style and suavity of manner to charm and convince. Hence it requires the best talent of the nation to prevent possible or even *probable bloodshed*. The prosecutor who fills the bill perfectly will be immortal.[54]

It was hardly to be expected that such a paragon should be willing to serve for the meagre salary offered. George Caesar Bates, of Chicago, who was commissioned on October 28, 1871, failed to answer the above description. He had, however, a certain gift of rhetoric, for upon his arrival in Salt Lake City, he wired Akerman: "Here. Will do equal justice though the heavens fall." [55] A few days later he expanded his sentiments in writing:

---

[52] Whitney, *op. cit.*, II, 598–600 quotes the opinion *in extenso*.

[53] *Cf.* Benjamin H. Bristow, Solicitor General (Acting Attorney General) to McKean, October 24, 1871 (N. A., D. J. Letter Book).

[54] J. H. Wickizer, special postal agent at Salt Lake City, to Akerman, October 9, 1871 (N. A., D. J. MSS, Utah).

[55] Bates to Akerman, December 1, 1871 (N. A., D. J. MSS, Utah—telegram).

This morning I have called the criminal calendar . . .
and as Brigham Young was frightened away, and as it
is my purpose to try him first for murder, and then under
the charge for lewd and lascivious cohabitation, and as
trial is likely to create excitement throughout this region
and the whole Union, I asked the Court to fix them for
January 9, when I shall be completely prepared to do
equal and exact justice, and try him with such candor
and fairness as shall compel endorsement of even the
Prophet himself, but still with all the zeal and energy I
possess.[56]

The indictment of the Mormon leader and several of his
followers for murder "in the first degree" had issued from the
grand jury on October 28.[57] Evidence leading to this had been
furnished by the confession of William Hickman, an unsavory
character, who in earlier days had served as a scout for Brigham
Young. Later, he had fallen from official favor, and was probably
inspired by motives of revenge in the effort to implicate his former
employer and others as accomplices before the fact.[58] According
to Hickman's statement, the murders had been committed by him
during the Utah War at the behest of Young and the Mormon
high council. Whatever might be thought of the value of the
bandit's testimony in the light of subsequent investigation, at the
time it was considered of sufficient weight by the grand jurors,
all of whom could not have been knaves or fools, to justify indictment.

Inasmuch as the Church President had left the city for a tour
of the southern settlements, warrant could not be served on him
at once.[59] Of his accused associates, Mayor Wells of Salt Lake
City was released on bail in the interests of public order, but the
rest were placed in the custody of Colonel Morrow at Camp

---

[56] To the same, December 5, 1871 (N. A., D. J. MSS, Utah).

[57] Whitney, *op. cit.,* II, 639. Hempstead objected to this definition of degree by the grand jury, since that was the province of the petit jury.

[58] *Ibid.,* pp. 629–638. Hickman, during his imprisonment at Camp Douglas,
wrote or dictated a manuscript account of his exploits, published as *Brigham's
Destroying Angel* (Salt Lake City, 1872). A local anti-Mormon publicist,
J. H. Beadle, of Corinne, edited the book, which is of extremely doubtful
value. Charles Kelly, *Holy Murder* (New York, 1934), presents the case
from the viewpoint farthest removed from Whitney's.

[59] Whitney, *op. cit.,* p. 642.

Douglas.[60] That the court was willing to believe that Young had absconded—or was desirous of creating that impression—was evidenced, on December 4, when his trial for violation of the statute on public decency was suddenly called. Prosecution forthwith demanded forfeiture of bonds, but finally agreed upon postponement until January 9. As for Young's non-appearance to answer summons on the second indictment, Bates telegraphed Akerman, December 7, "Brigham Young will come if allowed large bail. I advise it earnestly. Do you approve?" Benjamin Bristow, acting for the attorney general, replied: "I would make no terms with anyone under indictment who has not submitted himself to process." [61]

In his annual message to Congress, Grant reviewed the Utah question:

> In Utah there still remains a remnant of barbarism repugnant to civilization, decency and to the laws of the United States. Territorial officers, however, have been found who are willing to perform their duty in a spirit of equity and with a due sense of sustaining the majesty of the law. Neither polygamy nor any other violation of existing statutes will be permitted within the Territory of the United States. It is not with the religion of the self-styled Saints that we are now dealing, but their practices. They will be protected in the worship of God according to the dictates of their consciences, but they will not be permitted to violate laws under the cloak of religion. It may be advisable for Congress to consider what, in the execution of the law against polygamy, is to be the status of plural wives and their offspring. The propriety of . . . passing an enabling act authorizing the Territorial Legislature of Utah to legitimize all born prior to a time fixed in the act, might be justified by its humanity to the innocent children.[62]

At the instance of United States Attorney Bates, a bill, sponsored by Senator Aaron H. Cragin of New Hampshire, and

----

[60] McKean to Attorney General Williams, November 12, 1873 (N. A., D. J. MSS, Utah).

[61] Bates to Akerman, December 4, and December 7, 1871 (N. A., D. J. MSS, Utah) ; Bristow to Bates, December 8, 1871 (N. A., D. J. Instruction Book C, p. 82).

[62] James D. Richardson, *Messages and Papers of the Presidents* (New York, 1897), XI, 4105.

designed to put teeth into the act of 1862, was modified by the incorporation of a provision calling for the payment of the mooted federal court expenses, but the bill failed of passage.[63] Bates' letters to Akerman and his successor, Attorney General George H. Williams, who took office shortly after the beginning of 1872, became increasingly nervous.[64] For the benefit of the Senate Judiciary Committee, Bates caused a brief, dated Salt Lake City, December 30, 1871, to be drawn up and printed, forwarding it to the chairman, Lyman Trumbull.[65] Clearly, Bates was losing his nerve, and with it, his head.

The unexpected return of Brigham Young to the city, January 2, was followed by his appearance in McKean's court armed with a physician's statement that his recent absence had been necessitated by his declining health. Bates met the application for bail with the astounding demand that it be set at $500,000, whereupon opposing counsel rejoined that the amount fixed upon in the case of Jefferson Davis was only $100,000. McKean, however, refused the plea, and remanded the prisoner to the custody of the marshal, granting Young the privilege of confinement within his own home.[66]

With the approach of January 9, Bates' excitement grew. On the 5th, he wired to the Attorney General: "Politicians striving to make me unjust, vindictive. Fiat Justitiam [sic] Ruat Coelum. Postpone trials here until March and let me report to you." On

---

[63] Akerman to Bates, December 14, 1871 (N. A., D. J. Instruction Book C, p. 90), and December 18, 1871 (*Ibid.*, p. 110). A letter from Congressman John Taffe, of Nebraska, chairman of the territorial committee, to Akerman, December 16, 1871, regrets that it is too late to push through legislation during the current session. "Upon the reassembling of Congress I will endeavor to have a bill passed either providing for the payment of expenses in the cases referred to, or clearly defining the powers and duties of the federal officers." (N. A., D. J. MSS, Utah).

[64] Bates to Attorney General Williams, December 16, 1871 (N. A., D. J. MSS, Utah).

[65] Enclosed in letter to Williams, January 4, 1872.

[66] Bates to Williams, January 3, 1872 (*Ibid.*). And Bates remarked: "There is no excitement here now, and my course is approved by all just and fair men. . . ." General Connor, who met Brigham Young while the latter was returning to Salt Lake City, apparently offered to go bail for his former antagonist to the amount of $100,000. "History of Brigham Young" (MS) 1871, II, 2101–2102.

the 8th, he wired again: "Have not money to get ready for trial tomorrow. Order me to continue them until March and report at my own expense."[67] Yielding, it would seem to the importunity of the prosecution, McKean ordered postponement.

It is indicative of the confusion of his course that the mercurial Bates, relieved of immediate responsibility, began at once to enlarge the horizon of his exploits. On January 11, 1872, he wrote to the Solicitor General, Bristow:

> I hold in my hands a sworn statement by a perfectly reliable Mormon witness of all the facts, circumstances and details of the Mountain Meadow Massacre in 1858. [*sic*] There . . . 122 men, women and children were killed . . . under the written orders (as the commanding officer stated to witness) of Brigham Young himself. There is no reason to doubt its truth, and it can easily be corroborated. This witness is ready to come into the Court at Beaver and give his testimony before the Grand Jury . . . whenever he can be protected from outrages. He saved the seven children, all that were saved, but fired one shot at the helpless crowd. He was then a Mormon Bishop and on his evidence, with others at hand, we can convict this crowd of murderers.
>
> How you will ask? I answer, I., by holding a court at Beaver in May next, and preliminary thereto having a camp of two companies of soldiers to aid the U. S. Marshal, to arrest defendants, defend jurors and witnesses from assault, and to enable a United States Court to enforce its mandates.
>
> II., By furnishing the U. S. Marshal with means to pay witnesses. . . . By these means only, suggested by General Conner [*sic*] just from there, Judge Hawley, . . . and myself, can these most foul murders . . . ever be punished or avenged.[68]

As the event proved, the glory of conducting the Mountain Meadows trial was not for Bates to enjoy. Relations between

---

[67] Bates to Williams, January 5, 1872. On the 8th he wrote Williams: "Had I dreamed what I should be called upon to do, I never should have come, but being here I will fight it out to the end, and while thus harassed and vexed to death, spending *my own money* and working for nothing, . . . a clique of politicians, who have no real interest here, are discussing my 'soundness' because I will not go to trial against Brigham Young . . . *without proper preparation.* . . ." (N. A., D. J. MSS, Utah).

[68] Bates to Bristow, January 11, 1872 (N. A., D. J. MSS, Utah).

Chief Justice McKean and the attorney had reached breaking point. Bates went to Washington, reported to Williams, and on January 19 instructed his deputy, James L. High, that it was the desire of the Department of Justice that all the prisoners be admitted to bail.[69] This the doughty chief justice refused to do:

> There are eleven prisoners charged with murder under the Territorial laws. Six of them are in custody of the city without expense to the Government, the other five are held at Camp Douglas. . . . Some of the murders were committed under circumstances of great mystery and atrocity, and some were committed openly in the face of mankind, and some of the prisoners are known, even before trial, to be most desperate characters.
> Were these prisoners now to be turned loose upon society, before they are acquitted by a jury, it would be an act without a precedent in criminal jurisprudence. . . . And, besides, there are reasons which cannot be made public why these prisoners should not be admitted to bail—reasons which District Attorney Bates cannot have communicated to Attorney General Williams, and to which Mr. Bates seems quite indifferent. Indeed he is known by the Court to have made, in other particulars, serious misstatements in regard to affairs in Utah.[70]

Soon after, McKean himself hastened to Washington to defend his interests and to neutralize the effects of various petitions addressed to the President and Congress for his removal, signed by alleged Gentile partisans of Bates.[71] It was during his sojourn in the capital that the Supreme Court upset his judicial apple-cart by the decision in the Englebrecht case. As read by Chief Justice Chase, April 15, 1872, voicing the unanimous opinion of the Court, the decision enlarged upon the general theory that in the formation of territorial government the federal power had deemed

---

[69] J. L. High to Williams, February 1, 1872.

[70] *Salt Lake Daily Tribune,* February 1, 1872.

[71] L. A. Gobright, (agent, New York Associated Press) to Williams, February 4, 1872. "Much indignation was expressed here today upon discovery that despatches Associated Press sent from the west have been tampered with by parties in Mormon interest. Report that most of leading Gentiles in this city condemn Judge McKean's decision . . . utterly false. Resolutions of citizens at their meeting yesterday endorsing Judge McKean's decision were signed today by over 1500 persons. . . ."

it wise to leave to the inhabitants all the powers of self-government "consistent with the supremacy and supervision of national authority." In the particular case of the Utah statute of 1859 investing county courts with the duty of registering jury lists, and the territorial marshal with that of empaneling the juries, the Court remarked that the failure of Congress to reject that provision at the opportune time, implied approval by that body. As for the action of the district court in summoning a jury by open venire through the agency of the United States marshal, the decision found this to be an error both of theory and fact, based upon the proposition, which it had previously rejected (American Insurance Company *v.* Canter, 1st Peters, 546) that the courts which the district judges of the Territories were authorized to hold were courts of the United States. As a result of this decision, all indictments pending in the Utah dockets were voided. Once again, Brigham Young was released from the vexations of the law.[72]

Governor Woods took it upon himself to express the chagrin of the radical Gentiles. To President Grant he wrote, April 18, 1872:

> The news of the decision of the US Supreme Court in the Englebrecht case strikes consternation into the ranks of the Gentiles in Utah. Under the law as laid down by the Supreme Court, a Mormon Marshall [*sic*] will summon a Mormon jury to try Mormon Criminals, each, and all, of whom regard their duty to the Church as above all law. The Marshall and Attorney General are both polygamists, and the former is a criminal. . . . Henceforth, . . . law will be a farce and the officers of the government mere ninnies. . . . Their triumph in the Supreme Court makes the Mormons very jubilant, arrogant, insolent, and they feel, now, that all power is in their hands. . . . Were it not that they want to be on their good behavior with the hope of gaining admission as a State, I would expect trouble with them, and indeed, it may come anyway. . . . There are more than twenty murderers in Salt Lake City alone, who committed some as dark and diabolical crimes as darken the annals of human depravity, who are to be turned loose upon the community. . . .

[72] 13 Wallace, 659–663.

Bates has been in constant, confidential communication with your enemies—writing and telegraphing of the "situation" to Brigham Young's attorneys, with as much zeal as tho he were Counsel for Defense. . . . I do hope he may never come to Utah again.[73]

Bates' resignation was called for by the Department of Justice on March 2, 1872. A new United States attorney was not appointed, however, until the following year. In the interval, legal matters remained quiescent. Bates toyed with the idea of reviving prosecution under the Act of 1862 and wrote to Bristow that the Mormon defense would probably claim immunity on the score that the Treaty of Guadalupe-Hidalgo guaranteed religious freedom in the ceded territory.[74] Later, he made another effort to bring to issue the Mountain Meadows trial, informing the Attorney General that he was possessed of abundant evidence, and that the judge of the second district, Cyrus Hawley, would appoint him as special prosecutor.[75] Hawley, getting wind of this, promptly wrote:

This was a surprise to me: for, allow me to say, I never made any proposition or suggestion of the kind. Under our present laws, an attempt to prosecute the leading perpetrators of that atrosity [sic] would be but a farce and a mockery.[76]

Nothing came of all this, and on January 8, 1873, William Carey, of Illinois, succeeded Bates. With vindictive fury the latter wrote to Williams, accusing McKean, Strickland, and the other federal officials of all manner of judicial crimes, "money grabbing, peculation" and of being "in the ring" with Dr. Newman, the Senate chaplain, allegedly the evil genius of the President in his attitude toward the Mormons.[77]

---

[73] Woods to Grant, April 18, 1872 (N. A., D. J. MSS, Utah).

[74] Bates to Bristow, May 21, 1872.

[75] Bates to Williams, September 23, 1872.

[76] Hawley to Williams, November 30, 1872.

[77] Bates to Williams, August 8, 1872. ". . . I can furnish witnesses to prove every charge herein contained, if the President will send an honest man here to investigate the charges. Unless he does so, I shall come to Congress in December to prefer all these charges to that body."

Possibly impelled by rumors of these charges, McKean sat down to compose a lengthy *apologia pro vita sua,* addressed to the Attorney General (November 12, 1873). After a heated denial of the charge that the late indictments for murder had been based exclusively on the testimony of Bill Hickman, he outlined his general policy:

> Impressed from the first that my duties involved considerations of public policy greater than those which usually devolve upon a judge, I have constantly asked myself the question,—how can a hundred thousand deluded ———(?) oppressed, alien people, be disabused, liberated, and brought into harmony with American ideas and institutions? Keeping this problem in mind, I permitted Brigham Young, though indicted for murder, to occupy his own house and to take exercise in his own carriage. . . . I permitted Mayor Wells, also indicted for murder, to go on bail. . . . Thus, with mingled firmness and lenity, I have sought to secure the supremacy of, and respect for, Federal authority.
>
> One day, while these prosecutions were in progress, the door of the hay-loft in which my court was in session, was opened with a violent slam, and in rushed twenty or thirty stalwart men wearing pistols. They stood for some minutes in an insulting and menacing group near the middle of the room; but as they seemed not to be noticed, they gradually took seats. They were the organization known as "Danites." They returned to my court several days in succession, but as the desired effect was not produced, a different attempt at intimidation was resorted to. One Clawson, a son-in-law of Brigham Young, and the Adjutant General of the "Nauvoo Legion," had previously bought of the United States authorities one thousand muskets and bayonets, and one hundred and fifty thousand rounds of fixed ammunition. . . . For several days and nights thereafter, I frequently met on the streets squads of men. . . . I did not adjourn my court. These demonstrations continued, until, one evening two companies of Federal troops stepped off the cars, marched through the city and reinforced Camp Douglas. The next morning, not a musket was to be seen on the streets. . . .

In the esteem of the disgruntled chief justice, the Englebrecht decision was a woeful mistake. Men who should have been on trial for murder were holding "important civil offices." The probate courts were in actual control; justices of the peace assumed the right to sit in judgment in land grant cases; town corporations had enlarged their holdings so as to seriously restrict the gubernatorial authority.

> The elective system is unknown here. The Established Church nominates its candidates; all the church members are required to vote for those candidates on pain of excommunication, persecution, and damnation. Each voter's name is numbered on the poll lists; the same number is written on the back of his ballot, and thus a record is kept of his . . . vote. I was present in the great "Tabernacle" and heard Brigham Young, in the presence of more than ten thousand people deride and denounce the system of opposing candidates and contested elections. To illustrate his views he said "Lucifer tried to get up an election in heaven, and led off one third of the angels. But there was no counting of ballots there—they put him out."

As for his own career, McKean asserted, nothing would please him more than a full investigation. In penury, suffering the injustice of a wretched pay, he had struggled on, striving as best he could to uphold the banner of American civilization; his thanks had been the indifference of Congress.

> I have done. If, in any age, there was ever a part of a Christian land so utterly abandoned to the leadership of imposters, criminals and traitors, as is this Territory, I have never heard of it.[78]

---

[78] McKean to Williams, November 12, 1873 (N. A., D. J. MSS, Utah). On June 15, 1874, McKean again importuned the President:

"Brigham Young is very rich—made so by the most high-handed impositions upon his deluded people. Of late years he has become rapidly richer. He has repeatedly boasted in public of what he has claimed to have done in Washington with money. It is known that he keeps emissaries there during every session of Congress. Within the last few years the Cullum [sic] bill, the Voorhees bill, the Logan bill, the Frelinghuysen bill, and the McKee bill have all gone to their graves, and now the Poland bill seems to be dying.

"I respectfully ask your Excellency to call an extra session of Congress, to secure legislation for Utah. . . .

"The Federal Courts have again been excluded from the Court-Rooms of the Mormon authorities of this city. My District Court stands adjourned to Marshal Maxwell's Office. . . .

Unfortunately for his own reputation, McKean had not quite done. There remained one serio-comic act in his administration of the third district court of Utah. This was the divorce case of Young *v.* Young, filed July 28, 1873. Ann Eliza Webb Young, plaintiff, was a native of Nauvoo, Illinois, and a resident of Salt Lake City since 1848. By marriage with a man named Dee she had two children; on the dissolution of this union, in 1868, she had become the polygamous wife of Brigham Young—the nineteenth according to common estimation. The *Daily Alta California* (San Francisco, November 10, 1875) was unkind enough to remark that at the time of her second marriage "she was no 'Spring chicken' to be 'caught with chaff.'" The same journal, reviewing the case, indicated that "following her discovery of polygamic isolation . . . in the course of time Ann Eliza became acquainted with 'Gentiles' among whom was a brilliant young lawyer from the Pacific Coast. With his two associates . . . of the Salt Lake Bar, he saw a *cause celebre.*" Her "next friend" in the case was Brigadier General George Maxwell, Patrick's successor as United States marshal, and a fire-eating anti-Mormon. The bill, alleging cruelty and neglect, with no mention of the fact that the marriage was a polygamous union, asked for a liberal settlement in view of the defendant's great wealth, payment of alimony at the rate of $1000 per month *pendente lite* and of attorney's fees.[79]

The case was protracted. On August 25, 1874 the answer of the respondent was filed, showing that Brigham Young, although by his admission he had a lawful wife living, had indeed married Ann Eliza Webb as a plural wife according to the rites of the Church of Jesus Christ of Latter-Day Saints, April 6, 1868. Subsequently, the brief claimed, it was discovered that the plaintiff had never been divorced from Dee.[80]

While the trial pended, Ann Eliza, apparently a resourceful lady, capitalized her dubious celebrity. She toured the eastern

---

"Some years ago, when I held court in a hay-loft, over a livery stable, Atty. Gen'l. Akerman decided that the Federal Government would pay the rent of that place only when it was used for the trial of United States cases. . . ."

[79] *Daily Alta California* (San Francisco), November 10, 1875.

[80] Whitney, *op. cit.*, II, 758–759.

states, lecturing on the horrors of polygamy, and earned the plaudits of the Gentile press:

> Mrs. Ann Eliza Young, the eloquent advocate of liberty for her sex in Utah, will arrive on this evening's train from the East. Her return from a glorious mission among the people of the States, where she told the story of her wrongs to listening thousands, should and will be made the occasion of a popular reception at the Walker House by her numerous friends in Salt Lake City. In the great struggle at Washington, during the session of Congress just ended, Mrs. Young's influence, more than any other, aided in securing the enactment of a salutary law. The discarded wife of a tyrant became the honored guest of the best and noblest in the land.[81]

At long last, on February 25, 1875, McKean rendered his decision on the question of alimony, *pendente lite*. The plaintiff was awarded attorney's costs to the amount of $3000 and $500 per month alimony dating from the opening of the case. President Young appealed to the territorial supreme court; notwithstanding, the chief justice, at the expiration of the allotted time for the payment of a designated portion of the judgment, cited Young to appear before him to show cause why he should not be held in contempt of court. The aged man, venerated as a patriarch by his followers, again entered McKean's court to hear sentence passed upon him:

> Since the Court has not one rule of action where conspicuous and another where obscure persons are concerned; and since it is a fundamental principle of the Republic that all men are equal before the law; and since this court desires to impress this great fact . . . upon the minds of all the people of this Territory:
> Now, therefore, because of the said contempt of Court, it is . . . ordered and adjudged, that the said Brigham Young do pay a fine twenty-five dollars, and that he be imprisoned for the term of one day.[82]

---

[81] *Salt Lake Daily Tribune,* July 15, 1874. Ann Eliza Young later wrote a pot-boiler, *Wife No. 19* (Hartford, 1876), which is of little historical worth.

[82] Quoted in Whitney, *op. cit.,* II, 761 ff.

If triumph it was, McKean's enjoyment of it was brief. Young indeed spent the night in the penitentiary under circumstances that made it rather a civic reception than an incarceration. And a week later the rumored removal of the chief justice was confirmed.[83] David P. Lowe, of Kansas, was named to his office. Certainly no legal luminary, the displaced jurist, in spite of his acknowledged sincerity and crusading zeal, had done little to advance the Gentile cause in Utah. The Ann Eliza case, with its ludicrous implications and its attempt to embarrass in his age a man for whom the nation, with all its disapproval of his moral code, felt a certain respect as a pioneer and a colonizer, was undoubtedly a blunder in the worst taste.

A few days after his arrival in the Territory, Lowe overruled the plaintiff's plea for action to secure payment of alimony and arrears, amounting then to $9,500, declaring that the validity of the marriage in question had never been established. However, Lowe soon resigned, and Judge Jacob Boreman, of the second district, who had come to Utah in 1873 and whose anti-Mormon bias was fully equal to that of McKean, occupied the third district bench *ad interim.* Seizing the opportunity, attorneys for the plaintiff applied to him for a writ of contempt. This he issued, leaving the place of Young's confinement to Marshal Maxwell's discretion. The latter simply stationed a guard at the President's residence.[84]

As soon as word of this reached Washington, Attorney General Edwards Pierrepont wrote District Attorney Carey, November 2:

> It has been communicated to this Department that
> Judge Boreman has imprisoned Brigham Young because

---

[83] The removal of McKean called forth numerous protests from his friends. One George F. Prescott, manager of the Tribune Publishing Company, wired Grant, March 17, 1875, "The removal . . . is equivalent to a national recognition of Mormon supremacy in Utah. The man of Shiloh, Vicksburgh, and Appomattox could not make this unconditional surrender to Brigham Young." A Methodist missionary, C. P. Lyford, wired Senator Logan: "For God's sake try to induce our old commander to reinstate Judge McKean. His removal and the conduct of our new Governor Axtell disheartens every loyal man in Utah." On the other hand, George Bates communicated his joy to the President: "Justice herself, Angels of Justice, God of Justice, all honest Republicans, bless and thank you. Justice, law and order assured."

[84] *Daily Alta California,* November 10, 1875.

he had not paid some $9000 of alimony ordered to be paid by the Judge's predecessor. I am informed that the alimony was allowed to a woman who claimed in her bill to be the Seventeenth wife of Brigham Young, and that it appears on the face of her bill that she could not have been the lawful wife at any time. . . .

This is a matter of much importance and requires immediate attention. Consult with Judge Boreman at once. Show him this letter and suggest to him . . . that he act discreetly. . . . It would be unfortunate if an illegal imprisonment should be made.[85]

Carey replied, November 12, enclosing pertinent papers and a letter from Boreman, in which the latter took vigorous exception to the statement that the bill read as Pierrepont supposed:

It would hardly be necessary for me to say that no respectable court could for a moment entertain, nor any respectable attorney file, such a bill as the one in this cause has been represented to be.

The pleadings and papers speak for themselves; and I do not fear to have my action scrutinized. . . . My decision is based on sound law. . . . I did not examine the matter hastily.[86]

Young was released from custody within a few weeks by the new Chief Justice, Alexander White, but the case itself hung fire until April 20, 1877, when a final court decree pronounced the union polygamous, and cancelled the alimony award *pendente lite.*[87] It is difficult not to agree with the editor of the *Alta California* that "it must be clear . . . that there is running through all this litigation a streak of vulgar fraud. To deplete the treasury of Brigham Young . . . is simply to strengthen in the Mormons their accusations against the Gentile Judge of willful persecution. . . ."[88]

---

[85] Pierrepont to Cary [*sic*], November 2, 1875 (N. A., D. J. MSS, Utah).

[86] Boreman to Carey, November 10, 1875, enclosed in Carey to Pierrepont, November 11, 1875.

[87] Whitney, *op. cit.,* II, 767.

[88] *Loc. cit.,* November 10, 1875.

CHAPTER IV

THE GHOSTS OF THE MOUNTAIN MEADOWS

PRESIDENT GRANT, betrayed and bewildered, entered upon his final years of office with slackening interest in the affairs of Utah. As a successor to Woods, who resigned his post in December, 1874, he was content to nominate a man mild enough in temperament and demeanor to be acceptable to the Saints themselves. In so doing, however, he failed to reckon with the fact that there existed in Utah a vociferous minority which would be satisfied with nothing less than a governor after its own pattern. Samuel B. Axtell, a native of Ohio, had been sent to Congress by the Democrats of his adopted state, California, in 1867. Prudently revising his political creed, he was appointed governor of Utah Territory December 28, 1874, and made his entry into his capital city the following February.[1]

His first act in office was to issue a certificate of election to George Q. Cannon, the polygamous candidate for Congress who, during the previous August, had won a smashing victory over his Gentile opponent, General George Maxwell. Governor Woods had refused to give him the certificate, foreshadowing a more famous incident involving the same Delegate Cannon in 1880. The Gentile reaction to Axtell's alleged "weakness" was prompt and vitriolic. The Salt Lake *Daily Tribune* faithfully mirrored this feeling:

> He has been one week amongst us, and has set about his unholy work with an ardor and audacity that fill the mind of every honest citizen with alarm. The wise course pursued by Gov. Woods tended strongly to repress defiant lawlessness . . . and aid the loyal citizens of Utah in the assertion of their political rights. . . .
> The useful labors of that honest Executive, his un-

---

[1] Edward H. Anderson, "Territorial Governors—Samuel B. Axtell," *Improvement Era,* IV, No. 7 (May, 1901), 481–483.

worthy successor . . . is now perfidiously engaged in overturning.[2]

Soon the Gentile press was pleased to dub him "Bishop" Axtell, and to enlarge upon his subserviency to the commands of Brigham Young. Mining interests, it was reported, would be chary of risking investments in Utah, knowing that the chief executive, as a "mere tool" of the Mormon hierarchy, might well be prevailed upon to "use his official position to tax the mines out of existence." [3] His movements were watched with coldly critical eyes:

> Axtell, acting in the capacity of Brigham Young's Governor, took a spin around the city yesterday, in Brigham's royal carriage. George Q. Cannon, with one of his women, occupied the front seat, while Axtell, and one of Brigham's women, were snugly ensconced in the back seat. Thus our "best society" aired themselves, and thus did this man who was sent out to enforce the laws . . . insult the law-abiding people of the Territory. How much longer is this bilk going to be permitted . . . to remain in our midst? [4]

No paragon of executive wisdom, apparently, Axtell was transferred to the governorship of the Territory of Arizona, June 8, 1875, and his successor, George W. Emery, simultaneously named.[5] The exultation of the radical faction in this putative victory was short-lived, inasmuch as Emery proved himself to be a moderate administrator, more interested in the development of the territorial resources than in Mormon-baiting.[6] Born in Maine, in 1833, he

---

[2] *Daily Tribune,* February 12, 1875.

[3] *Ibid.,* March 21, 1875.

[4] *Ibid.,* April 15, 1875. On the occasion of a visit of James A. Garfield, June, 1875, the *Daily Tribune* announced:

"Bishop Axtell, at the command of his master Brigham, accompanied General Garfield to Ogden yesterday, to see the stalwart Babylonian fairly on his way home. The shrewd statesman allowed himself to be dined and wined by the gushing Mormon priesthood, including the latest acolyte, Bishop Axtell, but he kept his eyes open, and goes back home with a pretty clear comprehension of the whole unclean outfit." (*Daily Tribune,* June 8, 1875).

[5] N. A., D. J. Appointment File, 1873–1883.

[6] *Daily Tribune,* June 9, 1875. "Hallelujah! Bishop Axtell to Step Down and Aside! The Federal Government Has Not Yet Abandoned Us!

was graduated from Dartmouth College, and later was a legal associate of Benjamin Butler in Boston. Before receiving his appointment to Utah, he had served as collector of internal revenue in Tennessee.[7] Twenty-five years later he recalled his interview with Grant:

> I called on the President before leaving for Utah to thank him. I said, "I understand, Mr. President, that there are turbulent spirits in Utah as well as in the South." "Yes," he answered, "the Gentiles and 'Mormon' people seem to be having a lively time, but I think you will have little or no trouble." He added: "You go out there and look around, and I will come out and see you." [8]

It was during Emery's administration that the history of the Mormon Church passed a notable milestone with the death of its great leader, who, after a brief illness, passed away on the afternoon of Wednesday, August 29, 1877.[9] The *Daily Tribune* of that date, aware of his imminent dissolution, called no truce with its arch-enemy:

> . . . Brigham's rule has been unwise and oppressive, his vicious and criminal course has alienated the affections and destroyed the confidence of a large portion of the Saints, and the saying is very common among them that Joseph Smith's prediction has been fulfilled—Brigham Young having obtained the lead of the Church has led it to hell. . . .

With the Saints in mourning, the editor passed judgment over the corpse:

> He . . . has ruled over the Church with unquestioned sway, evincing a despotism nowhere equalled except in

---

The Chief Obstacle to Utah's Progress Obliterated! Now Let the Glorious Work Go On With Renewed Vigor! There's millions in It For the Citizens of Utah! Rejoice!!!"

[7] Anderson, *loc. cit.,* IV, No. 8, June, 1901, 561–563.

[8] *Ibid.,* p. 563. To Emery was paid the minor compliment of having an obscure county of the Territory named after him by the grateful Mormon legislature.

[9] Whitney, *Utah,* II, 845–849.

barbarous Turkey; . . . until the day of his death, he was a *de facto* Governor.

His habit of mind was singularly illogical, and his public addresses are the greatest farrago of nonsense that ever was put into print.

Yet we believe that the most graceful act of his life has been his death.   While Brigham lived and exercised his despotic sway there could be no material progress in Israel. . . . Now this man has gone, his pernicious rule will die with him.[10]

Certain it is that the administration of John Taylor, who succeeded Brigham Young, first as President of the Quorum of Apostles, and later as the sustained President of the Church, witnessed stormy days. The verdict of the American nation was that polygamy must be suppressed, and the process of carrying out that verdict was both painful and humiliating for the Saints. It must stand as a criticism of the political foresight of Brigham Young that he failed either to reckon with the strength of the popular abhorrence of the system which gave his people such unenviable notoriety, or to take measures to avoid the inevitable conflict. The Mormon viewpoint, of course, which regards polygamy as a matter of divine revelation and its final abrogation as the result of a special providential accommodation to the exigencies of the prevailing order, cannot accept this criticism. At all events, the determination of the Mormon leaders to stand by the doctrine of plural marriage for thirteen years after the death of Young gave to the Gentile minority, jealous of political and social supremacy in the territory, a golden opportunity to arouse the conscience of the nation, and incidentally, to garner its own harvest of political preferment.

The last years of Young's life, as already noted, saw the clouds gathering. If McKean had no immediate successor who regarded his judicial powers in the light of an instrument for the christianization of Mormondom, the arm of the law was nevertheless potent. The cases that awakened greatest interest during the latter half of the decade of the 1870's, and which quickened the antagonisms between Mormon and Gentile to greatest intensity, were the trials of John D. Lee for complicity in the Mountain Meadows Massacre and of George Reynolds for polygamy.

As a preliminary step in the business of bringing to justice the

---

[10] *Daily Tribune,* August 30, 1877.

perpetrators of the massacre, the War Department had been prevailed upon, as a result of the insistence of Associate Justice Hawley, whose judicial district was centered at Beaver in central Utah, to establish an army post at that village.

To the "Hon. P. H. Sheridan," Hawley had written from Chicago as early as June 3, 1871, insisting that unless military protection were afforded, witnesses would feel themselves too greatly imperiled by personal violence to testify willingly, nor could the guilty be brought to court:

> In my judgement, in order to secure the execution of the laws and for the protection of the loyal citizens, there should be a military camp of 2 or 3 companies at Beaver City. This city contains about one thousand people, and is about 25 miles east of the "Star Dist.," one of the richest silver bearing Dists. in the whole Territory, and which Dist. now contains about fifty miners in the actual working occupation thereof. Beaver . . . has the largest number of dissenting Mormons south of Salt Lake and who for the last six months have craved protection from the government. . . . Last fall (though this Dist. is the largest in Territorial extent of the three) the Marshal was unable to find more than six "Gentiles" who were eligible as jurors. . . . It will perhaps be remembered that the Mountain Meadow Massacre occurred in this District, and I regret to say that most of the leaders and principle men engaged in it are now and were at the time residents . . . and their influence is the controlling one. . . .
>
> It is true that "Knab," [Kanab] a new locality about 300 miles south of Salt Lake City and 100 miles due east of Parawan, is now the Gibralter for such persons whom the Church Authorities imagine will be liable to be proceeded against as criminals. It is in the fastnesses of the mountains and accessible only at one point. . . . Last fall several Mormons were indicted for murder, but their arrests have been prevented and it is believed that they have taken shelter in this place.
>
> During the last year I have been frequently interrogated by dissenting Mormons . . . to know when the government intended to extend to them protection. Now they are under a degrading Theocratic despotism. . . .[11]

---

[11] N. A., War Department MSS, File on Camp Rawlins, Utah (spelling unchanged).

Hawley reiterated his plea to General Ord, of the Department of the Missouri, and still later in a confidential note to President Grant. In May, 1873, the post was established, and was subsequently christened Camp Cameron. Whether or not the presence of the soldiery was the deciding factor, the long delayed prosecution was soon under way.[12]

Cyrus Hawley was succeeded in the second judicial district by Justice Jacob Boreman, a Kansan, who had signalized his arrival in Utah, April, 1873, by announcing that he would sooner go to an "animal show" than pay his respects to Brigham Young.[13] A grand jury was empaneled under the provisions of the Poland Act, and indictments found against nine persons, including John D. Lee, William H. Dame, and Isaac C. Haight, for participation in the massacre of 1857. A posse, under the direction of Deputy United States Marshal William Stokes set out to apprehend Lee, who for some years had operated a ferry across the Colorado River at the settlement which bears his name. After a wild odyssey, Lee was finally discovered hiding in the straw flooring of a chicken-coop at his residence in Panguitch, Utah, November 8.[14] Marshal Maxwell communicated the good tidings to Attorney General Williams two days later, with the information that Lee was then in custody in the guard room at Camp Cameron.[15] Colonel William Dame had given himself up prior to this, and the trials were set for the April term, 1875. Waiting developments, the Salt Lake *Daily Tribune* commented:

> Whatever may be the direct outcome of the trial, this much is certain, the active participation of the hierarchs of the Mormon Church in this wholesale butchery will be brought out so fully into the effulgence of daylight and published so widely to the world, that the whole corrupt outfit will be condemned by public opinion, and a retreat

[12] Hawley to Ord, January 12, 1872 (N. A., D. J. MSS, Utah) ; Hawley to Grant, February 24, 1872, *ibid.* Cf. Whitney, *op.cit.*, II, 718.

[13] Jacob S. Boreman, "Reminiscences of My Life in Utah, on and off the bench" (MS in the Huntington Library, San Marino, California, *circa* 1895), p. 11. Boreman probably owed his appointment to the fact that his brother was Senator Arthur Boreman, of Kansas. The jurist took a prominent part in establishing a Methodist mission in Beaver (pp. 27–28).

[14] Whitney, *op. cit.*, II, 783–784.

[15] Maxwell to Williams, November 10, 1874 (N. A., D. J. MSS, Utah).

outside the stake of Utah will be assiduously sought by
quite a number who now sit in the highest seats of the
Tabernacle.[16]

From the first, interest in the trial revolved around John D. Lee.
Difficulties encountered in obtaining witnesses caused the prosecution to plead for postponement until July, in the hope that the
evidence of a former bishop of the Cedar City ward, Philip
Klingensmith, who was finally located in California, would serve
not only to incriminate Lee, but the highest officials of the Church.
Klingensmith, who by his own admission had been an accomplice
in the deed, was given the benefit of a *nolle prosequi* when the trial
ultimately came before the court, July 22.[17]   The scarcely veiled
object of the prosecution was to extract from Lee a confession that
would afford grounds for an indictment of Brigham Young himself.   A few days before the opening of the trial, Lee made a statement, but its ambiguity in regard to the source of the plot to murder
the Arkansas emigrants was considered too great to be of value as
evidence to the State.   It remains a question whether Lee, though
cut off from the Church and anathematized by the ecclesiastical
authority, ever told all he knew.   The fact that he faced a firing
squad two years later without having added substantially to his
statement is rather strong evidence that the massacre was planned
and perpetrated without the direct knowledge of the Mormon
chieftains in Salt Lake City.[18]   The *Daily Tribune,* naturally, was
not convinced:

> The position of the Mormon press on Mountain
> Meadows is peculiar. . . .   For twelve years their voice
> was one of indignant denial that any Mormons were en-
> gaged in the affair.   Then a few hesitating admissions
> were made; and finally, in 1871, the whole Mormon peo-
> ple changed front as suddenly as a well-drilled regiment.
> All the papers and speakers who had furiously denounced
> us, in 1870, for saying that any Mormons were guilty,

---

[16] *Daily Tribune,* February 6, 1875.

[17] Whitney, *op. cit.,* pp. 786–797, *passim.*

[18] The best available bibliography of the extensive literature dealing with
the Mountain Meadows Massacre is to be found in "List of Works in the
New York Public Library Relating to the Mormons," *Bulletin of the New
York Public Library,* XIII (March, 1909), 183–239.

then furiously denounced Higbee, Haight and Lee for being guilty. The defense they then had for *all* the Mormons they now reserve for Brigham Young and the heads of the Church. If they were so badly mistaken in the former case, is it not just possible that they are mistaken as to Brigham's innocence? [19]

That the Lion of the Lord "knew of the massacre before it happened, and received a report soon after," that he directed the disposal of the loot, "that he employed all his power and cunning to hush the thing up as long as possible, and that he recognized the perpetrators as brethren and Saints," were charges stated with forthright conviction by the Gentile press. When the jury, four Gentiles and eight Mormons, disagreed as to Lee's guilt, August 7, the *Tribune* editor pronounced it "evident even to the most prejudiced jack Mormon that the existing system of government in Utah is an utter failure, as far as securing justice to the greater criminals is concerned." [20] Whitney, in his review of the case, charges that the prosecution deliberately courted a hung jury, in the expectation that later developments might pave the way for legal action against the Mormon leaders. [21]

On February 28, 1876, Colonel William Nelson, of La Crosse, Wisconsin, replaced Maxwell as United States marshal for Utah, and on April 25, Sumner Howard was appointed district attorney. [22] Howard's object, at the outset at least, was to wind up the trial of Lee, apparently without ulterior designs. [23] The case was reopened on September 14, in Beaver, Justice Boreman again presiding. [24]

[19] July 27, 1875.

[20] *Daily Tribune,* July 30, August 12, 1875.

[21] Whitney, *op. cit.,* II, 801–802.

[22] N. A., D. J. Appointment File, 1873–1883.

[23] Whitney, *op. cit.,* II, 805: "In the opening statement of the case Howard made the sensible observation that he had not come to try Brigham Young and the Mormon Church, but to proceed against John D. Lee for his personal actions."

[24] The same writer, *Ibid.,* pp. 803–804, cites a petition dated September 1, addressed to Governor Emery by a group of the Gentiles of Beaver, requesting him to use his influence to prevent the removal of one of the troop contingents at Camp Cameron. Weakening of the military arm might induce a Mormon uprising, in which the Indians would be glad to participate. "The Indians are cajoled and baptized into the Mormon Church and told that they are 'battle axes of the Lord,' many of them were encamped about this place

Dissatisfaction with Howard's plan of campaign was promptly registered:

> With the kindliest feelings . . . it is our duty to inform him that he is allowing his zeal to run away with his discretion. He announces with unmistakable emphasis that his business in prosecuting John D. Lee is to connect him with the crime of which he is charged, and not to try the whole Mormon priesthood. He is correct in this; but he should bear in mind that he is not the first prosecuting officer who has undertaken this difficult and important task. Last year ex-District Attorney Carey, . . . placed this same red-handed criminal on trial, and brought out evidence to convict him . . . if the jury had rendered an honest verdict. It is true the prosecution also sought to elicit evidence to inculpate men higher up in the Mormon Church; a perfectly legitimate and meritorious aim, because it was convincingly apparent that the bloody deed was done under "orders" and the whole mystery will not be unravelled until it is made apparent from whom those orders emanated.[25]

At this second trial the counsel for defense took the position that Lee, in participating in the massacre, had simply acted as an instrument of his "superiors." To offset this implied charge, Howard produced an affidavit signed by Brigham Young, asserting the latter's complete ignorance of the details of the affair. Admitting that he had interviewed Lee in Salt Lake City shortly thereafter, Young declared that he had interrupted Lee's narration, "as from what I had already learned by rumor I did not wish my feelings harrowed up with a recital of the details." The singular delicacy of the Mormon leader on that occasion has never seemed wholly convincing.[26]

On the morning of September 20 the charge was delivered to the jury, composed entirely of Mormons, and within a few hours

---

during the trial of Lee, and on several occasions inquired when the Mormons and 'Mericats' were going to war. The very fact that we cannot understand all the Indian movements, concurring with other events, such as the trial of John D. Lee, makes our suspicion all the stronger. . . ." Whitney terms these statements "malicious falsehoods."

[25] *Daily Tribune,* September 19, 1876.

[26] Whitney, *op. cit.,* II, 806–810.

Lee was pronounced guilty of murder in the first degree. Marshal Nelson, writing to Attorney General Alphonso Taft, expressed his complete satisfaction with the verdict:

> . . . The result seems to be displeasing to certain factionists here who have heretofore conducted this case and those connected with the "Mountain Meadows Massacre" with reference more to outside matters than to the cause at bar. It has been their public boast that the former trial of John D. Lee in July 1875 was not for the purpose of convicting the prisoner, but to fix the odium of the . . . butchering upon the Mormon Church. The result was the call for a large amount of public money and no result except the advancement of certain schemes and aspirations of local politicians whose attitude is that of uniform condemnation of the Administration and its appointees. In the trial just concluded the case of John D. Lee and that alone was tried. It became apparent early in the investigation, that there is no evidence whatever to connect the chief authorities of the Mormon Church with the Massacre. On the contrary, those authorities produced documents and other evidence showing clearly that not only was that great crime solely an individual offense on the part of those who committed it, but that the orders, letters, proclamations, etc., which issued from the central Mormon authority which was also at that time the Territorial authority, were directly and positively contrary to all shedding of blood, not only of emigrants passing through the Territory, but also forbade the killing of the soldiers of Johnson's [sic] Army which was marching on Utah. Being satisfied of this, the prosecution laid the case before the Mormon leaders and ask [sic] their aid in unravelling the mystery. . . . That aid was given and the horrid testimony is public from the mouths of eyewitnesses, convicting the prisoner without the shadow of a doubt. Those whose thunder is stolen by this conviction and the fixing of the crime where the evidence places it, and who failed in the same prosecution before, are exceeding angry, and are making to the public such misrepresentations as their malice suggests and are said to be also forwarding certain of their statements to Washington. . . . The loss of political capital will drive men into strange postures.[27]

---

[27] Nelson to Taft, September 22, 1876 (N. A., D. J. MSS, Utah). Taft, of course, was father of the future President.

Justice Boreman, passing sentence on Lee, left no doubt in the minds of his hearers that he was personally convinced that the real guilt lay "with others, and some in high authority." These, he said, had "inaugurated and decided upon the wholesale slaughter of the emigrants," and he referred to the fact that for nineteen years, "there has been throughout the entire Territory, a persistent and determined opposition to an investigation of the massacre." [28] Pending the appeal of the case to the territorial supreme court, where the judgment of the second district court was upheld on February 10, 1877, District Attorney Howard disclosed his plans in a letter to Taft, October 4, 1876. He indicated that these involved the risk of incurring the enmity of the Gentile faction in order to lull the suspicions of the Mormons. The next step was to be the arrest of Haight, Higbee and Stewart, all under indictment for complicity, and who were in hiding in the mountains. However, Marshal Nelson's moves were being watched too carefully to render his assistance feasible. A "first class detective" was needed:

> We have "driven the opening wedge" into this diabolical transaction by the conviction of Lee. Now if we can have such assistance as we ask, our final success will be assured.
> The conviction of Lee, his abandonment by the Mormon authorities and the apparent acquiescence in his conviction is working its *intended* results. Now I want to take advantage of the situation to arrest the others, who are nearer the "seat of power" than Lee ever was, and thus gradually work our way to the core of rottenness.[29]

Taft promptly commissioned a special agent of the Justice Department for the services suggested by Howard.[30] However, neither the resourcefulness of the detective nor the offer of a reward of five hundred dollars for the apprehension of any of the men wanted, which Attorney General Charles Devens, Taft's

---

[28] Boreman, *Reminiscences*, p. 67; *Daily Tribune*, October 10, 1876.

[29] Howard to Taft (Confidential), October 4, 1876 (N. A., D. J. MSS, Utah).

[30] Taft to Howard, November 3, 1876 (N. A., D. J. Instruction Book G, p. 71).

successor, after much discussion, finally authorized the district attorney to make,[31] succeeded in securing their persons.

The execution of John D. Lee was Marshal Nelson's dramatic moment. Preserving discreet silence until a few days prior to the date set for the exaction of the penalty, March 23, 1877, he transported the condemned man to the scene of the massacre itself. On a Friday morning, Lee, denying his guilt and charging Brigham Young with sacrificing him "in a cowardly and dastardly manner," faced the firing squad with stolid composure.[32]

The *Daily Tribune* made the most of Lee's final testimony:

> The first victim to outraged justice, who fell yesterday, declares that he has been betrayed in a shameful and dastardly manner. Brigham Young, he declares, is teaching the people false doctrines, and his life is sacrificed through following dishonest leaders. Intercourse with the world, the increase of gentilism in Utah, the execution of the United States law, and the utterances of a free press and pulpit, have served to show this miserable being how he has been misled.

Ominously, the editor added: "The execution of Lee will be a useful subject for the brethren to ponder."[33]

As matters turned out, Lee was the only one of those indicted who was brought to trial. Howard himself was soon engaged in explaining to the attorney general certain features of his conduct in regard to Lee during the latter's incarceration in the penitentiary in Salt Lake City. Charges were made by Edwin Gilman, a former deputy United States marshal of Utah, that the district attorney, after wringing from Lee a confession, had suppressed vital portions implicating the President of the Church. Howard was called to Washington, where he apparently had little difficulty in

---

[31] Devens to Howard, March 14, 1877, April 4, 1877 (N. A., D. J. Instruction Book G, p. 192).

[32] Whitney, *op. cit.*, II, 825–829. Nelson's request to Taft to secure permission from the Secretary of War for a company of soldiers from Camp Cameron to carry out the sentence, was rejected, although the soldiers did act as guard on the occasion. Nelson to Taft, (telegram) February 2, 1877 (N. A., D. J. MSS, Utah) ; Taft to Nelson, February 23, 1877 (N. A., D. J. Instruction Book G, p. 174).

[33] *Daily Tribune*, March 24, 1877.

refuting the allegations.[34] In the meantime, the district attorney made a final effort to carry the investigation to the door of the dying patriarch:

> In the years 1856–7 Brigham Young as Governor and Ex-officio Indian Agent of Utah received a large sum of money from the United States for supplying the Indians of the Territory with farming implements, etc., etc. I think it can be proven that very much of the property taken from the Emigrants murdered at the Mountain Meadows was by Lee and other agents of Brigham Young turned over to the Indians—vouchers taken from the subagents for the same as though he (Young) had actually bought and paid for the property out of the money in his hands for that purpose. I desire to call your attention to this matter and suggest that the accounts and vouchers of Brigham Young with the Indian Department for the years above named be copied and sent to me.
>
> I have very good evidence that in the manner indicated Young had the benefit of the property of the murdered Emigrants and defrauded the United States to the amount of the vouchers returned covering said property.[35]

Devens took steps to secure the desired information, but was forced to indicate to the zealous Howard that the annual appropriation for the conduct of the territorial courts had been wholly expended, and that the comptroller had refused to pass his accounts as charged to the general fund for the expenses of the United States courts.[36] If the district attorney found anything in the transcript of the accounts of Brigham Young as Indian Agent to confirm his suspicions, by the time he could act the Mormon chieftain was dead.

Disappointment likewise dogged Howard's attempt to lend legal aid and comfort to the Liberals of Utah by an investigation of the

---

[34] Devens to Howard, April 11, 1877 (N. A., D. J. Instruction Book G, p. 220) ; Howard to Devens, April 16, 1877 (N. A., D. J. MSS, Utah). Seemingly, the former district attorney, George Bates, was behind Gilman in pressing the charges against Howard. Devens to Bates, April 16, 1877 (D. J. Instruction Book L).

[35] Howard to Devens, April 26, 1877 (D. J. MSS, Utah).

[36] Devens to Carl Schurz, May 3, 1877 (N. A., D. J. Executive and Congressional Letter Book E, p. 397) ; Devens to Howard, May 16, 1877 (N. A., D. J. Instruction Book G, p. 267).

certificate of naturalization which had been issued to George Q. Cannon, the congressional delegate. The information filed, as he wrote to Devens, May 1, 1877, alleged that Cannon's naturalization papers had not been issued in open court, and that fraud was found in the application, Cannon not having fulfilled minimum residence requirements at the time.[37] Devens returned a cool answer, stating that the fact that Cannon had already been recognized by the House of Representatives could hardly be overlooked.[38] During the summer, when Howard was in Washington to clear his record, Devens apparently prevailed upon him to annul the proceedings. On his return to Salt Lake City, he informed his superior that he had "followed your instructions to the letter, although it was very distasteful to me." Bungling of this sort did not endear Howard to the rabid anti-Mormon politicians of Utah, and Robert N. Baskin, Cannon's Liberal opponent, broke off relations with him.[39]

Checked on one front, Howard found evidence that in his opinion furnished a solution for another of Utah's "mysteries," the Morrisite "War" of June, 1862. Joseph Morris, a fanatical visionary, had joined the Mormon Church in England and had followed the Saints to Zion. In 1860, however, Morris quarreled with Young when the latter refused to accept the authenticity of his revelations. A number of followers accepted the religious and social leadership of the dissenter, and with a group numbering about five hundred he established his headquarters not far from the city of Ogden, at the mouth of Weber Canyon, there to await the coming of the day of judgment, which Morris predicted for the immediate future. Failure of the day to arrive seemingly did not diminish his ascendancy over his flock, but difficulties with the Mormon farmers, whose stocks were preyed upon by the Morrisites, resulted in open conflict. On May 10, 1862, Chief Justice Kinney issued a warrant to Colonel Robert T. Burton, of the Nauvoo Legion, for the apprehension of Morris and his chief counsellors, notably one John Banks. In executing this commission Burton, whether by necessity or design, precipitated a passage at arms in which Morris and several of his adherents—two of them

---

[37] Howard to Devens, May 1, 1877 (N. A., D. J. MSS, Utah).

[38] Devens to Howard, May 10, 1877 (N. A., D. J. Instruction Book G, p. 263).

[39] Howard to Devens, July 28, 1877 (N. A., D. J. MSS, Utah).

women—were killed and in which Banks sustained wounds which shortly resulted in his death. Seventy-six Morrisites were taken into custody, and at the March, 1863, term of the third district court, presided over by Kinney, they were tried. Seven were convicted of murder in the second degree and sentenced to prison terms, while the remainder were fined. Governor Harding, however, with the backing of the California Volunteers, issued two proclamations, dated March 31, 1863, extending executive clemency to all. Received at Camp Douglas, they were subsequently provided with armed escort to the vicinity of Soda Springs, Idaho, near which point Colonel Connor had established a military post bearing the name Camp Conness. The Mormon jury, which had passed judgment on the Morrisites, retaliated with a strong censure of Harding's action which the sympathetic Chief Justice Kinney allowed to be officially "spread on the books." [40]

Now, fifteen years after the incident, District Attorney Howard was convinced that he had proof of Burton's guilt. To Devens he wrote, July 28, 1877:

> The work before the Grand Jury has been productive of great results. . . . In the case of the murder of John Banks and Joseph Morris I ascertained that a witness— one S. D. Sirrene—was living in California. It was, up to a few weeks since, thought that he was dead; that he had been murdered by order of the Mormon authorities, to "put him where he could not talk." . . . He is an intelligent, and I believe a reliable man. His testimony is not only positive as to the killing of Banks and Morris, but he has given me the names of other witnesses, some of whom I have already produced before the Grand Jury, and who gave most valuable, and, it seems to me, conclusive evidence that this horrible crime was committed by the direct order of Brigham Young. . . .

According to Sirrene's version, the order to "break up the Morrisites" emanated from Young himself, and Burton was under orders that neither of the two leaders of the sect should be brought back alive.

---

[40] George B. Arbaugh, *Revelation in Mormonism* (Chicago, 1932), pp. 183 ff. *Cf.* Whitney, *op. cit.*, II, 48–59, 99–103. John Banks, "A Document History of the Morrisites in Utah" (Thesis, MS, University of Utah, Salt Lake City, 1909), an account by a descendant, is of little value.

> . . . Burton took three pieces of cannon, planted them near Morris' camp, and while the people were holding religious services, fired upon them, killing several men, women and children. Morris, after standing the siege for some time, caused a white flag to be raised and surrendered. Burton rode into the camp. All the weapons and arms of the Morris party were stacked, taken possession of by Burton, and an unconditional surrender made. After all this was done, and while there was no show of resistance, . . . Burton called Morris out and, sitting on his horse, shot him four times with his revolver and until he fell dead at his feet. At the same time John Banks was shot in the back of the neck, but was injured only slightly. A woman, (Mrs. John Bowman) standing by and seeing Burton shoot Morris, said to him "This is cold-blooded murder." Burton shot her dead. Another woman characterized the transaction as "another Mountain Meadow Massacre," and Burton shot her dead.

The gruesome recital continued with the details of the murder of Banks, who was alleged to have been brought to Burton's camp, and dispatched by Dr. Jeter Clinton, Young's coroner and later an alderman of Salt Lake City. Clinton assertedly severed Bank's spinal cord with his scalpel.

> Now, this is not conjecture nor speculation. Neither does it rest upon the testimony of Sirrene alone. I have taken the evidence of at least six witnesses as to the killing of Morris and the two women by Burton and established the fact, beyond a doubt, that it was done in the manner above stated. . . . For these murders Burton is indicted.
>
> I have also very strong corroborating evidence . . . as to the killing of Banks by Clinton, and Clinton is indicted.

According to "Territorial practice," Howard continued, the concurrence of twelve of the fifteen grand jurors was necessary for indictment. "On the present Grand Jury there are but two Mormons." Even so, "knowing that the action of the Grand Jury would be immediately reported to Brigham Young . . . I anticipated the indictment in these cases and caused the arrest of the accused by Commissioner's Warrants. Otherwise they would have been in the mountains before their indictments were found." Mormon resentment flared up:

On bringing Burton before the Commissioner, the room was immediately filled with Mormon policemen (all Danites and several of them murderers whose crimes are being inquired into by the Grand Jury). One D. H. Wells, the Lieutenant General of the Nauvoo Legion and Brigham Young's second Counsellor, rushed into the room in great excitement, and with threats and menaces informed me that "These investigations and arrests of their best men must stop or I would see trouble. That the Mormon people were excited and that I would bring on a crisis quicker than I wished or contemplated."

This conduct is significant in view of the recent denials of the Mormons of any purpose on their part to interfere with the administration of Federal authority through officers of the courts. It is also very significant that Gen. (?) Wells, their military leader, should be the man to first show a disposition to "bulldoze the Courts.

An increase in the military forces in Utah Territory, concluded Howard, would alone save the day. "You will remember that I stated to President Hayes and yourself that I did not fear an outbreak except at the time when the Mormon leaders were to be arrested for their crimes. That time has come." [41]

Devens, alarmed by this report, penciled on the back of the letter: "Marshal not to proceed to make arrests until there is military force. Not to bring on collision until military is ready to sustain you and in sufficient force to aid you." He wrote at once to Secretary of War George W. McCrary (August 3, 1877):

I am informed by letter from the United States Attorney for Utah . . . that there is great reason to believe that if certain arrests are made of persons indicted by the Grand Jury . . . there will be resistance, riot, and perhaps bloodshed. Mr. Howard is also of the opinion that the number of United States troops at present in Utah is not sufficient to afford sufficient aid in enforcing the process of the Courts.

I have instructed Mr. Howard to direct the Marshal not to proceed with such arrests until he can be fully sustained by the military. I have, therefore, respectfully to request you to instruct the Commander of the troops in Utah to sustain the Marshal in the service of his process, and if they shall be called upon to act as his posse; and

[41] Cited above, July 28, 1877.

further that a larger number of troops be sent to that Territory . . . unless you shall be fully satisfied that the United States civil authorities, with . . . the military authority now there are capable of executing the process of the courts. . . .[42]

From the available evidence, it would appear that the War Department was skeptical of this request. Investigation led it to believe that the military force then stationed in the Territory was capable of dealing with any situation that might arise.[43] Howard maintained a steady correspondence with the attorney general, formulating plans for further prosecutions, suggesting legislation to limit the powers of the Mormon probate courts, and above all, insisting on the difficulties of administering justice in Utah under existing circumstances.[44] On February 6, 1878, Howard was replaced as district attorney by Philip T. Van Zile, of Michigan, who owed his appointment to the interest of Senators Isaac P. Christiancy and Thomas W. Ferry, of that State, both of whom were active in the formulation of anti-Mormon legislation.[45]

On taking office, Van Zile made every effort to continue the policies of his predecessor. To Attorney General Devens he wrote, requesting a statement as to general plans. The latter could only reply that he could offer none, though he suggested the prosecution of "worth-while cases" only.[46] In Van Zile's esteem, *The People v. Robert T. Burton* was eminently worth-while, and he regaled the patient attorney general with another full-length account of it.[47] The case finally came to trial on February 20, 1879 before Chief Justice Michael Schaeffer of the Salt Lake district court. Sirrene, Howard's reputed star witness, did not appear, and a mixed jury of Mormons and Gentiles agreed upon Burton's acquittal (March 7, 1879).[48]

---

[42] Devens to McCrary (N. A., D. J. Executive and Congressional Letter Book E, p. 557).

[43] *Cf.* Whitney, *op. cit.,* II, 824.

[44] Howard to Devens, November 8, 11, December 7, 1877 (N. A., D. J. MSS, Utah).

[45] D. J. Appointment File, 1877–1883.

[46] Devens to Van Zile, April 5, 1878 (N. A., D. J. Instruction Book H, p. 21).

[47] Van Zile to Devens, April 18, 1878 (N. A., D. J. MSS, Utah).

[48] Whitney, *op. cit.,* III, 35–44. In the Appointment Clerk's File, Depart-

At the same time that these rather fruitless efforts to settle past scores were being made, contending interests in the Territory were equally absorbed in the trial of a Mormon Elder, George Reynolds, for violation of the anti-Polygamy statute. When, in 1874, the Poland bill was enacted into law, and it became possible, at least in those sections of Utah where a Gentile minority existed, to secure mixed juries, it was realized that sooner or later a test case of the constitutionality of the anti-polygamy statute would have to be made. The circumstances which led to the indictment of Reynolds are shrouded in obscurity. In 1874, when the case was brought to bar, the defendant was a man of thirty-two. A native of England, as were so many of the prominent figures in the Mormon Church during this period, he had come to Utah in 1865, and for some years had acted as private secretary to Brigham Young. On August 3, 1874, he entered into polygamous relations with one Amelia Jane Schofield, the ceremony being performed in the Salt Lake Endowment House by Daniel H. Wells and witnessed by other high-ranking Mormon officials.[49]

The Mormon historian and apologist, Orson F. Whitney, has stated that during the summer of 1874, the district attorney, William Carey, entered into "negotiations" with the Church authorities, with the proposal that if they would provide the subject and witnesses necessary for a test case, proceedings against other alleged violators of the statute would be dropped, and further, that the penalty inflicted in the case, should judgment be adverse, would be purely nominal. Whitney's volume, containing this allegation, appeared in 1898.[50] In 1914 Robert N. Baskin, the Gentile attorney

---

ment of Justice (N. A.) an interesting correspondence was discovered, throwing light on the political career of General Lew Wallace. Under date of August 9, 1878, F. A. Dockray, an attorney of Salt Lake City, wrote Devens, asking him to delay the matter of appointing a chief justice for the Utah supreme court until he could present Wallace's name. Wallace himself wrote to introduce Dockray as "a most estimable gentleman." On August 13, 1878, Devens noted "Hon. Wm. P. Rice has shown me a letter addressed to Senator Conover by F. A. Dockray to effect that if Gen. Wallace appointed Ch. Jus. of Utah he would appoint him (D.) Clerk—worth $10,000 a year— that he could raise $2000 on the app^t and that $1000 of it was at Sen. Conover's service." It would be interesting to know if the author of *Ben Hur* were privy to this attempted bribery.

[49] Whitney, *op. cit.*, III, 47.

[50] *Ibid.*, III, 46–47.

long associated with the Liberal party, essayed, in his *Reminiscences of Early Utah,* to refute Whitney's interpretation. Though advanced in years when he wrote, Baskin, who had been a close associate of Carey and an eye witness of the trial, presented an able rebuttal. He denied flatly that any convention was agreed upon, contending that the case was entirely open, and that the attorneys for the defense made use of every legal means to vindicate their client.[51] The papers dealing with the Reynolds case, transmitted by Carey's successor, Sumner Howard, to Attorney General Taft, and received at the latter's office July 26, 1876, give no indication that would support Whitney's statement.[52]

The facts of the indictment and trial are clear. Reynolds' polygamous marriage was notorious. Information bearing thereon was submitted to the grand jury at the September term, 1874, and the indictment was drawn on October 23. Reynolds surrendered, was released on bail, and was summoned to trial on March 31, 1875, Justice Philip Emerson presiding. The testimony of the second Mrs. Reynolds, freely given, it would seem, clinched the case, since she admitted the facts stated in the indictment. Whitney has insisted that Daniel Wells testified that he had officiated at the polygamous rites; Baskin is emphatic and circumstantial in his denial that Wells made any such admission.[53]

On April 1, 1875, the jury returned a verdict of guilty, recommending the prisoner to the mercy of the court. Justice Emerson gave sentence nine days later, imposing one year at hard labor at the Utah Penitentiary and a fine of three hundred dollars. However, on appeal to the territorial supreme court, the decision of the lower court was set aside, on the technical grounds that the grand jury of indictment was an illegal body since it was composed of more than sixteen men as limited by law.[54]

In the following autumn the case was revived, and after due process, Reynolds was again convicted, December 21, 1875, receiving a heavier penalty of two years imprisonment at hard labor and a fine of five hundred dollars. In this second trial, the defendant's plural wife, Amelia Schofield, could not be found by the process

---

[51] Baskin, *Reminiscences,* pp. 61–72.
[52] Howard to Taft, (enclosure) July 26, 1876 (N. A., D. J. MSS, Utah).
[53] Whitney, *op. cit.,* III, 48; Baskin, *op. cit.,* p. 62.
[54] Utah, 266.

servers. The court, thereupon, admitted witnesses of the former
trial to testify as to the facts of her previous admission.[55]   The
territorial supreme court sustained the verdict of the district court
on June 13, 1876, and the case was finally appealed to the Supreme
Court of the United States on a writ of error.[56]

Arguments were heard by that tribunal on November 14, 1878.
Attorney General Devens addressed the Court, stressing the constitutionality of the Anti-Polygamy statute of 1862. The report of
the proceedings caused Dr. Seymour B. Young, nephew of the
late Mormon leader, to take up an unaccustomed pen:

> To his honor general Devans, Atorney general of the
> United States.
> Sir in your argument before the supreme court in the
> case of the people vs. George Reynolds of Utah you have
> rehashed credit Mobilier Colfaxes shallow nonsense
> wherein you state in relation to poligamy being an article
> of faith or religion with the Latter Day Saints a colony of
> Thugs might settle in any portion of the republic and com-
> mit murder and claim that it was part of their religion.
> Permit me to state that I believe you to be a man well
> read and learned in the law, nay, perhaps a very "Daniel
> come to Judgment" and that you will not admit even to
> yourself, the quotations from the too wellknown Smiler,
> to be good logic or sound law.
> It certainly is very unjust to make a comparison of two
> principles that are not in the least analogous and thereby
> create an opinion or influence to lead the Supreme court
> of the United States, beyond whom there is no appeal, to
> do an injury to an inocent party. You very well know
> that the Sacrifice of human life among the Hindoes and
> the plural mariage of the latter Day Saints are two prin-
> ciples diametrically opposed to each other. While murder
> or Thugism is abhorrent to man and the command of God
> is expressly against it, plural mariage on the contrary
> is a divine principle one which God has commanded his
> people to obey and is productive of life and when lived
> up to as it will be by God's people will be productive of
> vast good to the human family.
> Could you not have argued the case directly on its
> merits or at least left out those "oderous" (Mrs. Parting-
> ton) comparisons or if you must make comparisons not

---

[55] Baskin, *op. cit.*, pp. 63–64.
[56] 98 U. S., 145.

give us a rehash of that Superanuated bilge but try and
get up Something original.[57]

After two days of argument, during which Ben Sheeks, Gentile
attorney of Salt Lake City, ably defended Reynolds, the case was
taken under advisement. On January 6, 1879, Chief Justice Mor-
rison R. Waite spoke for a unanimous Court, which upheld the
validity of the statute in question and sustained the decision of the
highest territorial court:

> In our opinion, the statute immediately under con-
> sideration is within the legislative power of Congress.
> It is constitutional and valid as prescribing a rule of ac-
> tion for all those residing in the Territories, and in places
> over which the United States has exclusive control. This
> being so, the only question which remains is, whether those
> who make polygamy a part of their religion are excepted
> from the operation of the statute. If they are, then those
> who do not make polygamy a part of their religious belief
> may be found guilty and punished, while those who do,
> must be acquitted and go free. This would be introducing
> a new element in criminal law. Laws are made for the
> government of actions, and, while they cannot interfere
> with mere religious belief and opinions, they may with
> practices. Suppose one believed that human sacrifices
> were a necessary part of religious worship, would it be
> seriously contended that the civil government under which
> he lived could not interfere to prevent a sacrifice? Or, if
> a wife religiously believed it was her duty to burn herself
> on the funeral pile of her dead husband, would it be be-
> yond the power of the civil government to prevent her
> carrying her belief into practice.
> So here, as a law of the organization of society under
> the exclusive dominion of the United States, it is pro-

[57] Young to Devens, November 18, 1878 (N. A., D. J. MSS, Utah). The
reference to Colfax reflects Mormon resentment against the campaign the
former Vice President was then making against polygamy. The Colfax MSS
in the Library of Congress contain several of his letters to the editor of the
Salt Lake *Daily Tribune,* indicating the nature and extent of his anti-Mormon
activity, as well as rough drafts of a number of his speeches on the subject,
which are excessively bitter and ill-tempered, and contain a number of com-
parisons between Mormonism and Thugism, etc., which Devens may well
have read and borrowed. A half-sister of Colfax was the wife of Ovando J.
Hollister, collector of internal revenue for the Territory, and a prominent
anti-Mormon.

vided that plural marriages shall not be allowed. Can a
man excuse his practices to the contrary because of his
religious belief? To permit this would make the professed doctrines of religious belief superior to the law
of the land, and in effect, to permit every citizen to become a law unto himself. Government could exist only
in name under such circumstances.[58]

In Utah, the outraged feeling of the Saints found ample expression. The Salt Lake *Herald* was certain that "There is but
one really Supreme Court in the United States, and that is the
people of the whole country. . . . Compared with this august
court, the Washington tribunal is a petty affair, and its judgments
are liable to be unhesitatingly overruled, as was the case in the
Dred Scott matter." Congress was appealed to as the expression
of a higher will "to restore that desirable harmony between the
declared principle of the government and the action of the legislative, the judicial and the executive departments of the same."
Monogamy itself was declared imperiled. "What real security
then has monogamy since the Supreme Court's decision that religious 'actions' are suppressible by congress?" Van Zile, who was
reported from Washington as stating that on the very day of the
Reynolds decision, seventy-six polygamous marriages took place in
the Salt Lake Endowment House, was roundly scored: "He has
declared himself an enemy of the people, and if the telegraphic
report can be relied upon, he is . . . both vicious and unprincipled." [59] Eliza Snow, a Mormon lady of literary bent, interpreted
to her satisfaction the animus of the Supreme Court:

> Yea, let us cause thousands of honorable, loving wives
> to be stigmatized as prostitutes, and their offspring as
> bastards.
> Let us desecrate their homes and exterminate the only
> people of whom our nation can truly boast as protectors
> of purity and innocence, lest their virtuous and honorable
> example shall, in the present reign of corruption, rise up
> before us as a burning reproof.
> Instead of the Territory of Utah as it now is—a theme
> of boast as a nucleus of peace, good order and happiness,
> let us, through our crushing policy, exhibit it to the na-

[58] 98 U. S., 145, at page 162.
[59] Salt Lake *Herald,* January 18, 25, 30, 1879.

tions abroad, as a spectacle of confusion, desolation and woe.[60]

Subsequently the Supreme Court instructed the territorial supreme court to modify the "hard labor" clause in Reynolds' sentence. He was incarcerated in the Nebraska State penitentiary in June, 1879, but on representations made by Delegate Cannon that the prisoner was in poor health, the attorney general instructed Marshal Michael Shaughnessy of Utah to transfer him to the territorial penitentiary in Salt Lake City.[61] Later, Devens telegraphed the marshal: "Examine Reynolds case. He is a convict sentenced for punishment, and should be subject to prison discipline and not permitted to receive frequent visitors. . . . Reported that he has had unusual privileges." [62] At the expiration of his term, shortened for good behavior, in January, 1881, Reynolds was accorded an impressive ovation by his co-religionists, to the disgust of the local Gentiles.[63]

It is not the purpose of this study to recount the various individual prosecutions for polygamy which followed upon the Reynolds case. While it is true that these judicial proceedings were a reflection of the local antagonism between Mormon and Gentile, the element of national interest figured more dominantly. There was abroad the feeling that the "great crusade" against polygamy was at last to be launched by America as a whole. Van Zile informed Attorney General Devens, July 11, 1879, that, "There never was a time when opportunities were so flattering as now. And a few more convictions of the 'big fellows' would settle the matter of polygamy." He suggested that the Justice Department place at the disposal of the district attorney's office "a fund . . . upon which . . . I could employ a detective to look up the proofs" for pending cases.

> I think if I could say to some appostate [sic] Mormons here that I know of I will give you $100 if you will look up the proofs that will convict certain bishops and

[60] *Deseret News,* January 21, 1879.

[61] Devens to Shaughnessy, June 23, 1879 (N. A., D. J. Instruction Book I, p. 240).

[62] Devens to Shaughnessy, September 5, 1879.

[63] Whitney, *op. cit.,* III, 57.

influential Mormons that I could make Mormonism shake
in her boots before next January.

Van Zile took special pleasure in confiding to his chief that he had
penetrated the mysteries of Mormonism: "I have succeeded in
getting hold of the secret endowment house ceremony together with
the clothing worn a suit of which completed I have in my office." [64]
    With the coming of the Eighties, an echo of the lamented Judge
McKean was heard from the bench of Chief Justice John A.
Hunter, identifying himself with the Gentile minority, and appeal-
ing for a fourth district judgeship in the Territory:

> I hope you will remember that we are a suffering com-
> munity having to deal with the most intolerant bigots, and
> are fighting a battle such as does not compass any other
> section of the country. As a means to the end of the
> Church Hierarchy, full protection to the legal rights of
> the Gentile element should be given. In the present state
> of the judicial force such protection is not offered. . . .
> All of us understand that as long as this people adhere to
> their Mormon teachings, the Territory will not be ad-
> mitted as a State, and it certainly seems proper that the
> Gentile element which has come here, and by its presence
> and influence, given moral force to the interests of the
> general Government, should have, in return, this aid.[65]

Though Reynolds had been convicted, it was clear to the Utah
Gentiles that the necessary preliminary to a successful campaign
to destroy polygamy was a tightening of the law. While the law
admitted of loopholes, the Mormons, with the aid of clever attorneys, would make full use of them. Eagerly the congressional horizon was scanned for indications of the disposition of
the national legislators to exercise their power over the Territory.
In 1874, the Poland bill was hailed as a step in the right direction,
providing, as it did in its fourth section, that the jury lists should
be drawn by the clerk of the district courts as well as by the justice
of the local probate court in the jurisdiction of which the district
court was sitting. When the bill passed the House of Representatives, late in May of that year, the Salt Lake *Tribune* voiced the
minority sentiment:

---

[64] Van Zile to Devens, July 11, 1879 (N. A., D. J. MSS, Utah).
[65] Hunter to Devens, February 2, 1880 (N. A., D. J. MSS, Utah).

> The very necessity of such legislation . . . is a ser-
> mon of deeper significance to the masses of Utah than any
> ever preached by their once-powerful, but now doubted
> leader.
> The same men who have long labored to excite hos-
> tility between the people and their government will now
> take the Poland bill for a text upon which to rekindle the
> fires of hatred. They will preach that a Gentile crusade is
> aiming to overthrow the Saints and deprive them of their
> homes. . . .[66]

However, experience showed the weakness of the very provision which had seemed to afford greatest leverage against Mormon
domination. The Gentile press was soon complaining that the fact
that the Mormon probate judges could draw half the panel meant,
invariably, "a dead-lock in all trials of offenders in which the Mormon Church is interested." [67]   General Maxwell and Robert N.
Baskin, representing the Gentiles in Washington, lobbied zealously
for the passage of a bill sponsored by Senator Christiancy, the
point of which was "to declare ineligible for juror in any trial for
bigamy or polygamy the pious Saint who has polluted his household
with this filthy crime polygamy, or who has scruples of conscience
against finding a verdict of guilty where this offence has been
proved." [68]   But 1876 was an election year and the congressional
politicians had other matters to consider. The *Daily Tribune* could
only offer as consolation:

> But even if the passage of such an act be delayed a
> year, the steady gain we are making upon the Mormon
> Church will not be retarded, and sooner or later such an
> instrument must be placed in our hands to vindicate our
> inalienable liberties. . . .[69]

The "reform administration" of President Hayes was greeted
by the minority in Utah as the dawn of a better day, when Con-

---

[66] *Daily Tribune,* June 3, 1874. *Cf. Ibid.,* April 23, June 18, 24, 1874. The
last issue contained another paeon of praise: "Ad Majoriam [*sic*] Dei Glo-
riam! Polygamy and Murder No Longer Justified! Human Slavery Abolished Forever and Priesthood Rule Killed! . . . The Last Relic of Barbarism Extirpated from the Earth," etc., etc.

[67] *Ibid.,* January 22, 1876.

[68] *Ibid.,* January 22, 1876.

[69] *Ibid.,* June 16, 1876.

gress would "make atonement for the sin of omission that has long rested upon it." [70]   But Hayes' precarious victory over Tilden had its repercussions even in the Territory.   Anti-polygamy legislation of various degrees of stringency, debated frequently and at length in both Houses of Congress during the following four years, was thwarted, not, apparently, because the Democrats had any special love for Mormons or Mormonism, but because of political expediency.   It is apparent, moreover, that as Southern legislators began to make their influence felt in Washington, they, mindful of the indignities suffered by their states during the era of reconstruction, were slow to enthuse over measures that would serve to increase federal control over the territories.

Not until Garfield was in office, and the memory of Credit Mobilier, Star Route frauds and reconstruction had faded into the middle distance, did Congress reach agreement about the case of Utah Territory.   Typically representative of the New England conscience in politics, Senator George Edmunds of Vermont sponsored the bill to which he gave his name.   Embodying the provision of the Christiancy bill for the disfranchisement of Mormons practicing polygamy, it further provided for an electoral commission, to be appointed by the President under the customary conditions— senatorial consent and minority representation—to supervise the exercise of the ballot in Utah and to report to Congress, through the Secretary of the Interior, on conditions existing there.

Discussion of the bill, pending during the early part of 1882, displayed the dissatisfaction of the more radical Gentiles with the comparative moderation of its provisions.   Their cry, rendered strident by delay and disappointment, was for the disfranchisement, not only of those actually living in polygamy, but of all who believed in the doctrine.   Obviously, such an extreme demand went far beyond the Supreme Court dictum in the Reynolds case.   The commission these Gentiles wanted was not merely one to superintend local elections, but to rule the Territory with an iron hand. And with an eye to their own political welfare, they advocated the selection of such a commission from their own ranks, claiming that only a Gentile who had lived in Utah and who had experienced the

---

[70] *Ibid.,* March 8, 1877.

insidious power of the Mormon hierarchy could be equipped to deal with the problem realistically.[71]

Nevertheless, when the Edmunds bill, having been approved by the Senate, was passed by the House on March 14, 1882, by a vote of one hundred and ninety-nine to forty-two, there was exultation in the Gentile camp. The editor of the *Daily Tribune,* who had led the school of critics, echoed the theme of congratulation: "The Gentiles have scored a real triumph at last, the first . . . in a contest which has raged for twenty years." [72] The anti-polygamy crusade was at last prepared to take the offensive.

[71] *Ibid.,* January 26, 1882.
[72] *Ibid.,* March 15, 1882.

CHAPTER V

THE LIBERAL PARTY AND
GOVERNOR MURRAY

AGAINST THE odds of an overwhelmingly dominant Mormon population, strongly organized not only along religious lines but politically as well, the Gentile aspirations for control of Utah through the ballot seemed indeed a forlorn hope. The first feeble effort to contest an election with a Church candidate, in 1867, had underscored the cohesion of the Mormon vote and the pitiable ineffectiveness of the opposition. If the Saints were to be left in undisturbed possession of the franchise, it was fully realized that any effort to dislodge them from their political hegemony would of necessity be a tedious and disheartening task. Yet the Gentiles of Utah shared the boundless optimism of the frontier. Even in 1867 they echoed General Connor's conviction that the mineral wealth of the region would speedily attract a non-Mormon population sufficient to wrest the political sceptre from the Church.

The passing years failed to demonstrate the accuracy of that forecast, but there still seemed to be ways and means of turning the tide. There was, first of all, the possibility that the federal government might see fit to divest polygamists of the vote, and further, recognize the cogency of the Gentile argument that all who believed in "patriarchal marriage" as a divine ordinance must be classed as polygamists; again, there was the possibility that woman suffrage, as enacted by territorial legislation, might be rejected by Congress. The Gentile leaders were shrewd enough to understand that if the campaign were to be successful, it would call for their instancy, in season and out of season, in bringing the Utah situation to the attention of the country at large, whose interest in a distant and sparsely-settled territory would be, at best, fitful and capricious. Finally, there was always the hope, constantly reappearing in political debates of all kinds, under appropriate guise, that "Young

122

Mormonism" could be prevailed upon the desert the ways of the fathers and make common cause with the "liberal" Gentiles.

Thus, as its basic platform, the Liberal party could exploit the charges of ecclesiastical interference in politics as pernicious and un-American. That there was the closest connection between the "Peoples' Party" and the Mormon Church was too plain a fact to be convincingly denied. In the twenty years that followed their first plunge into territorial politics, from 1867 to 1887, when the Edmunds-Tucker bill became law, the Liberals became reconciled to a crushing series of defeats at the polls, but they kept their eye on the barometer of national opinion, as registering popular sympathy with their well advertised effort to throw off the weight of a thing so foreign to the American spirit as religion in politics.

Robert N. Baskin, as the leading spirit in the organization of McGroarty's contest with Delegate Hooper, did not allow the paltry one hundred and five votes received by his candidate to dampen his ardor. In December, 1869, encouraged no doubt by the rapid increase in the Gentile population consequent upon the completion of the railroad and the immediate development of the mining industry, he began to agitate for a permanent political opposition, with a local habitation and a name, to underwrite an effort to disfranchise the polygamous Mormons:

> . . . In this same December, a few gentlemen gathered in Reuben H. Robertson's law office and prepared the Cullom bill, and Mr. Baskin went to the Capital with it, and on the 21st, Mr. Cullom, then chairman of the House Committee on Territories, introduced it in the House. It did away with Mormon usurpations and substantially divested the Mormons of the political privileges of citizenship, on the ground that they declined to perform the duties, and even to acknowledge the allegiance of citizenship. The bill was debated; it gave rise to considerable discussion in the press, it was protested against by the Mormons and all sorts of calamities threatened should it become law, and the attempt be made to put it in force. It passed the House by three-fourths majority, but was smothered by Senator Nye of Nevada in the Senate. When Mr. Baskin returned to Salt Lake his friends thought they had just grounds to fear his assassination. The schismatics of the December previous, called Godbeites, were in fear of the same all that winter

and on their behalf, Mr. Godbe went and saw the President.[1]

In July, 1870, Gentiles of a political bent met at Corinne, Utah, under Baskin's direction. Agreement was made that their former party affiliations should be discarded in the interests of their common cause. General George R. Maxwell was nominated as the Liberal party candidate for Congress, and in the August elections succeeded in gaining 1,469 votes as against Hooper's total of 21,-656.[2] A study of the election returns for the next twenty years would seem to indicate that, at that time, in proportion to their numbers, the Gentiles polled a higher percentage of votes than they ever succeeded in doing subsequently. The scattered character of the Gentile population, distributed in far-flung mining communities, added to the fact that many of the miners themselves were but slightly interested in local politics, and had no intention of establishing domicile in Utah for voting purposes, explains in a measure the relatively small vote obtained by the successive Liberal candidates for territorial offices.

On July 4, 1871, the Liberals inaugurated a custom of holding a separate patriotic celebration in Salt Lake City, to which they generally adhered until the dissolution of the party.

> The moral effect of the Liberal procession on the 4th will be mighty in Utah. While in numbers it was second to the Church turnout, in wealth, influence and in the social standing of its participants it was equal to the display made by the Theocracy.
> The capital never witnessed a gathering, so large as this, free and independent of the Church. . . .[3]

With anti-Mormon fire-eaters in the saddle, such as a certain Judge Dennis Toohy of Corinne, the Liberal party ran headlong into difficulties. The Godbeites, willing enough to see the Mormon

---

[1] Ovando J. Hollister, in the Salt Lake *Tribune*, November 4, 1888. The article cited is substantially accurate, though the purpose of Godbe's visit with President Grant was rather to plead for the employment of less drastic methods for the solution of the Mormon problem than those contemplated by the Cullom bill.

[2] *Ibid.*

[3] *Daily Tribune*, July 6, 1871.

hierarchy humbled, were sufficiently mindful of their own past affiliations with the Church and their present business interests with the rank and file of the Mormons to deprecate any extreme measures which were proposed. One of their number, Eli B. Kelsey, wrote to the *Tribune* editor anent a particularly violent Liberal convention:

> . . . The spirit of the proceedings in the Mass Meeting of the Liberal Party . . . convinced me that a portion of those who assume the lead are bent upon a war upon the people of the Territory on social and religious grounds. . . . I oppose the absurd assumptions of the Mormon priesthood . . . but because Brigham has shorn the flock, I do not, therefore, think we are justified in taking their hides also. . . .
>
> If there are individuals who aspire to the leadership of a liberal party in Utah, I hope they will have the wisdom to avoid the framing of an iron bedstead upon which to measure the people. . . . I trust that they will remember that the Mormons are a hundred thousand strong in Utah.[4]

The Corinne *Journal,* organ of the radicals, made prompt reply:

> With . . . hope and expectation, we have said many kind words for the Mormon Protestants. It seems that it was a false hope and we must part company. The personal convenience of three or four of these men is of more consequence to them than the cause of reform in Utah, or they imagine that the cause doesn't involve the abolition of polygamy. In either case there is enough said. It is a bad egg, and won't hatch our style of chicken at all.[5]

Weakened thus by internal dissension, the Liberal party failed to elect a single member of the territorial legislature in the campaign of 1871.

---

[4] Letter dated July 25, 1871; *Ibid.,* July 27, 1871.

[5] Corinne *Journal,* July 29, 1871, a file of which is preserved in the Bancroft Library. *Cf.* Whitney, *Utah,* II, 540: "Henceforth the Liberal Party was utterly devoid of the reform feature. It was anti-Mormonism unmixed, —bitterness and rancor to the heart's core. Elements of respectability from time to time have become attached to it, and at intervals have directed its policy; but one by one these are breaking away, leaving the party to die, poisoned by the exudations of its own encysted venom." Written in the nineties, this may be taken as a typical Mormon reaction.

Statehood, the goal of Mormon aspirations, was for the Liberals the thing to be feared most. It would mean, as the *Tribune* told its readers, "the recovery to Brigham Young and the Mormon priesthood of the absolute control of which they have been deprived by the Reformation and the incoming agencies which have arrived with the Railroad and the development of the mines." Until the Gentiles should be "sufficiently numerous to at least balance fairly with the fanatical class at the polls," the United States must hold the whip-hand. Early in 1872, a constitutional convention was called for by the territorial assembly. The Liberals sought unity in face of danger: "All minor points of antagonism to the Church and its leaders should be resolved into the one great purpose before us . . . whether Liberals shall migrate to the moon, or stay here and fight it out on this line. . . ." From the Church camp emanated the proposal that the convention should be composed of ten Mormons and nine Gentiles—a safe though not ungenerous attempt to quiet the strident Liberal opposition. But the Gentile press was not to be taken in: "This classification of the delegates . . . is a most treacherous one, . . . designed for show at home and effect abroad. There are only a few names in that list that have the Gentile value." [6]

The convention met on February 19, 1872, made short work of the objections of the Gentile minority to the wisdom of the proceeding, and adopted a constitution based upon that of Nevada. The fifth article of the ordinance and bill of rights for the proposed State of Deseret contained the provision:

> That such terms, if any, as may be prescribed by Congress as a condition of the admission of the said State into the Union, shall, if ratified by a majority vote of the people thereof . . . thereupon be embraced within . . . this ordinance.

Since this, even by implication, was the sole reference to a solution of the paramount issue of polygamy, the Gentiles would have

---

[6] *Daily Tribune,* December 9, 1871; January 15, 1872; February 5, 1872. Among the non-Mormons elected was the Hon. Thomas Fitch, formerly congressman from Nevada, who seems to have intrigued with the Mormons, and was rewarded by election to the United States Senate by the hopeful Utah assembly.

none of it. Baskin, Henry W. Lawrence and Joseph R. Walker were sent to Washington by the Utah Liberals to oppose the results of the convention in Congress. In this they were successful.[7]

As a consequence of this maneuvre, ill-feeling between the two groups became even more pronounced during the summer of 1872. The *Utah Mining Journal* poured its ridicule upon the Mormon politicians :

> The Church "Mass Meeting," on Saturday, in the Tabernacle, to select candidates to fill the various offices becoming vacant this year, was so characteristic . . . of the Priesthood of the so-called Latter-Day Saints, that it did not fail to attract the attention . . . of the sensible portion of the community. . . . The ticket was made up by Brigham Young, Wells, *et al.*, submitted to and approved by the School of Prophets, an idle form, and then, under the thinnest possible pretense, laid before the people. What the people had to say may be judged from the simple fact that the *Evening News* . . . issued long before the "convention" had adjourned, or even fairly discussed the names of the candidates, published in full the ticket gotten up in the Lion House, as adopted by the mass meeting ![8]

George Q. Cannon, astute politician and a practicing polygamist, was the choice, however indicated, of the Peoples' Party for congressional delegate. The Liberals, meeting again in Corinne, July 25, reaffirmed their faith in General Maxwell, "Though we have little reason to hope that the party nominated by the Convention today . . . will be elected to Congress, yet we are not to view the Convention as a failure." Progress, all good Liberals were assured, was being made more rapidly than was believed. In a Liberal victory reposed the only hope of the territory.[9]

The campaign subtracted nothing from the heat of a Utah summer. The *Tribune* considered that "Non-Mormons throughout the Territory should now distinctly understand that it is the policy of the Church party to have a full-blooded Mormon and a practical polygamist full of the Priesthood" represent the people, and, "With such a bitter Gentile-hater as Geo. Q. Cannon in Con-

---

[7] Whitney, *op. cit.,* II, 692 ff., 721.

[8] July 15, 1872. File in the Salt Lake Public Library.

[9] *Ibid.,* July 25, 1872.

gress, can any one for a moment imagine that any outsider's interests would be consulted?" [10]   The climax came on the night of August 3, when a Liberal meeting in front of the Salt Lake House was broken up by an excited mob.   Seeking refuge in Independence Hall, the embattled Liberals vented to their injured feelings.   In the morning the anti-Mormon press reviewed the incident: "It was a deliberate outrage on the Gentiles of Utah and an insult to the American people. . . .   If we have rights, they are worth fighting for.   Let us then hereafter meet force with force." [11]   On the following day the Liberals polled nearly two thousand votes, but failed to carry a single county against Cannon's overwhelming majority.[12]

Mormon sentiment, so far as the national election of 1872 was concerned, was solidly behind Horace Greeley, both because he carried the banner against the Grant regime and because he had spoken kind words of them in past years.   The Liberal explanation that it was their expectation of Greeley's victory that impelled the Church leaders to manipulate the election of Cannon, was probably close to the truth.[13]   In full confidence that the House of Representatives would refuse to seat a polygamist, the Liberals determined to contest the election.   Maxwell, therefore, as the defeated candidate, lodged a protest with the sympathetic Governor Woods on the grounds that his opponent was constitutionally disqualified. Cannon replied by swearing that he was not guilty of the charges alleged against him.   The *Utah Mining Journal* interpreted this as a denial of his polygamous marriages:

> Good for George Q. We have long thought it would come to this. But what form of pity can we express for the women who have during long years of . . . submission . . . been known as Mrs. Cannon No. one, No. two, No. three, and so on? . . . How easily, after all, has the Utah problem been disposed of by this sublime act of re-

---

[10] *Daily Tribune,* August 2, 1872.

[11] *Utah Mining Journal,* August 4, 1872.

[12] For a few days it appeared that Beaver County might have had the distinction of being the first to register a Liberal victory. However, the votes of a number of miners were declared invalid, and the People's party emerged triumphant (*Utah Mining Journal,* August 9, 16, 1872).

[13] *Daily Tribune,* November 6, 1872.

pudiation, as witness the signature of Mr. Cannon to his emphatic denial of the revelation.[14]

Hooper's term of office did not expire until March 4, 1873; Cannon, consequently, did not apply for his seat until December 1 of that year. Woods reluctantly issued the certificate of election. When Congress assembled, Representative Clinton Levi Merriam, of New York, acting on behalf of Maxwell, offered a resolution to disqualify the Mormon delegate. The resolution was tabled, however, and Maxwell's subsequent effort to secure action through Representative George C. Hazelton, of Wisconsin, was rebuffed by the Committee on Elections.[15] The unexpected had happened, and the Gentiles were forced to reckon with the fact that the "Theocracy" had scored a pointed victory. A hint of discouragement found expression:

> We are still bound with the chains of a dominant priesthood. Our children are denied the privilege of education ("I am opposed to free schools," says the Prophet, "and to legislation in favor of free schools"). And our Legislative Assembly are mere registers of His Mightiness' edicts. We have no voice at the polls, no returns of the use made of our money, and justice is denied us in all the Courts of the Territory . . . the Council Chambers are closed to a free press. . . .[16]

With commendable resiliency, the Liberals again prepared to contest the congressional election of August, 1874. A strong effort was put forth by the Gentile press to attract the allegiance of "Young Mormonism," urging it "to do battle with the old fogies." [17] Robert N. Baskin was chosen as the Liberal standard bearer, and

---

[14] *Utah Mining Journal*, November 25, 1872.

[15] *43rd Congress, 1st Session, House Miscellaneous Document, No. 49* (Washington, D. C., 1872), 151 pp. Hazelton's address was subsequently printed, *Speech of the Hon. Geo. C. Hazelton, against Permitting Polygamy to be Represented in Congress . . . April 18, 1882* (Washington, D. C., 1882), 15 pp.

[16] *Daily Tribune*, January 15, 1874. The *Tribune* reporter, a short time previously, had been denied entry into the Salt Lake City council chambers because of the alleged scurrility of that paper's treatment of the city fathers.

[17] *The Daily Press*, July 13, 1874. An incomplete file of this journal, strongly Democratic in national politics, is in the Salt Lake Public Library.

on August 3, ran up a vote which amounted to nearly one-fifth of that cast for the incumbent Cannon by the People's party.[18] In Salt Lake City, the balloting was marked by disorders, calling forth the comment that "the conspirators against the public good made their last fight in opposition to the will of the people." [19]

Tooele County, to the west of Salt Lake City, was carried by the Liberal ticket during the same election. The feverish activity of the mines had brought into the district a considerable number of prospecters and Cornish and Irish laborers. The territorial election law for county officials made no provision for registration, but reckoned the list of those eligible from the tax rolls. It was discovered that the number of ballots cast, particularly in the Gentile mining centers, far exceeded the number of local taxpayers. Obviously, fraud had been practised, but Governor Woods, disregarding the findings of the canvassing board, issued certificates to the Liberal candidates, and Chief Justice McKean, to whom the cases were appealed, gave the defeated Mormon claimants short shrift. Until 1879 Tooele County remained under the control of the Liberals, earning, in Gentile circles, the title "Republic of Tooele." That the Liberal regime, in the hands of transients and adventurers, rather than of settled inhabitants, was inefficient and financially disastrous for the county, as Whitney charges, is hardly surprising.[20]

True to form, Baskin resolved to contest the election of his opponent. In this, as has been noted previously,[21] he enjoyed the cooperation of Governor Woods, who in view of his own imminent resignation from office, had nothing to lose by refusing to grant a certificate of election to Delegate Cannon. But Governor Axtell, succeeding Woods, was more amenable to the will of the Mormon majority. Nevertheless, the defeated Liberal was on hand in Washington for the opening of the Forty-fifth Congress. "This gentleman," wrote the editor of the *Tribune*, "goes at his

---

[18] Cannon—24,864, Baskin—4,598. *Cf.* Hollister, *loc. cit.*, November 4, 1888.

[19] *Daily Tribune*, August 4, 1874. In the melee, Mayor Heber M. Wells was arrested by Marshal Maxwell for "inciting to insurrection," but the charges were later dropped.

[20] Whitney, *op. cit.*, II, 740–755; III, 131–134.

[21] *Vide supra*, p. 94.

own expense and neglects a lucrative law practice to battle for the enfranchisement of this benighted and priest-bound Territory." [22] Congress was not particularly interested in the tribulations of Mr. Baskin, but the Liberal leader would not permit official indifference to dampen his enthusiasm. Throughout the session he remained on Capitol Hill, working behind the scenes with Senator Christiancy of Michigan for the formulation of the territorial election bill which in substance was enacted into law as the Edmunds Act of 1882.[23]

With the threat of congressional action framing election laws designed to disqualify polygamists hanging over them, the Mormon leaders were forced to compromise on one point, the marked ballot. The original act of the legislative assembly, approved January 3, 1853, provided in its fifth section that:

> Each elector shall provide himself with a vote containing the names of the persons he wishes elected, and the offices he would have them fill, and present it neatly folded to the judge of election, who shall number and deposit it in the ballot box. The clerk shall then write the name of the elector, and opposite it the number of his vote.[24]

Clearly, the possibilities for interested parties to keep check on the popular vote were open to valid criticism. The Liberals made the most of the opportunity, using the "iniquity" of the law as a talking point in their campaign to revise the law so as to disfranchise as many of their opponents as possible. President Grant, on the occasion of his visit to Salt Lake City, October 4, 1875, was "posted" on the matter:

> . . . The President, on his return to Ogden, sought the company of two or three staunch Gentiles, and retiring into his private car, asked many questions in regard

---

[22] *Daily Tribune,* November 30, 1875.

[23] *Ibid.,* February 18, 1876, November 27, 1877. Senator Christiancy's abnormal behavior when, at the age of sixty-four he married a girl of nineteen, was embarrassing for the Liberals waging the fight against polygamy. The Mormon press was not slow to make capital out of the vagaries of the elderly opponent of patriarchal marriage. *Cf. Deseret News,* February, 1876, *passim.*

[24] *Compiled Laws of the Territory of Utah* (Salt Lake City, 1876), p. 84.

to the working of the present jury laws and the manner
of conducting elections in Utah. When fully informed
upon these subjects, the President said he should again
recommend legislation for this Territory in his forthcoming message.[25]

The *Utah Evening Mail,* one of the Gentile organs, professed
to regard the secret ballot as a Mormon interpretation of "omni-
present Jesuitism" whose "leaven of ecclesiasticism not only
penetrates and poisons the social and domestic relations, but also
strikes a deadly blow at personal liberty and republican institutions." [26]

Early in February, 1876, the Utah Liberals forwarded a petition to Congress praying that body to take action to secure a secret
ballot for the Territory.[27] Senator Christiancy made a point of
including appropriate legislation bearing thereon in the anti-Mormon bills which he sponsored before the Senate. To forestall
radical measures, the territorial legislature enacted a new election
law, February 22, 1878, which did away with the marked ballot,
provided for the appointment of three judges of election by the
county courts, and insisted upon proof of "stability of residence." [28]
While the bill was under discussion, the *Daily Independent,* another of the multitudinous Gentile papers of Salt Lake City, expressed the opinion of the minority:

> It is simply ridiculous to pretend that the object of
> the marked ballot in Utah was to protect the ballot-box
> from fraud, or that it ever has been an auxiliary of
> freedom. At the time this precious boon was conferred
> upon the free and independent citizens of Utah, they
> were all, presumably, of one heart and one mind, or if
> not, the opposition was so trifling as to amount to noth-

---

[25] *Daily Tribune,* October 13, 1875.

[26] February 3, 1876. File in the Salt Lake Public Library.

[27] *Daily Tribune,* February 3, 1876. The call to the meeting read: "It is
expected that no Mormons nor jack-Mormons, nor any milk-and-water Gentiles or Apostates will be there. They are not wanted. Nothing but the
true-blue will do for this occasion, and all others are invited to stay away.
Let none but free men rally!"

[28] *Laws, Memorials and Resolutions of the Territory of Utah . . .
Twenty-third Session of the Legislative Assembly* (Salt Lake City, 1878),
pp. 28–37.

ing, and the aim was *to keep them so.* The people of
this Territory have been literally forced by every means
within the control of an unscrupulous, heaven-ordained
hierarchy, which centered in one narrow-minded but
strong-willed individual, to be united. The republican
form or some approach to it had to be maintained for the
sake of decency . . . but it has been a sham republicanism from the beginning. . . . The spy-ballot system
. . . is about "played out." [29]

However, that the territorial legislature, Mormon in personnel
and sympathy, should remedy the disorder was precisely what the
radical Liberals did not want. It stripped them of too valuable
an argument for the necessity of a federal law which could be
framed to reach much farther. Moreover, the insistence upon
residence qualifications would obviously bear most heavily upon
the migratory miners, from whose vote the Liberals principally
drew whatever strength they had. Hence, meeting in Independence Hall, February 27, 1878, the party chieftains resolved:

We, the freemen of Utah and citizens of the United
States in convention assembled declare our unalterable
opposition to said election law and record our undis-
sembled grief at its enactment. This law gives to the
Mormon priesthood the power to provide the machinery
to work the plan and the engineers to operate the machinery. It in effect disfranchises a large majority of the
Liberal voters, while it throws wide open the doors to
the wives, be they many or few or alien, to vote at the
beck and under the covering mantle of their Citizen Lord.
    Resolved, that the freemen of this Territory anx-
iously look to Congress for the enactment of an election
law that will secure them in their constitutional rights
as citizens of the United States and of this Territory,
and that they will amend this Utah burlesque on the Utah
frauds. [30]

The matter was brought to the attention of Attorney General
Devens, who discussed it at a meeting of the Cabinet, March 15.

---

[29] February 13, 1878. File in Salt Lake Public Library.

[30] Baskin to Joseph C. Hemingray, Washington, D. C., February 28, 1878
(N. A., D. J. MSS, Utah). Hemingray, a Salt Lake attorney and a friend
of Christiancy, was in the national capital at the time, substituting for Baskin
as the Liberal lobbyist. (*Daily Tribune,* November 27, 1877.)

From the almost illegible outline he left of his oral report, it is apparent that Devens was not impressed with the cogency of the Liberal argument. He noted the law as "a substantial improvement," although recognizing that "the difficulties . . . will be more felt by the non-Mormon population who are miners and who change their residences oftener than the Mormons." [31]   Until the Edmunds bill was enacted into law (1882), the Liberals were perforce content with their pyrrhic victory.

As indicated in the preceding chapter, Governor Emery failed to measure up to the demands and expectations of the radical Gentiles. His determination to do all in his power to keep peace in the Territory became a source of constant irritation to them, and they lost no opportunity to decry him as a "jack-Mormon," the generic term for a Gentile who was disposed at all costs to live on terms of cordiality with the Saints.[32]   Playing Roland against Oliver, the Liberals fomented discord between the governor and Territorial Secretary George Black, a pronounced anti-Mormon who had served under Governor Woods and who undoubtedly felt aggrieved because he had been passed over in the succession.[33]

Emery's loyalty to Grant, and his support of the current third-term proposal, did nothing to improve his relations with the local die-hards:

> Emery, relying on Grant, has lost face. So has Grant. . . . Two years ago, no more loyal supporters of President Grant could anywhere be found than the non-Mormons of Utah. . . . But . . . he has alienated all the friendship that was felt for him in this Territory; his repeated acts of tyranny, arrogance and injustice have

---

[31] N. A., D. J. MSS, Utah.

[32] The term "jack-Mormon," first used in the above sense, at the present time bears the connotation of a non-practising Mormon; an interesting example of change in definition.

[33] *Daily Tribune,* April 22, 1876. The Utah Republicans—most Liberals belonged to that party so far as national politics was concerned—sent Secretary Black as a delegate to the convention of 1876, to the evident discomfiture of Emery. "We hope his Excellency has not gone off mad, but he no doubt has a clear prevision that the Ides of March will bring a radical change in the official life in Utah." Black was removed from office the following spring.

so turned the hearts of the people against him that there
is none so poor to do him reverence.[34]

It may be suspected that the feeling against Grant was caused
not by these alleged shortcomings, but by his loss of interest in
the Utah question.

In 1876, the biennial contest for the post of congressional
delegate was again fought between George Q. Cannon and Robert
N. Baskin. The *Tribune* led off with the attack:

> "Our honored Delegate," as the Church journals ef-
> fusively call the many-wived Apostle, returned to Salt
> Lake City last evening, and was received with immense
> gush by his brother infallibles and the long-neglected
> inmates of his harem. For three years . . . this man has
> been allowed to retain his seat in Congress without his
> fitness to sit in that body being once brought to a vote,
> notwithstanding it has been shown to the committee on
> privileges and elections, to whom his case was referred,
> that he is an unnaturalized alien and an acknowledged
> felon—cohabiting openly with four or five concubines.
> This shameful dereliction of duty on the part of Congress
> the craven Mormon prints hail as a great victory. . . .[35]

The election, held at the regular time in November, was quiet
and orderly; neither candidate received a record vote, but Cannon's
victory was again impressive, 20,850 to Baskin's 3,833.[36] The
defeated Liberal failed to file notice of protest within the statutory
time, but early in the following April unexpectedly informed
Governor Emery that he was ready to attend the canvass of votes.
Emery, who had already issued the certificate of election to Cannon, was nonplussed. It is doubtful whether Baskin had any
legal justification for his belated demand, but he had the backing
of the Gentile press, the sting of whose lash the governor had
already felt. Ultimately Emery yielded to importunity, ordered
a re-canvass, and allowed the protest to be recorded. Money was
raised by the Liberal committee to send Baskin, with former Chief

---

[34] *Ibid.,* May 26, 1876.
[35] *Ibid.,* August 22, 1876.
[36] Hollister, *loc. cit.*

Justice McKean and District Attorney Sumner Howard to Washington.[37] But Congress, with more important matters on the calendar, was not particularly interested in their case.

The spring of 1877 was not a happy time in Utah. The execution of John D. Lee and the threatened legal proceedings against Brigham Young, added to the general bitterness of feeling, made Emery's task wholly unenviable. It would seem that he made an earnest effort to keep matters under control. While acceding to the demand of the judiciary and the radicals to apply to the War Department for military reinforcements, he was accused of making the request in disarmingly temperate terms.[38] When General George Crook, after his investigation of affairs in the Territory, concluded that an increase in the army personnel would merely benefit the local speculators, Emery bore the brunt of Liberal chagrin:

> His Excellency the Governor, it seems, cannot lead a straight-forward official life. Since he came to Utah he has appeared in all the characters known upon the stage of trickery. He was a square Gentile at first and saved the little town of Corinne from an attack of Mormons and Indians. Before long he was found hobnobbing with the Mormon priesthood. . . .[39]

The hue and cry was raised for his removal. With another session of the legislative assembly in prospect, "composed of two-score polygamous bishops and apostles," the radical feeling was "that it would be fatal to our liberties and ruinous to the material interests of this Territory to have Governor Emery retained in office. . . ."[40] However, with the support not only of the Mormons but of the conservative Gentiles, particularly those whose business interests were bound up in the peaceable solution of local difficulties, Emery held office until December, 1879. On November 13, 1877, Chief Justice Michael Shaeffer wrote Secretary Carl Schurz in reply to inquiries made by the latter concerning the actions and qualifications of the Governor:

---

[37] *Daily Tribune,* April 6; April 13; May 9; May 23, 1877.
[38] *Ibid.,* May 25, 26, 27, 1877; June 16, 1877; June 27, 1877.
[39] *Ibid.,* May 29, 1877.
[40] *Ibid.,* October 3, 1877.

I do not know that Governor Emery is "inclined to use his official influence to advance the interests of the Mormons at the expense of the more enlightened sentiment of Utah," but it is generally known that he is, I think, imprudently intimate with some of the leading Mormons here, and is not very popular with the Gentile portion of the community. Nothing can be truthfully said against the Governor's moral character, but he is naturally reticent and non-communicative, which may give rise to unfounded suspicions, and has a tendency to render him unpopular. . . .

There are two extreme elements here—the Mormons and the ultra anti-Mormons; and a government official is constantly between these two fires, and subject to their respective criticism and fault-finding, as I myself know from personal experience. A strong, self-reliant, independent, firm, but conservative man would, in my judgment, be an improvement in the Governorship of this Territory; but an extremist would not.[41]

As an estimate of Emery, Shaeffer's analysis was probably accurate. For his successor, instead of the "firm, but conservative man" specified, President Hayes was prevailed upon to nominate one who was in almost every respect a direct antithesis. On January 20, 1880, the Salt Lake *Tribune* carried a Washington press dispatch issued the previous day:

General Murray, whose name is sent in as Governor of Utah, entered the Federal army in 1861 as a boy of eighteen years.

He is personally very handsome, but aside from his soldierly dash and fine presence, has not made any particular impression among those who know him in Washington. On the contrary, he appears to be generally considered a man of large personal vanity and small intellectual ability. The President, in making this appointment has overruled the almost unanimous wish of his Cabinet for Governor Emery's retention.

Handsome in a flamboyant style Eli H. Murray undoubtedly was. Thirty-seven years of age, this Kentuckian had served in the Union forces, taking part in Sherman's march to the sea as commander of the Fifth Corps. Brevetted Brigadier General at

[41] Copy printed in the *Salt Lake Herald,* February 20, 1878.

his discharge, he studied law and established himself at Louisville.[42]
Governor Thomas Theodore Crittenden of Missouri was a half-
brother of the new nominee whom the Senate obligingly confirmed.
This may have explained Hayes' choice. Into the drab history of
the territorial politics Murray, with his genial, shallow personality,
injected a note of color:

> Lofty and sour to them that loved him not;
> But to those men that sought him sweet as summer.

The *Tribune* promptly climbed on the gubernatorial band-
wagon. Emery was gone: "Thank God, this is all over, and the
Liberals of Utah can breathe in peace again." Murray was
described as "a chivalrous Kentuckian, generous and open-hearted,
with an honorable record as a soldier and citizen, and a staunch
supporter of the Administration." [43] Duly installed in office, Governor Murray made no attempt to disguise his antipathy to all
things Mormon, and correspondingly, his overt support of the
Liberal party.

1880 was election year; the spirit of the new governor infused
fresh energy into the minority opposition. Calling upon the Gentiles to register, August 12, O. J. Hollister reminded them that
the census returns showing 32,000 out of the 144,000 inhabitants
as non-Mormons, proved that they held the key to the future. At
the Liberal rally in Independence Hall, on the 18th, General Connor took the chair:

> It was my privilege to start and maintain for years the
> first Gentile newspaper in Utah. This I did at the ex-
> pense of thousands of dollars. I twice represented the
> Gentiles of Utah in Washington, making two trips to
> that city at my own expense, endeavoring to secure anti-
> Mormon legislation from Congress. Latterly, I have
> seemed to slacken my efforts, but it was only because I
> had impoverished myself in the cause.
>   I feel now like again taking up the fight with renewed
> vigor. . . .

---

[42] Edward H. Anderson, "Territorial Governors; Governor Murray," in
Improvement Era, IV, No. 9, July 1901, 641–642; Louisville *Courier-Journal*,
January 19, 1880.
[43] *Daily Tribune*, January 20, 1880.

Unity was the cardinal principle. The temptation of the Democrats to strike out for themselves was sheer madness, "because the Church party will take possession of the Democratic organization as they did years ago, and swamp it. . . . For a generation, the opponents of ecclesiasticism will be forced to act together in Utah." The rally ended with words of commendation from Governor Murray, who assured his gratified hearers that "he would support whatever might be determined upon by the meeting in favor of liberty." [44]   A month later the party caucus nominated Allen G. Campbell, a wealthy mine owner of Beaver, as candidate for Congress, in opposition to the perennial George Q. Cannon. The Liberal platform excoriated polygamy and Mormon interference in politics and concluded with a forthright demand for the suspension of local representative government:

> Resolved, That our experience in Utah satisfies us that any reform in these vital questions through the local legislature is not practicable, and we affirm the conviction that the true and only remedy for the evils we have communicated lies in a repeal of the legislative power now possessed by the Utah Legislature, and in transmitting it to a tribunal to be provided for by Congress and the National Executive.[45]

Early in September, President Hayes and his lady, with General Sherman and others of the official family, visited Salt Lake City. Murray's adroit handling of the program practically excluded the Mormon civic and territorial leaders from any contact with the chief executive. "While R. B. Hayes is President of the United States," the *Tribune* lectured, "he cannot officially recognize a little kingdom with the Republic. . . ." [46] Hayes was properly impressed; back in Washington he incorporated into his annual message, delivered December 6, probably the strongest presidential statement ever made on Mormonism:

> The political power of the Mormon sect is increasing. It now controls one of our wealthiest and most populous Territories, and is extending steadily into other Terri-

---

[44] *Ibid.*, August 19, 1880.
[45] *Ibid.*, September 23, 1880.
[46] *Ibid.*, September 5, 1880.

tories. Wherever it goes it establishes polygamy and sectarian political power.

. . . To the re-establishment of the interests and principles which polygamy and Mormonism have imperilled, and fully reopen to the intelligent and virtuous immigrants of all creeds, that part of our domain which has been in a great degree closed to general immigration by the immoral institution, it is recommended that the government of the Territory of Utah be reorganized. It is recommended that Congress provide for the government of Utah by a Governor and judges or commissioners appointed by the President and confirmed by the Senate, or a government analogous to the provisional government established for the Territory northwest of Ohio by the Ordinance of 1787. If, however, it is deemed best to continue the existing form of local government, I recommend that the right to vote, hold office, and sit as jurors . . . be confined to those who neither practice nor uphold polygamy. If thorough measures are adopted, it is believed, within a few years the evils which now affect Utah will be eradicated, and the Territory will in good time be one of the most prosperous and attractive of the new States of the Union.[47]

Not unnaturally, the Mormon press received the message with emphatic disapproval. The *Deseret News* branded the proposal as wholly unconstitutional, suggestive of a "monstrous mutiny" in the President's mind, and proclaimed that such "tyranny" as that contemplated would never be permitted by the American people.[48]

The results of the campaign in Utah were disappointing and humiliating for the Liberals, whose candidate, Campbell, in spite of an energetic struggle, polled only 1,357 votes, as against Cannon's total of 18,567. The usual procedure of contesting the election was followed, but this time with intense interest. As the Liberals had planned and hoped, Governor Murray, improving on the methods of his predecessors, not only refused the certificate to Delegate Cannon, but granted it to the Liberal candidate. The *Tribune* was at pains to explain the action:

Governor Murray . . . has not questioned the legality of the votes cast for Cannon, nor the fairness of the

---

[47] James Richardson, ed., *Messages and Papers of the Presidents*, X, 4458.
[48] *Deseret News*, December 7, and *passim*.

election. He has simply taken cognizance of two facts which the contest brought out, and which are, first, that George Q. Cannon, being foreign born, and never naturalized, is not a citizen, and second, that it is not possible for Cannon to cure his disabilities and become a citizen before the fourth day of March next. But some may say "it is a fearful thing in a Republic, to overthrow the will of a majority of the people, as expressed through the ballot box." The answer to that is, that while it is a matter greatly to be deplored, the fault is not with the Governor who but executes a trust under the guidance of the law, but with the men who, through their ignorance or cunning, forced the alternative upon him.[49]

Acknowledging that "my action on this question is not final," and that the House of Representatives must ultimately judge the case, Murray prudently went East, leaving Secretary Thomas to deal with the irate Cannon. Thomas stood by the decision of his superior, but yielded so far as to issue a statement certifying that the Mormon Apostle had actually polled an impressive majority of the votes. Armed with this, the delegate presented himself on the floor of the House and was duly enrolled by the clerk, who took the obvious position that it was not a territorial governor's business to pass upon the qualifications of elected members of Congress.

Murray and Campbell hastened to Washington to offset the effects of this move. To President Garfield, who had stated in his inaugural address that "The Mormon Church not only offends the moral sense of mankind . . . but prevents the administration of justice through the ordinary instrumentality of the law," [50] Campbell wrote, March 31, 1881:

> I have read with much pleasure your recently reported statement that you wished to carry out the views expressed in your inaugural, by making the stamping out of polygamy one of the leading features of your administration, . . . Circumstances have made me the representative of principles, and have brought me forward as the opponent of a system, which, I believe, is undermining our Western States and Territories. . . . I would not for a moment, with the light vote polled for me claim the seat but for the fact that my only opponent was an alien,

---

[49] January 9, 1881.
[50] Richardson, op. cit., X, 4601.

and that he cannot attempt to cure this disability without bringing to the front the fact that he is also a polygamous lawbreaker.[51]

The Cannon-Campbell controversy was dragged through the session of Congress which convened December 6, 1881. On January 10, 1882, it was voted to refer the matter to the Committee on Elections. Not until February 25 were the resolutions reported, denying the right of both contestants to a seat in the House, and declaring the post vacant. Cannon's ineligibility was predicated plainly upon the fact that he was a polygamist, rather than upon the technicality of his doubtful naturalization. The committee took the stand that territorial delegates, strictly speaking, were not members of the House; as a result, while monogamy was not a constitutional qualification for a seat, the House itself could exclude a delegate for violation of a congressional statute. On April 19, after Cannon had been accorded the privilege of addressing the House, the resolutions of the committee were read, and the polygamous delegate was declared a private citizen.[52]

Purely from the point of view of political expediency, it is strange that the Mormons should have persisted in returning a known violater of the law as their representative, especially at a time when they must have realized only too well that the tide of public opinion was running strongly counter to their peculiar institution. It is equally strange, and perhaps illustrative of the political morality of the period, that Cannon was not without friends in both party camps. At all events, the same Congress which ratified the Edmunds bill could hardly, with any degree of consistency, have handled this case otherwise. The Utah Gentiles failed in foisting Campbell on Congress, as, indeed, they probably anticipated. Their immediate object, the humiliation of the Mormon leaders, was temporarily satisfied.

In the meantime, Murray had thrown himself vigorously into the struggle to secure Gentile supremacy in Utah. In his first annual report to Congress (1880), he minced no words:

---

[51] Quoted by the *Daily Tribune*, April 7, 1881.

[52] Cannon's speech is reported in *Congressional Record*, April 19, 1882, pp. 3036–3070. A digest of all the official documents bearing on the Cannon-Campbell case is in *Congressional Record*, December 6, 1881, pp. 33–43. *Cf. 47th Congress, 1st Session, House Miscellaneous Documents, No. 25.*

> . . . as long as Utah is allowed to remain with her present practices, organizations and laws, it cannot be said that this government deals out equal and exact justice to all its citizens. . . . The church dictates, suggests, or its influences control all things spiritual or temporal among its people. The officers of the church, and those in polygamy, to a great extent fill the offices of the Territory, enact its laws and execute them. . . .

The lassitude of Congress in neglecting to implement the Act of 1862, he complained, had "put a premium on crime." With what he intended as fine irony, he suggested a law "constituting this an independent polygamous State, a thing apart from the 'wicked people' of the United States." His remedy—the possible source of President Hayes' inspiration—would revive the Northwest Ordinance, or provide a government similar to that of the District of Columbia, in order to bring the Territory "in unison with American civilization." [53]

The governor's relations with the territorial legislature were fully as strained as those which characterized the colonial governors of Massachusetts and New York before the outbreak of the Revolution. When the twenty-fifth session assembled in January, 1882, his message, read in his absence by Secretary Thomas, was anything but conciliatory. It was for the lawmakers of Utah, he told them, to open the territory to American influences. The Mormon Church he denounced as a malign influence:

> . . . In no sense—even in the slightest degree—is the sovereignty of church over state in unison with the language or spirit of the Constitution or your country's laws.
> That political power is wielded by church authority throughout Utah is a fact.
> That officers of church exercise authority in temporal affairs is a fact.
> That the sovereignty of the Church is supreme and its practices followed, the laws and courts of the United States to the contrary, is a fact.

The patience of the nation was rapidly nearing exhaustion, he warned the legislators; it was theirs to choose between remedying

---

[53] *Report of the Governor of the Territory of Utah for the Year 1880* (Washington, 1880), pp. 8–9.

the conditions themselves or accepting a remedy thrust upon them.[54]

Although a federal law, as it appeared in the Revised Statutes of the United States (1875), deprived territorial governors of an absolute veto, as permitted in the Utah organic act of September 9, 1850,[55] Governor Murray made free use of whatever veto power remained to thwart the ambitions of the assembly. An appropriation to provide the University of Deseret with needed buildings and equipment fell under his executive ax, for he insisted, not without reason, that the school, in all but name, was a sectarian institution.[56] His efforts to vindicate an interpretation of the organic act, which left large discretion in territorial appointments to the governor, were less successful.[57]

With the Edmunds bill enacted and the Mormon leaders in growing danger of receiving the prescribed penalties, the Church press broke out in violent attacks upon the governor and his coterie as the authors of the mischief. His earlier career in Kentucky was scrutinized for evidence damaging to his character, and his occasional indiscretions, while posing as the champion of righteous monogamy, were thoroughly aired. The Gentile press hastened to his defense:

> We know of nothing in all the history of partisan hate and malignity that compares in downright cussedness with the course pursued by the newspaper organs of the Mormon Church in connection with . . . the unproven charges aganist Governor Murray. . . . Finding himself confronted by a system openly and undeniably hostile to the nation of which he is the representative, he points out in emphatic terms in his official messages, the . . . offensive positions deliberately taken by the dominant Church and State party in this Territory. The malignity with which the scribes and pharisees of this Latter-day institution go about outside to manufacture testimony

---

[54] *Governor's Message and Accompanying Documents, 25th Session of the Legislative Assembly of the Territory of Utah, 1882* (Salt Lake City, 1882), pp. 9–10.

[55] McKean to Williams, November 16, 1874 (N. A., D. J. MSS, Utah); Williams to McKean, November 27, 1874 (N. A., D. J. Judges and Clerks Letter Book I, p. 83).

[56] Whitney, *op. cit.*, III, 200–202; *Daily Evening Chronicle,* March 17, 1884.

[57] *Ibid.*, pp. 197–200.

against Governor Murray, and trump up old and exploded charges, offensive with age as they originally were in the rascality which gave them birth, shows conclusively that the Governor's indictment against the politico-ecclesiastical power which curses Utah is true in all its essential points.[58]

In his report to the Secretary of the Interior for the year 1885, Murray dwelt at length upon the operation of the Edmunds law in Utah. He found much in that statute to criticize, particularly the fact that it left the non-polygamous Mormons unhampered and in control.

. . . The man who holds a woman while another ravishes her is alike guilty. This being true, it follows that a monogamist Mormon is not deserving of as much consideration as a polygamist, for the reason that, where two men claim to believe that polygamy is divinely appointed, the one who follows that belief into a conscientious practice is the honester of the two. If you punish the honester one, you at least should disfranchise the other. . . .

Reiterating his plea for the abolition of representative government in the Territory, Murray displayed his wounds: "I have stood for nearly six years in the midst of a storm, and in kindness am attempting to stay the people from rushing headlong to their own destruction." [59]

Whether in good faith or solely for political effect, Murray made persistent attempts to persuade the federal government to obviate the peril of a Mormon uprising by increasing the military strength at Fort Douglas. With intensified prosecutions, unrest, indeed, had become noticeable. Local incidents lent some color to his plea:

Recent occurrences in Utah, such as the half-masting of the flag of the United States July 4, 1885 and the excitement growing out of it, the late threatening harangue

---

[58] *Salt Lake Evening Chronicle,* February 4, 1884.

[59] *Report of the Governor of the Territory of Utah to the Secretary of the Interior for the Year 1885* (Washington, 1886), pp. 6, 14 ff. See also, "Remarks on the Way Out of the Difficulty, by E. Murray" (MS, Bancroft Library, 1884).

against the Government and the officers charged with the
execution of the laws, notably that of Apostle Heber J.
Grant at the Logan conference . . . the assault a short
time since in the night time upon the homes of U. S. Attorney Dickson, Assist. U. S. Atty. Varian, and U. S.
Commissioner McKay, by unknown persons . . . indicate a strong feeling . . . that may result in conflict.[60]

On the night of November 28, 1885, a shooting fracas occurred
in the heart of Salt Lake City, in which a deputy United States
marshal, Henry Collin, was allegedly set upon by a group of young
Mormons resentful of his behavior in recent arrests of those
charged with violation of the Edmunds act.   Murray acted immediately, telegraphing President Cleveland that the Territory was
on the brink of revolt and that martial law was imperative.   As a
result, a company of soldiers, dispatched from Omaha by order of
General Alexander McDowell McCook, arrived in Salt Lake City
on December 7.   Murray's haste in the matter was his own undo-
ing; the fact that his estimate of the situation was ludicrously exaggerated was promptly demonstrated, and the Mormon press was
quick to play up the blunder as an illustration of his unfitness for
office.[61]

John T. Caine, the non-polygamist successor of Cannon as
delegate, wrote to Cleveland enumerating the grievances of his
constituents against Governor Murray:

That the object of the Governor is to cause anarchy
in the territory . . . can scarcely be doubted by those
who are familiar with his past conduct and aware of his
bitter and unconcealed hostility to the great majority of
the people of Utah. For years past, he and an insignifi-
cant but active and unscrupulous minority of the non-
mormon population have been intriguing and scheming
to have the present . . . government overthrown, and
that of a Legislative Commission substituted therefore. . . .
I submit, Sir, that you have had irrefragable evidence
of the untruthfulness and unscrupulousness of the Governor. He deliberately deceived you in December last in
regard to the probability of mob violence and popular

---

[60] *Ibid.*, pp. 10–11.
[61] Whitney, *op. cit.*, III, 447–453.

turbulence in Salt Lake City. His representations to you on that occasion were in accordance with a conspiracy entered into by himself and other unscrupulous persons at a meeting held at the Walker House, in Salt Lake City, and the purpose was to create public apprehension of a Mormon uprising. Reputable gentlemen who were invited to be present at this gathering . . . left in disgust after denouncing it as infamous. The sensational telegrams which were sent to the Eastern and Western press enlarging upon and magnifying the statements made to you were inspired by and . . . sent by the Governor and his co-conspirators.[62]

Not long afterwards, on March 16, 1886, word came to Governor Murray from Secretary L. Q. C. Lamar that his resignation would be acceptable. As a Southern Republican, it is possible that his removal had already been decided upon. The *Tribune* set down the action to "Mormon hate and the hate which has come down in the embittered soul of Lamar."[63] From the pen of Mrs. Angie Newman, leader in the Gentile woman's anti-polygamy crusade, came impassioned words:

His Excellency, Eli H. Murray, Governor of Utah.
Permit me, sir, still to say in very justice, "His Excellency." Utah never had but one Governor. The dignity of that administration has so enwrapped the actor in ermine robes, no hand can remove the royal garment. But as the white snow has fallen on every leaf and shrub—rests like a dead weight upon every material thing—so, upon every loyal heart in this Territory has fallen this morning the frost of defeat, at the announcement of your resignation. Who can paint the heart's emotion? Who can still the tumult? God reigns! That is all our hope. Perhaps we have trusted in an arm of flesh. But we have felt that arm well-nigh omnipotent, and therefore, our sense of helplessness. You will, I feel sure, permit me this individual expression of the homage of grateful hearts, in recognition of the high service you have rendered Woman in your attempt to break the chains of this self-enslaved race. When the history of this decade of the American people is written, the one grand

---

[62] John T. Caine to Cleveland, February 22, 1886 (N. A., Department of the Interior, Utah File).
[63] *Daily Tribune,* March 17, 1886.

heroic figure of the period must be that of Governor Eli
H. Murray. The record of his official action will be the
one stainless page in that volume of the ages.

But, without waiting for posthumous honors, allow
me, this morning, to lay upon you this one laurel wreath,
woven by many hands, the thanksgiving of loyal women
for the work you have wrought. This wreath will not
wither with the years. Night cannot always linger in
Utah, for the luster of this one star will diffuse itself
through the gloom until the day breaks.[64]

Thus the territorial governor whose term had been the longest
since that of Brigham Young, and whose distrust of the Mormons
was the least dissembled, passed from the scene. In him, the
Liberals lost their outstanding champion.

Neither the adverse decision of the House of Representatives
in regard to the seating of Apostle Cannon, nor the operation of
the Edmunds act, disfranchising all those who confessed to or
were convicted of polygamous relations, served to break the grip of
the People's party on elective offices in the Territory, outside of
the few mining communities where the Gentiles were in the
majority. On the eve of the election of 1882, in which John T.
Caine, an able Mormon attorney free from the taint of polygamy,
was candidate of the Church party, in opposition to the United
States district attorney for Utah, Philip T. Van Zile, favorite son
of the Liberals, the territorial central committee of the latter
faction submitted a "Memorial of the Non-Mormon People of
Utah" to President Arthur and the Houses of Congress. Explaining that, "We are variously styled by our opponents 'Gentiles'
and 'Outsiders,' but the name 'Liberals' has been adopted by ourselves as a designation sufficiently distinctive for our purposes,"
the memorialists claimed to represent "thirty thousand loyal American citizens in Utah . . . who . . . pay more than one-third of
its taxes." The arraignment of Mormon political control followed
the usual arguments, with stress laid on the fact that the normal
development of the area had been hindered and obstructed by the
bigotry of religious zealots. "In a word, it has made Utah a land
of disloyalty, disaffection and hatred toward the Government; has
retarded its growth, prosperity and advancement, . . . made its

---

[64] *Ibid.*, March 24 (Dated March 16, 1886).

history a reproach to the Nation." The Edmunds act was sharply criticized. While, as they admitted, "it indicates an intention to strike at the vital point, the political power of the Mormon Church, we are in truth compelled to say that in its practical operation it has not effected and will not effect the desired reforms." The estimated disfranchisement of sixteen thousand polygamists served no real purpose. "The disfranchised portion dictates the course of those who are not disfranchised as completely and absolutely as before. . . ."

Recurring to the scheme of an appointive legislative council, the document disavowed Liberal designs upon the government:

> We do not ask that the government of the Territory be turned over to the minority of its people (although that might be eminently proper where as in this case only the minority acknowledge, and in good faith yield allegiance to the National authority) but we do ask that the Nation itself resume its authority over Utah, take back the power delegated to and abused by the Territory. . . .
>
> . . . Thus far the "Liberals" of Utah have on this picket line of civilization, maintained the local struggle against overwhelming odds. They have reached a point where discouragement must ensue unless your honorable bodies provide measures whereby the same laws may be made and enforced in Utah as in other States and Territories of the Union.[65]

In the campaign, Van Zile, attempting obvious strategy, challenged Caine to a series of debates to be staged throughout the Territory. The Mormon candidate bluntly refused:

> I propose conducting my campaign in the interests of my friends, the party who nominated me, and not in the interests of my opponents, and I do not propose to furnish the latter with audiences they could not otherwise obtain. . . .[66]

Caine's victory, 23,239 to 4,908, was a heavy blow to the vaunting ambition of the Liberals, and was only partially compensated for by the consolation they derived from the increased effectiveness of the

---

[65] *Memorial of the Non-Mormon People of Utah, October 7, 1882* (printed copy, n. d., in the Utah file, N. A., Department of the Interior), pp. 1–4.

[66] *Daily Tribune,* October 18, 1882.

legal crusade to stamp out polygamy and to force the Mormon leaders into flight or submission.

During the remainder of the decade the local political situation varied little. Delegate Caine was able to retain his congressional post even through the stormiest days of the persecution of the Saints, and the Mormon majority was safeguarded in the territorial legislature. A few minor breaches in the wall of ecclesiastical domination were the most that the Liberal party could boast. Summit County, northeast of Salt Lake City, where productive silver mines had created an almost wholly Gentile community in Park City, returned a Liberal to the territorial legislature on August 3, 1885, following a spirited battle with the candidate representing the scattered Mormon farming centers of the area.[67] Not until 1889 was Ogden, second city of the territory, and an important railroad junction, carried by the Liberals. The following year, in the face of emphatic protests from the Mormons, coupled with charges of corruption and chicanery, a Gentile mayor was installed in Salt Lake City.[68] But the changing political complexion of its largest cities, where the non-Mormons tended to concentrate, was hardly indicative of a lessening of the loyalty of the overwhelming mass of the Latter-Day Saints to the party which represented their interests.

Not until statehood, granted in 1896, saw the merging of the conflicting parties—Liberal and People's—into the traditional organs of American political opinion, was it possible for a Gentile to receive a majority vote on a statewide canvass.[69]

---

[67] *Park Mining Record,* August 6, 1885.

[68] Whitney, *op. cit.,* III, 687–711, gives a lengthy account of this event.

[69] Whitney, *op. cit.,* III, 517, makes mention of the establishment, in 1886, of the "Loyal League," a secret political organization, founded for the purpose of combatting the movement for statehood. Sporadic mention of the activities of the League are to be found in the Salt Lake *Tribune* and the *Park Mining Record.* Probably the league was no more than the "inner circle" of the Liberal party. Its principal activity seems to have been the raising of funds to maintain lobbyists in Washington—R. N. Baskin in particular.

CHAPTER VI

THE TORCHBEARERS

THE RELIGIOUS impulse which had launched an evangelical crusade to save the Mississippi Valley from the clutches of "Popery," which had lashed the abolitionists into the demand that the slavery issue be arbitrated by the appeal to arms, which had poured its generous millions into the evangelization of the "lesser tribes without the law," moved ineluctably toward the liquidation of the "twin relic of barbarism." By one of the strange anomalies of American religious history, Mormonism, itself a by-product of the restless New England conscience, became the stumbling-block of offense to the conformist heirs of that tradition. Congregationalists, Methodists, and Presbyterians, together with other evangelical sects, came to regard Mormonism, and particularly its doctrine of polygamy, as a challenge both to American morality and to their missionary zeal. The twenty years between 1870 and 1890 were filled with the clamor of their denunciation. Utah's religious problem assumed an increasingly prominent place in the moral concern of the home missionary societies, which began to feel, as the editor of the *Vedette* had suggested, that there was very little reason for worrying about the conversion of Booriboola-Gah while the Mormons preached and practised plurality of wives in our own Rocky Mountains.

In the sixties, the Reverend Norman McLeod had sounded the tocsin. Though the evangelical churches did not begin their campaign in Utah before 1870, his brief career was fairly symptomatic of what was to come and of the methods to be used to achieve victory. In the meantime, Christian effort in the Territory was confined to Protestant Episcopalianism and Roman Catholicism, groups to which proselytism, though not foreign, was of less importance than the spiritual welfare of their own adherents.

Encouraged by the response accorded his appeals by friends in

151

the East, Bishop Tuttle went ahead with plans for the construction of a suitable cathedral church in Salt Lake City. The corner-stone was laid with appropriate ceremonies on July 30, 1870, and ten months later the congregation abandoned Independence Hall which had served them as a chapel for four years. St. Mark's Cathedral, freed of debt, was consecrated on May 14, 1874, a monument to the Bishop's financial ability and his sympathy with the gothic revival.[1] Under Episcopalian auspices the first regular hospital in the city was founded in the spring of 1872, occupying for some years an adobe building on the corner of Fourth South and Fifth East Streets.[2] St. Mark's school, inaugurated by the first missionaries, enjoyed a gratifying growth, and in 1873 was housed in a new building, reputed to be the finest of its kind in the Territory.[3] The school continued to be frankly a missionary venture, over three-fourths of the students receiving free tuition provided by eastern benefactors.[4] As the *Daily Tribune* was quick to point out:

> Being deprived of an efficient school system in Utah by the obstinacy and obstructiveness of our divinely inspired hierarchy, the only resort for the education of our children, is to the efficiency and faithful services of our teachers, aided by the liberality of the various religious bodies in the United States.[5]

Episcopalian missionaries spread out from Salt Lake City, establishing churches and organizing congregations in Ogden, Corinne,

---

[1] Tuttle, *Reminiscences*, pp. 392–393. He remarks that this was one of the last buildings designed by Upjohn the elder. Its cost was about $80,000, no small sum for the time and place. According to Cordelia Allen Smith, in *World's Fair Ecclesiastical History of Utah* (Salt Lake City, 1896), p. 203, the parish was canonically organized November 15, 1870.

[2] *Ibid.*, pp. 394–405. *Utah Mining Journal*, July 8, 1872.

[3] *Cf.* Smith, *World's Fair History*, p. 195, where it is described as "a large and commodious structure, containing a large chapel, and a sufficient number of class rooms. . . . It was the finest educational building in the territory." In his last report as Bishop of Utah, 1886, Tuttle stated that up to that time the school had educated 3000 boys and girls, of whom more than 300 had come to him for Confirmation. *Ibid.*, p. 197. The school closed in 1892.

[4] Salt Lake *Daily Tribune*, May 25, 1876.

[5] *Ibid.*, August 31, 1875.

Logan and elsewhere, although growth was painfully slow.[6] As late as 1881, the denomination could claim but three hundred and seventy-five communicants in the Territory, with five ministers attending half-a-dozen churches.[7]

Broad Church in tendency, Bishop Tuttle did not scruple to admit to communion any baptized Christian, but he drew the line on Mormons,—

> Members of the Church of Jesus Christ of Latter-day Saints we cannot admit to our altar. It is true they have been baptized . . . but they admit so much pernicious error into their doctrine that it would not be fit for an evangelical Church to affiliate with them.[8]

In a more dignified and less spectacular way than McLeod, the good Bishop spoke his mind on polygamy. Commenting on one of his sermons, the *Daily Tribune,* for which all was grist brought to its mill, remarked:

> It was an able dissertation on the domestic relation of man, including in it a discussion of monogamy and polygamy. It would have done the believers in the pretended revelation of celestial marriage great good to have heard this Christian minister disprove the divinity of the practise among the people of Utah.
> It is certainly gratifying to see the Christian Churches of this Territory making war on polygamy. . . .[9]

Toward the close of 1876, Tuttle, reporting to the Board of Missions, indulged in the prophecy that the anticipated death of Brigham Young would change the complexion of things in Utah:

---

[6] *Cf. Ogden Standard Examiner,* March 5, 1939. Chauncey P. Overfield, "The Church and the Mormons" in *Living Church* (Milwaukee), XCIV, No. 14, 417–420.

[7] There is some confusion in the various estimates. Thus, the *Daily Tribune,* June 1, 1881, gave the above figure. On January 11, 1882, it reported only 350 members. But one year later, at the time of the first Convocation, May 2, 1883, the number had jumped to 650.

[8] *Daily Tribune,* January 9, 1876.

[9] *Ibid.,* February 20, 1877.

> If I forecast aright, we are not too soon on the ground
> with our schools and churches. Men's minds and souls
> in the Territory will be as rudderless ships on a disrupted
> sea. And it will be the duty of civilization and humanity,
> as well as the glory of the Church, to provide nearby for
> them anchors of truth and the havens of peace Christianity
> offers.
>
> What troubles me is this, that although we have four
> schools and three churches in Utah, and in the former six
> hundred pupils, yet we ought to have many more, at Provo,
> Fillmore, Beaver, Grantsville, Plain City, and all the larger
> Mormon towns and centers. . . .[10]

Occasionally, Tuttle's comparative moderation was gall and
wormwood to the Gentile zealots. The *Tribune* pounced upon
him when it learned that in a sermon delivered in the Church of the
Holy Sepulchre, New York City, he had spoken fairly of the virtue
of many Mormons:

> Bishop Tuttle might truthfully have put in a word
> for the honest followers of the Church, but as a Christian
> minister . . . it was incumbent upon him to set forth in
> clear language the flagitious character of the Mormon
> priesthood. It cannot be, as Pope has declared, that
> "Priests of all religions are the same." We have no re-
> proof to make for such recusancy, as the Bishop has al-
> ready had his reward. Our malicious *Grandmother,* see-
> ing that this Christian minister had laid himself open to
> censure, hastened to slime him over with her blighting
> pestilential praise.[11]

Obviously, it was no easy task for a missionary in Utah to save
himself from falling between two stools. Nevertheless, until he
accepted the bishopric of St. Louis, Missouri, in 1886, Tuttle man-
aged to remain on reasonably cordial terms with all parties. On the
morning of his departure from Salt Lake to assume his new charge,
the *Deseret News* saluted him:

---

[10] *Ibid.,* November 9, 1876.

[11] *Ibid.,* November 11, 1877. Returning to the attack a few days later, the
editor opined that "it is a mere exhibition of folly or disingenuousness for any
man to condemn the Mormon religion as worse than heathenism, and then in
the same breath proceed to celebrate their social and domestic virtues. (November 15). *Grandmother,* of course, was the Mormon paper.

. . . We respect a consistent antagonist. . . . Bishop
Tuttle is not only frank enough to express freely his dis-
sent from the doctrines of the "Mormons" while among
them, but brave enough to speak in defence of that unpopular people when in the midst of enemies. There are
few prominent men who dare do this. Many declare themselves averse to the unfair course pursued toward the
"Mormons." . . . But public sentiment is so strong
against them that they . . . are afraid to utter their defense openly for fear of being accused of being "influenced by the Mormons." [12]

A year later, in a communication to the *Spirit of the Missions,*
Tuttle hailed the dawn of Gentile victory in Utah—a false dawn,
as time was to show:

Twenty years ago . . . I entered Main Street, Salt
Lake City, in one of the old stage coaches of the plains.
. . . I am now almost the oldest non-Mormon resident
here. . . . I have lived to see the imperious arrogance
of Mormonism bite the dust, although deep-seated ob-
stinate rebelliousness still remains. Its chieftain is in hiding, and has been for two or three years, and many of the
leaders are skulking with him.[18]

Masonry, as a common denominator of the Protestant Gentiles,
endeavored to keep pace with territorial expansion. By 1875 six
lodges had been organized, although the three largest of these were
in Salt Lake City. With the opening of a new Masonic hall, the
availability of a popular library on Mormonism was advertised:

Only a few of the numerous works published on the
Mormons are now lacking to make the collection complete,
and of these is the history of Joe Smith, by himself, which
the Church authorities, since his death, have ordained de-
stroyed. On behalf of the brotherhood, we ask anyone
who may have this volume and is desirous of putting it

---

[12] *Deseret News,* August 31, 1886. Although translated to the diocese of
Missouri, Tuttle returned to Utah the following year to govern the missionary
district pending the acceptance of the mitre by his successor. The Right Reverend Abiel Leonard was finally prevailed upon to accept the post, and was
consecrated in St. Louis, January 25, 1888. (Allen, *loc. cit.,* p. 207.)

[18] Quoted from *Daily Tribune,* September 11, 1887.

where it will do the most good, to send it to the Free
Mason's Library. . . .[14]

The Odd Fellows were reported, at that time, to number three
hundred members, grouped in five lodges and one encampment.
It was observed that, "the Hebrew Gentiles as a rule belong to the
Odd Fellows more than to the Masons." [15]

Catholics, numerically the largest of the Gentile religious bodies,
pursued a quiet course, and took but little part in the prevailing
conflict. With the transfer of the Territory to the spiritual jurisdiction of the Archbishop of San Francisco, Father Foley, who
had conducted services in the improvised chapel on "Second East,
opposite Wells, Fargo's old stage depot," left for Denver on
May 31, 1871, having succeeded in bringing together "a congregation which bids fair to be largely increased." [16] Within a few days
Patrick Walsh, a priest of the San Francisco Archdiocese, had
taken up residence as pastor of the parish whose limits were
coterminous with the territory.[17] Corinne, at that time flourishing,
was made a regular mission, and plans were laid for the erection
there of "a free school for children independent of all sectarian
bias." [18] Nothing came of this, however, and Walsh turned to
the problem of providing a fitting church for Salt Lake City. The
corner-stone was laid on September 24, 1871, and its dedication,
under the title of St. Mary Magdalene, November 6, 1872, brought
the Right Reverend Joseph Sadoc Alemany from the coast to preside at the ceremonies.[19]

On August 14, 1873 the Reverend Lawrence Scanlan arrived
in the Mormon metropolis as successor to Father Walsh. A man
of great physical and moral courage, he is still revered by Catholics in Utah as the architect, under God, of the Church in what is
now the Diocese of Salt Lake. His long pastorate saw the main
influx of Irish miners to work the lodes buried in the Utah mountains. With few assistants he endeavored to keep the faith alive

---

[14] *Daily Tribune,* November 17, 1876.

[15] *Ibid.,* July 13, 1875.

[16] *Ibid.,* April 30, 1871; May 30, 1871.

[17] W. R. Harris, *The Catholic Church in Utah.* (Salt Lake City, 1909)
p. 284.

[18] *Daily Tribune,* June 22, 1871.

[19] Harris, *op. cit.,* p. 284.

by unremitting missionary labors. His parochial foundations were not numerous because of the unpredictable impermanency of the mining camps. Thus, Ophir, where he erected a church, and where the famous Paulist priest, Walter Elliott, preached a mission, was soon a ghost town.[20] This, too, was the fate of Silver Reef, where, in December 1878, he opened a hospital and built a mission chapel.[21] Stockton, Corinne and Frisco had resident priests during their boom periods, but the work of the Church was perforce abandoned in such localities when mining ceased to be profitable and Catholic miners sought labor elsewhere.[22]

In 1875, in answer to Scanlan's earnest request, the Sisters of the Holy Cross came from their mother-house, Notre Dame, Indiana, to assist him in his western mission. Under the direction of Mother Augusta Anderson, a woman of high intelligence and marked ability,[23] Catholic education was launched. Academies for girls and younger boys were opened in Salt Lake City (1875) and Ogden (1878). Parochial schools were established in Silver Reef, Park City, and Eureka. Hospitals were soon in operation in the capital city and in Ogden, the latter being a railroad hospital staffed by the sisters under contract.[24] To provide for the education of young men, he built, in 1886, All Hallows' College in Salt Lake

---

[20] *Daily Tribune,* June 17, 1875.

[21] Mark A. Pendleton, "Memories of Silver Reef," in *Utah Historical Quarterly,* III, No. 4, October, 1930, 99–100.

"Fond memories rushed upon me as I paused at the foundation of the Catholic Church where I had often heard Father Scanlan preach and where the Sisters' School was held. Sister Bonita, the kind, the cultured, has been a blessed memory all these years, and Father Scanlan was beloved by all.

"There was no mistaking the basement of the hospital. On this site the Sisters of Mercy [actually, Sisters of the Holy Cross] had served humanity. . . ."

[22] *Cf. Daily Tribune,* April 17, 1880; April 29, 1881: "Rev. Father Smith, who has for two years past had charge of the Catholic Church at Ogden, where he has greatly endeared himself to the community . . . leaves this morning for Frisco, to take charge of the church at that point."

[23] References to the work of Mother Augusta are to be found in Sister M. Eleanore, C.S.C., *On the King's Highway* (New York, 1931), *passim.* See also Sister M. des Victoires, C.S.C., "History of Catholic Education in Utah" (MS, M.A. thesis, University of Notre Dame, 1929).

[24] Sister M. Eleanore, *op. cit.,* pp. 415–416; Archives of St. Mary's, Holy Cross, Indiana, "St. Lawrence's Hospital, Ogden, Utah." (MS)

City, confiding its direction to several of his priests until 1889, when the Marist Fathers assumed charge.[25]

Father Scanlan was appointed Vicar General of the Archbishop of San Francisco shortly after his arrival in the Territory, with jurisdiction extending, apparently, over all of Utah. On September 14, 1886, advance notice of his appointment as Vicar Apostolic was published in the *Daily Tribune*.[26] He was at that time forty-three years of age. The Catholic population of the vicariate was variously estimated at between three and five thousand. The largest parish, St. Mary-of-the-Assumption, Park City, numbered eight hundred souls; that of Salt Lake City mustered only a scant four hundred.[27] Paying tribute to Scanlan's apostolic labors the *Tribune* editor wrote:

> Such work as this, under the most adverse circumstances, amid a hostile people, and with money always hard to get, deserves recognition. Thousands of miles has he ridden by stagecoach and rail, and many times has he deprived himself of necessaries that others might be benefited thereby.[28]

Consecrated Bishop of Laranda, June 27, 1887, in St. Mary's Cathedral, San Francisco, Scanlan was placed in charge not only of Utah but of the eastern half of Nevada as well. On his return to Salt Lake City he was accorded an enthusiastic welcome by all

---

[25] *Daily Tribune*, August 22, 1886. "The members of the Catholic Church, and in fact all interested in educational matters in this city, have reason to be proud of the new college building which is now nearly completed. . . . The building . . . is one of the most beautiful, architecturally, of any of Salt Lake's few public buildings." Ninety students were enrolled on its opening day, September 19, 1886.

[26] *Daily Tribune*, September 14, 1886. "The Roman Catholics of Utah will be pleasantly surprised today on learning that Rev. Father Lawrence Scanlon, rector of St. Mary's Church and leading priest in Utah has been made by the Pope Titular Bishop and Vicar Apostolic of the Territory. . . . A *Tribune* reporter was the first to carry the news to the clergyman by calling at All Hallows College and congratulating him on his appointment. Bishop Scanlan could not believe the news, so entirely unexpected was it, and even after some ten minutes suspected there must be a large colored gentleman in the ecclesiastical wood-pile. . . ."

[27] Robert W. Sloan, *Utah Gazetteer and Directory* (Salt Lake City, 1884), p. 211.

[28] September 14, 1886.

groups, and the territorial governor, Caleb West, headed the reception committee.[29]

While it cannot be said that Bishop Scanlan was silent on the subject of polygamy, it is evident that he confined his remarks to his own pulpit in moral discourses to his own people,[30] and chose rather to cultivate amicable relations with individual Mormons, some of whom still recall his friendly spirit toward them during the periods of sharpest antagonism. Alone among the Gentile religious groups, the Catholic Church in Utah was substantially able to maintain its organization without special financial aid from outside sources.[31] The Catholic schools, unlike the Protestant mission institutions, were supported by tuition, and in spite of occasional blasts from Latter-Day Saint leaders, they were largely patronized by children of Mormon parentage.[32]

---

[29] The irrepressible *Tribune*, May 25, 1887, relative to Scanlan's titular see: "It is a jolly combination, this union of Asia and Utah, and one quite familiar to the minds of those posted on local affairs; but in the present instance, happily, the joinder is for decency and not the reverse." Mormonism was "Asiatic," due to the practice of polygamy, which seems to have suggested Asia to the anti-Mormons.

"Rt. Rev. Bishop Scanlan arrived home from his consecration at San Francisco last evening, and was welcomed at the depot by many friends, led by Governor West, Secretary Hall, W. S. McCornick and Dr. Fowler." (July 9.) The Bishop was presented with a "fine top, Brewster side-bar, Studebaker buggy, fully equipped with whip, Angora rug and handsome duster; also a fine set of harness."

[30] On the occasion of the visit of Dom Pedro of Brazil to Salt Lake City, April 24, 1876, Scanlan "preached a controversial sermon, which was in effect a reply to Apostle Pratt's discourse in the Tabernacle. . . ." The editor of the *Tribune* smelled blood: "Whatever views the Brazilian Emperor may have carried away of these diametrically opposed doctrines, he leaves the two champions of the oppugnant faiths occupying their pulpits to fight the controversy out on this line. The Catholic priest has opened his well served batteries upon the Mormon citadel. . . ." However, no controversy developed; nor did Scanlan advocate Mormon-baiting on the part of his priests.

[31] The Irish miners, many of whom became wealthy, were characteristically generous toward their Church. Before his death, in 1915, Bishop Scanlan could boast a building achievement remarkable for a diocese so small numerically.

[32] "Archives of Saint Mary-of-the-Assumption, Salt Lake City, Utah, from its Foundation by Mother M. Angela in 1875" (MS, College of St. Mary-of-the-Wasatch, Salt Lake City, Utah), p. 6:

"The new Academy was named Saint Mary-of-the-Assumption. School

Far different were the relations between the evangelical sectaries and the Saints. The echoes of McLeod's vituperation had scarcely died away when Mormondom was aroused to a high pitch of controversial heat by the arrival of the Reverend John Phillip Newman from Washington. During 1869, this Methodist minister, chaplain of the United States senate, had engaged in a newspaper controversy with a prominent Mormon apologist, Orson Pratt. The point at issue, polygamy, was dragged through the columns of the *New York Herald*.[33] On July 30, 1870, the *Daily Tribune* announced that Newman, en route to California, proposed to debate the question in Salt Lake City with none other than Brigham Young himself. Apparently Newman labored under the impression that a challenge to such a debate had been given by the Church President, though the provenance of his impression is not altogether clear. On August 6, he addressed a note to Young stating his readiness to answer the challenge by publicly discussing the question, "Does the Bible sanction Polygamy?"[34] Young immediately answered that the alleged challenge was unknown to him and disclaimed responsibility for the appearance, in the *Salt Lake Telegraph*, a pro-Mormon sheet, of an article which Newman had accepted as an authoritative statement.[35]

A wordy correspondence ensued, Newman broadly suggesting

---

opened September 6, 1875, the classes being taught in the new building.

"On the Sunday previous, the Mormon Bishop proclaimed from the pulpit that no Mormons would be permitted to send their children to the Sisters' school under the penalty of being cut off from the church. Consequently but few of them returned, although many of the better class, anxious for better educational facilities, had made arrangements for their daughters to attend. In after years many of their children attended the school and the Sisters experienced much kindness from the Mormons with whom they came in contact.

"The Catholic population of the city consisted of nine or ten families but so generous was the non-Catholic patronage that at the end of the first week of school there were one hundred day pupils and six boarders."

[33] Whitney, *History of Utah,* II, 440–441. Whitney's treatment of this episode, pp. 440–486, is worth reading. *Cf. Daily Tribune,* July 30, 1870.

[34] The *Daily Tribune,* August 13, reprinted the correspondence in full.

[35] The *Salt Lake Telegraph* was founded July 4, 1864, by T. B. H. Stenhouse, during his Mormon days. It was discontinued December 22, 1869, but was revived by a certain M. A. Fuller, of Chicago. No files of this revived issue are extant. See Alter, *Early Utah Journalism,* pp. 340–349.

that the Lion of the Lord was reneging in cowardly fashion. Irritated, Young made answer:

> . . . I . . . ask, what must be the opinion of every candid, reflecting mind who views these facts as they appear? Will they not conclude that the distortion of the truth in accusing me of disclaiming and declining a challenge, which I never even contemplated, is unfair and ungentlemanly in the extreme and must have been invented with some sinister motive? Will they not consider it a paltry and insignificant attempt on your part to gain notoriety, regardless of the truth? This you may succeed in obtaining; but I am free to confess, as my opinion, that you will find such notoriety more unenviable, than profitable, and as disgraceful, too, as it is unworthy of your profession.
>
> If you think you are capable of proving the doctrine of "Plurality of Wives" unscriptural, tarry here as a missionary; we will furnish you the suitable place, the congregation, and plenty of our Elders, any of whom will discuss with you on that or any other scriptural doctrine.[36]

Newman refused to accept substitute respondents, and the *Deseret News* promptly interpreted this as evidence of Newman's own wish to get out of the difficulty.[37] Matters having reached this pass a group of Salt Lake Gentiles prevailed upon him to agree to terms of debate with his former antagonist, Orson Pratt.[38] The Mormon Tabernacle was offered to the contestants, and August 12 was fixed upon as the opening day.

For three days the great debate continued, listened to breathlessly by the thousands who crowded into the vast, unlovely structure. Newman, whatever his qualifications as chaplain of the Senate or his merits as an orator, proved neither a scripture scholar nor an apt debater, and his anthropology was both strange and wonderful. Pratt, a clever, though equally shallow, polemist,

---

[36] Dated August 6. (*Tribune,* August 13.)

[37] August 8, 1870.

[38] August 9, 1870. "But as I came here in full faith to debate the question with him, regarding myself as the challenged party, and as he endeavors to escape by denying that he has ever challenged me, I will put the matter now beyond dispute by sending him a challenge."

scored heavily.[39] The results were inconclusive: the Mormons retired certain of their victory; Newman's admirers felt satisfied
that he had demonstrated that the Old Testament gave no warrant
for polygamy. Some years later, C. P. Lyford, a fellow Methodist
missionary in the Territory, wrote:

> Dr. Newman made the most of the Bible argument
> against polygamy and utterly defeated his antagonist, but
> in the estimation of the masses in Utah he himself was
> defeated, and for two reasons: first no argument could
> have weight with his auditors upon that subject, inasmuch
> as one cannot argue with fanatics; and secondly, because
> he addressed himself to his audience as he would have
> done in Washington or New York City.[40]

Between the Methodists and the Mormons, in a special manner,
ill-feeling mounted high, aggravated by the fact that the leading
figures in the anti-Mormon crusade of the seventies, Governor
Shaffer and Chief Justice McKean, were ardent members of that
sect.[41] In November, 1869, the Board of Missions took action to
provide a missionary for the Utah field.[42] In the spring of the following year the Reverend Gustavus Marshal Peirce arrived in Salt
Lake City, and began to conduct services in Faust's hall on Main
Street. The *Daily Tribune,* June 9, reported:

> The Rev. Mr. Pierce [*sic*] has met with marvelous
> success in the few weeks he has been in Utah, and has
> many reasons, we think, for saying that his lines have
> fallen in pleasant places. He got an admirable start from
> friends in Syracuse, New York, to come here: was only a

---

[39] The debate showed a tendency to wander off into Hebrew roots, about
which it is extremely doubtful whether either contestant had more knowledge
than he could bone up the night before.

[40] C. P. Lyford, *The Mormon Problem, An Appeal to the American People*
(New York, 1886), p. 176.

[41] Whitney, *op. cit.*, II, 541–544. Shaffer's funeral services were conducted
by the Rev. Mr. Peirce, shortly after the latter's arrival. McKean's declining
years were largely devoted to Methodist work. He died in Salt Lake in 1879.

[42] Henry Martin Merkel, *History of Methodism in Utah* (Colorado
Springs, Colo., 1938), pp. 56–57. The Reverend Lewis Hartsough was appointed superintendent of the Utah area in December, 1869, but due to ill
health, failed to establish any mission centers. He withdrew in the spring of
1870.

few hours in the city before he began to greet "brethren and sisters" among the most respectable of our "Gentile'" citizens, and with that indefatigable labor characteristic of the earnest missionary he has probably already seen every person Methodistic in education and tendency in the Territory.

Under Peirce's direction a church was built in Corinne, and was dedicated on September 20, 1870.[48] A pretentious and costly structure, erected in Salt Lake City in the following year, plunged the small congregation into unmanageable indebtedness, from which it had to be rescued by the Home Missionary and Extension Society.[44] A revival, staged during the summer of 1871 brought "a mammoth tent and fifty clergymen" to convert the Mormons, but signally failed to achieve its goal.[45] With seven clergymen in attendance the Rocky Mountain Conference of the Methodist Episcopal Church was organized on August 8, 1872, to include the Territories of Utah, Idaho, Montana, and the western portion of Wyoming. The statistical report for that year reckoned, for the entire conference, one hundred and six members and four churches.[46] Within a short time, missionaries were at work in Tooele, Ophir and Provo.

Presbyterian beginnings in Utah date back to the visit of the Reverend Sheldon Jackson to the village of Corinne, early in 1869, as superintendent of the missions of his church in the inter-mountain area. He found this "Gentile town" a suitable place for a mission church.[47] On June 13 of that same year the Reverend Melanchthon Hughes came as resident pastor. Two years later Jackson returned to organize the Presbyterians of Salt Lake City, and on September 28, 1871, the Reverend Josiah Welch was called as minister of the new congregation.[48]

After a lapse of six years, Congregational work was revived

---

[43] At the present time (1941), this is the oldest Gentile church building in use in Utah.

[44] Merkel, op. cit., pp. 155–156. Mrs. W. B. Mabry, in World's Fair Ecclesiastical History of Utah, pp. 261–262.

[45] Daily Tribune, April 19, 1871; June 9, 1871.

[46] Merkel, op. cit., pp. 59–60.

[47] Emma J. McVicker, "Presbyterian Church," in World's Fair Ecclesiastical History of Utah, pp. 221–222.

[48] Ibid., p. 222.

with the return of the Reverend Norman McLeod to the scene of his earlier conflicts.   Independence Hall again rang with his oratory, and the Gentile press gave excellent publicity to his on-slaughts on Mormon theology.   Prominently identifying himself with the cause of the Liberal party, he made his chapel the political headquarters of the faction during the heated campaign of the summer of 1872,[49] and repeatedly took the stump himself:

> That gallant patriot, Rev. Norman McLeod, who has proven himself a fearless upholder of right and a Christian gentleman, will deliver a lecture at Independence Hall on Saturday evening next, on the theme, "Mormons and the mob spirit."   Such a subject by such a man will be ably handled.   Let every American turn out and hear him.[50]

"Brighamism" was next announced as his pulpit topic, and on October 7, he promised to divulge the awful secrets of the Mountain Meadows Massacre: "He will give many facts of interest not known to newcomers.   People, after hearing Mr. McLeod, will know whether the Profit [sic] is celestially inspired or only a clever humbug in the religious line to make money for himself and family."   When he spoke on "Polygamy," the Daily Tribune sounded an ominous note:

> The hall was crowded.   The lecturer, in his opening remarks referred to some personal threats having been made, and remarked that if the opposition (Mormons) succeeded in taking his life they must remember that there were organizations in this City and Territory that would avenge his blood upon some of their most respected members.[51]

The record of McLeod's second spring closed with a final dramatic scene.   On the evening of October 28, 1872, he conducted memorial services for Dr. King Robinson, murdered six years previous.   "He left not a shadow of doubt in the minds of his hearers as to who instigated that terrible crime, as he traced it directly to the Mormon

---

[49] McLeod arrived in Salt Lake in May, 1872 (Daily Tribune, May 21, 1872).   Cf. Utah Mining Journal, August 5, 1872.

[50] Utah Mining Journal, August 8, 1872.

[51] Daily Tribune, September 9, 1872.

teachings." [52] Soon after, it would seem, McLeod left the Territory to return no more.

As the decade advanced, evangelical missionaries made strenuous efforts to penetrate the Mormon hinterland. Since the smaller agricultural villages and towns were almost wholly inhabited by members of the dominant Church, the problem presented was in certain respects analogous to that confronting the missionaries in pagan lands. It could not be a question of a church organization following the settlers, but rather of a deliberate attempt to establish a church, on the strength of Eastern capital, in the hope that conversions among the Mormons would multiply. As the principal means to attain this end, the Protestant sects endeavored to obtain aid for the foundation and support of schools. The fact that the territorial public school system, inadequately supported by taxation, was forced to maintain itself by tuition charges, served to attract the children of a number of Mormon families to the sectarian or mission schools, which generally offered tuition gratis. Moreover, the practical subservience of the common schools to the influence of the Church, which made them to all intents and purposes Mormon seminaries, was distasteful to some of the more "liberal" Saints.

At all events, mission schools were featured as a possible opening wedge to break into the embattled strongholds of the faith. By 1880, the campaign to establish "Christian" schools throughout the Territory was in full swing. From the scattered records available, it is evident that the Methodists, Congregationalists, Presbyterians, and to a lesser extent the Episcopalians and the Baptists, poured money in relatively large sums into the enterprise.[53]

---

[52] *Utah Mining Journal,* October 23, 1872. Baptist beginnings date from the autumn of 1872, when services were held in Richard's Hall, Salt Lake City, under the direction of G. W. Dodge, Indian Agent for the Territory (*Utah Mining Journal,* November 23, 1872). Work was not resumed until 1882, when the Reverend Dwight Spencer was appointed general missionary by the American Baptist Home Missionary Society. See Mrs. Henry B. Steelman, "The Baptist Church," in *World's Fair History,* pp. 276–288, and John D. Thornley, "The Baptist Church in Utah" (MS, 1940).

[53] *Report of the Governor of Utah to the Secretary of the Interior for the Year 1891* (Washington, 1891), p. 21 In this report Governor Arthur L. Thomas furnished much statistical data bearing upon the sectarian churches and schools. His figures show that up to the end of 1891 a total of $1,583,-019.00 had been spent in maintaining the mission schools (including the Cath-

The Presbyterians led off in this work with the establishment of the Salt Lake Collegiate Institute, opened in the fall of 1875 under the supervision of Dr. John M. Coyner.[54]   In spite of its ambitious title the school was only a preparatory academy.   In his report to the Rocky Mountain Presbytery, published in the *Daily Tribune,* April 16, 1876, the Reverend Josiah Welch reviewed progress:

> The Presbyterian Church, realizing the importance of the field, commenced active missionary operations some five years ago.   The Presbytery of Utah has been organized, churches have been planted, and schools established. Five Presbyterian ministers are now actively engaged in missionary work, and the probabilities are that four more will be added during the coming year.

He estimated the Gentile population of Utah at about 14,000 in a total population of 150,000.   Some three hundred children were enrolled in the Institute and in a mission school at Mount Pleasant in central Utah.   However, in order to attract Mormon children, he presented a plea to his eastern co-religionists for a "charity fund" of $3000 a year.

> With this we can educate one hundred pupils; . . . we appeal to the Sunday Schools of the Church for aid. Thirty dollars will pay the tuition and provide books for a pupil for a year. . . .   Can you not as a school take one or more scholarships?

Less happy was the lot of D. J. McMillan, Presbyterian minister and school-master of the village of Mount Pleasant.   Taking up his work there in 1875, he claimed to have one hundred and fifty Mormon children in attendance at his classes by the end of the year. Mormon authorities did not take kindly to his proselytism:

> The Stake of Zion has been in great commotion over Mr. McMillan and his school. . . .   That gentleman came

---

olic academies and parochial schools).   The expenditures for maintenance and improvement during 1891 alone amounted to $224,850.00.

[54] McVicker, *loc. cit.,* p. 225.   *Daily Tribune,* August 19, 1877; November 7, 1877.

here a year ago as a missionary of the Presbyterian
Church, and by his gentlemanly bearing and his uncom-
promising advocacy of pure faith and general diffusion of
intelligence, has gained hosts of friends, and has called
down upon himself the enmity and persecution of the
Church of Brigham Young of the Mountain Meadow
Saints. He has done more for Mount Pleasant and San
Pete County in a moral and educational way, than all the
red-handed officers of the dominant party from B. Y.
down, or rather up, to the humblest Saint.[55]

McMillan himself described the "persecution" in a letter read to
the Presbytery:

Brigham and a crowd of fellow ecclesiastics have been
here two days. The old slanderer has taken two turns at
abusing me, pronouncing me a vile, godless man, worse
than an infidel, teaching sedition, infidelity, spiritualism,
and free-love abominations. He warned the faithful that
unless they withdrew their patronage from me, and drive
me from their midst, sorrow and distress would reach
their homes through my villainy. The whole series of
Mountain Meadow blasphemers followed in their master's
train, each heaping vileness upon me. But I am in no
way discouraged.[56]

To prove his last statement, McMillan proceeded to organize
schools in other Mormon communities nearby. A foothold was
gained in Brigham City where "for the past ten years no Gentile,
nor even a Saint suspected of being weak in the faith, has been
allowed. . . ."[57] Reinforcements for the Presbyterian mission
schools were hailed by the Gentile press on their arrival:

Night before last fourteen young ladies reached Salt
Lake from the East, employed to come here by the Presbyterian Church Missionary Society, to engage in teaching. They will proceed immediately to their respective
fields, and ten new schools will at once be opened. These,
with the twelve schools already flourishing under the same

[55] *Daily Tribune,* March 7, 1876.

[56] *Ibid.,* April 23, 1876.

[57] *Ibid.,* October 17, 1877. Property for a school and chapel were said to
have been purchased from a "disgruntled Mormon."

auspices, make a commencement which is a fearful menace to the system which prevails in Utah.[58]

By 1885 the Reverend Robert G. McNiece, moderator of the conference, could submit to the territorial governor the following report:

> The Presbyterian denomination is now carrying on thirty-one day schools in Utah, in which about nine hundred children and youth are being educated, 75 per cent of them being of Mormon parentage. These schools are practically free, since the buildings and teachers cost the patrons nothing in most cases. With one exception, the local receipts are not sufficient to pay for the fuel and annual repairs. In these schools 53 teachers are employed . . . most of them from the East. Nothing of a denominational character is taught; they are simply American schools. It costs the Presbyterian denomination $26,000 a year directly from its treasury to maintain this educational work. . . . The American residents in Utah are taxed to support purely Mormon schools which they never patronize. The Government should at once take charge of the public school system in Utah by appointing an American as superintendent of public instruction and taking the school system out of the hands of the Mormon priesthood, who are training up the children and youth of the Territory to hate country and all American institutions.
>
> These American schools are bitterly opposed by the priesthood. In Mormon towns it is no uncommon thing for these school buildings to be stoned and besmeared with filth, and it is still less uncommon for the self-sacrificing women who have left their pleasant homes in the East to carry on this educational work to be publicly subjected to the vilest insinuations and slanders . . . in the addresses . . . in the Tabernacle.[59]

[58] *Ibid.*, September 17, 1880. "We take great pleasure in announcing that the new Presbyterian mission school at Fillmore, under the charge of Miss McKean, was opened last Tuesday morning with thirty scholars present.

"The Liberals have secured the old State building. . . . Through the generosity of kind friends in the East the school is entirely free from debt, and has quite a handsome sum in the treasury" (*Tribune,* February 17, 1881).

[59] *Report of the Governor of Utah Territory to the Secretary of the Interior for the Year 1885* (Washington, 1886), pp. 31–32.

The school question was agitated in the Territory throughout the period, with the Gentile press taking the lead in decrying the domination of the system by the Mormon Church. How could Utah maintain respectable common schools so long as Brigham Young continued to exact his exorbitant tithes, and thus keep his people in a constant state of impoverishment? What progress could be made along educational lines when the Church President actually objected to the literary training of Mormon children, and preferred that they remain in besotted ignorance?[60] These were stock charges, and the editors of the opposition made the most of them. The extraordinary blunder of the Mormon Church in attempting to introduce the "Deseret Alphabet," a simplified and semi-phonetic method of writing the English language, lent weight to the Gentile accusation of deliberate obscurantism.[61] The University of Deseret, nominally a territorial institution, but in reality a Mormon school, was known to have sponsored the absurd venture.[62] Nor does a study of early education in Utah bear out claims made by local enthusiasts that Utah led the West in educational advancement. However, by 1877 there were signs that the University was breaking away from its orthodox moorings:

> The Mormons never had but one institution worthy of the name of school, and this was known as the Deseret University, but it owes its very existence to the persistent labor of Dr. John R. Park, and not to the priesthood.
> . . . There is no disguising that a little knowledge is a dangerous thing for young Mormons, and that, there-

[60] *Daily Tribune*, January 8, 1874. "The *Herald* says the tax-payers of Utah cannot afford to pay for public schools. There is more truth than poetry in this declaration. The demands of Brigham upon his devout followers for tithes and other contributions so impoverish the community, that they have to deprive themselves of many necessaries to supply his wants." *Ibid.*, September 14, 1874: "Brigham Young bases his objection to educating the children of his followers upon the ground that an educated man will not work. . . . 'Educate a lad,' said he at the last conference, 'and he will want to become a Governor, a judge, and treasurer; you can get no useful work out of him. Free schools make lawyers, doctors, devils of our boys, and quite unfit them for any future usefulness.'"

[61] Andrew L. Neff, *History of Utah 1847 to 1869* (Salt Lake City, 1940) pp. 850–855, gives an adequate account of this educational freak.

[62] *Ibid.*, p. 851.

fore, the University has been a perfect breeder of apos-
tacy. Scores of young Mormons have left the institution
infidels in the gospel of Brigham, and the pious old fraud
has not been slow to see it. . . . The real trouble is that
Dr. Park and his assistants have not adopted the *Doctrine and Covenants* and other Church works as text
books. . . .[63]

A typical Gentile reaction to the ecclesiastical control of education is brought out in a letter from Justice Philip H. Emerson, of
the first district court, Provo, to Attorney General Williams, June
25, 1874:

> I have three children whose ages range from six to
> fifteen years—they are at school in Michigan, my wife is
> with them. The inhabitants of this place are almost en-
> tirely Mormons; out of 3000 inhabitants there are not to
> exceed 6 Gentile families. The schools are under the
> entire control of the Mormons, and I cannot think of
> keeping my children under such influences. Hence, I
> must keep them at school in Michigan. . . .[64]

The annual reports of the territorial governors to the Secretary
of the Interior returned again and again to the charge. That of
Governor Eli H. Murray, for the year 1885, is fairly representative:

> The public school system is very generally established
> over the Territory, but it is a source of great complaint by
> a large number of the people who are taxed for the sup-
> port of schools into which their children never enter.
> This is lamentable, and that control which tolerates
> schools by taxation of all the people, and into which all
> the children of the commonwealth may not for any reason
> enter is wrong, and should receive the attention of Con-
> gress. This condition of public education has stimulated
> effort to supply schools independent of Mormon control,
> and has resulted in the different religious denominations
> of the country establishing schools throughout the Terri-
> tory. The sum of it is, that the public schools receive as
> a body the Mormon children, and the schools established
> by the . . . denominations receive . . . the non-Mor-

---

[63] *Daily Tribune,* May 22, 1877.
[64] Emerson to Williams, June 25, 1874 (N. A., D. J. MSS, Utah).

mons. I am informed that many children of Mormon parentage, are taught in the latter-named schools, being preferred because the teachers are better qualified, and the schools, in fact, better.[65]

The Methodist attempt to win converts from Mormonism by education closely paralleled that of the Presbyterians. A seminary, or high school, was founded in Salt Lake City,[66] and grammar schools organized wherever possible. Incidental friction with the Saints became evident from time to time. Thus, the conference report of 1885 recorded that:

> Professor Copeland was well treated in Grantsville, other than having been turned out of his Mormon boarding house by the counsel of a Bishop, and hissed through the streets. . . . Miss Mills, of Rush Lake, has had a year of encouragement, notwithstanding the opposition, such as destroying books at St. John's, being turned out of her rooms, and accused of being a government spotter, and as giving Peg-Leg Davis away to the Deputy Marshals.[67]

Engaged in acrimonious debate with the *Deseret News,* in 1885, the editor of the *Daily Tribune* appealed to the Reverend Thomas Corwin Iliff, Methodist moderator, for statistics which would indicate the number of Mormon children under Methodist tutelage. Iliff's figures, for the school year 1884–1885, purported to show that of a total enrollment of 865 pupils in thirteen schools, 248 were from Mormon families, 178 from families that formerly had been Mormon. Less than one-third of the maintenance cost was derived from tuition; heavy subsidies were annually granted by the Woman's Home Missionary Society.[68] Four years later, the governor's report gave twenty-one as the number of schools supported by the sect, staffed by thirty teachers, with 1,396 children in attendance.[69]

---

[65] *Loc. cit.,* p. 17. See also *Report for the Year 1878,* p. 4.

[66] Merkel, *op. cit.,* p. 156; *Daily Tribune,* August 21, 1875.

[67] *Daily Tribune,* July 4, 1885.

[68] *Ibid.,* November 5, 1885.

[69] *Report of the Governor of Utah Territory to the Secretary of the Interior for the Year 1889* (Washington, 1890), p. 17.

As early as 1881 plans were drawn for a projected Methodist university in Utah. Eight years passed, however, before it was announced that funds had been made available from eastern sources and that the institution would be established in Ogden, then rising to importance as the second city of the Territory.[70] The anticipation was that Utah would benefit as had the Middle West from such foundations, radiating Christian culture distilled from Wesleyan evangelism. At the laying of the corner-stone, August 5, 1890, Governor Arthur L. Thomas dilated on the theme:

> . . . We regard it as one more agency established to help accomplish the emancipation of the majority of the people of the Territory of Utah from the thralldom of intolerance and bigotry. . . . A strange spectacle is presented to the people of the United States, and of the world by the attitude of the majority of the people of the Territory towards their Government. . . . Here a band of priestly leaders, many of them foreign-born . . . make their religious belief a political and business commodity and who claim the privilege under allegedly divine right to say what particular laws of the land they will obey. . . .[71]

The university, however, failed to materialize, due largely to the financial stringencies of the 1890's.

The Salt Lake Academy, under Congregational auspices, was opened in 1879 with O. H. Benner as headmaster.[72] To forward the success of this institution, and to launch Congregationalism into the work of "Christianizing" Utah, twenty-six leading clerics and laymen of the denomination met in Chicago in that year to found the "New West Education Commission" as an agency for supplying funds and furnishing competent teachers for schools in Utah.[73] Asserting complete freedom from all sectarian bias, the

---

[70] *Daily Tribune,* July 12, 1881.

[71] *Ibid.,* August 6, 1890.

[72] *Ibid.,* August 15, 1880. "Its aims are to fit young people for teachers, prepare them for college or the study of learned professions. . . . The school . . . is unsectarian. . . . It began a year ago with 100 students, now it has 150. . . . Remember, young men and young women of Utah, that of nearly $1,500,000 paid yearly to support a church, only a thirtieth part is devoted to the schools, and these schools are so poor that they in no wise fit students to occupy a fair or decent place in life. . . ."

[73] *Daily Tribune,* January 30, 1880. On December 25, O. J. Hollister, collector of internal revenue for the Territory, and a prominent Congrega-

commission went to work with commendable zeal, and by the end of the 1880's had twenty-four schools in operation, educating nearly twenty-five hundred children.[74] Probably the most ambitious of the Protestant educational efforts, the commission was reported by Governor Thomas, in his summary for 1891, to have expended annually an average of $40,000 during the preceding decade.[75]

During the painful years prior to the final submission of the Mormon authorities in the matter of polygamy, increasing pressure from the Gentiles made the Saints fearful that their control over the common schools was nearing its end. By provision of the Edmunds-Tucker Act of 1887, the office of territorial superintendent of schools, hitherto elective, and held, as a result, by Mormons, was made appointive, and therefore passed into Gentile patronage. Jacob S. Boreman, the retired jurist who had presided at the trial of John D. Lee, was named to this office. Reluctantly, the Mormons prepared to establish an independent parochial school system, as Boreman, in his school report for 1889, noted:

> . . . The District Schools of the Territory are not in a vigorous or flourishing condition. In a few localities where the influx of new people and the infusion of new life have caused a change the control of the schools is passing out of the hands of those who heretofore controlled them.
>
> The Mormon people do not show that independence of action that is so characteristic of the American people, but are obedient, even against their better judgment, to the will of their Church leader. . . .

tionalist, wrote from Chicago detailing a recent meeting of the commission, which recorded the following:

"Resolved, that we recognize with respect, a loyal and intelligent minority in Utah, and that we protest in advance against the admission of Utah as a State, at any time, without the consent of that loyal minority.

"Resolved, that Pres. James B. Angell, LL.D., of Michigan; the Rev. Pres. William M. Brooks, of Iowa; and John G. Jennings, Esq., of Ohio, be a committee to appoint a commission of five to proceed to Utah and make a careful and thorough investigation of Mormonism—its character, its temper and its purpose, and especially to examine the condition of Christian schools and ascertain their fitness as instruments for the weakening and ultimate overthrow of that gigantic evil; and make a due report to the churches, at their discretion; and to this Council."

[74] *Report of the Governor,* 1889, p. 16.

[75] *Report,* 1891, p. 21.

Those who control the mission schools and academies of other churches are anticipating that when free schools shall be established throughout the Territory, their mission schools will have to give way and be closed, and some of these Christian churches will be very glad when that time arrives. It is to be regretted that at this very juncture the Mormon Church should take the opposite course, and should endeavor to push forward a policy looking to the withdrawal of the Mormon children from the public schools.

This antagonism . . . has taken effective shape since the enactment . . . of a statute forbidding the use of sectarian books in the district schools.[76]

The year 1889 would appear to have marked the climax of the denominational school system. The Gentile sects then were operating ninety-three schools in Utah with 7,961 pupils enrolled.[77] Three years later the number of such schools had dropped to eighty-one.[78] Partly as a result of decreased income as an effect of the Panic of 1893, most of these free schools in the smaller Mormon communities were forced to close their doors. Today, they are hardly more than a memory. With statehood and re-adjustment, in 1896, the trend toward separate Latter-Day Saint schools declined, for the Mormon Church then controlled the situation and saw little wisdom in multiplying expenses.

While it goes without saying that the rank and file of the evangelical missionaries in Utah were men and women honestly intent upon bringing the truths of Christianity to the benighted Mormons, as they conceived them, many of them considered it their special vocation to take a leading part in the radical anti-Mormon campaign. To be "posted" on Mormon theology, and to deliver sermons the principal purpose of which was to expose the inconsist-

---

[76] *Report of the School Commission for 1889* (Salt Lake City, 1889), p. 3. *Daily Tribune,* January 14, 1890. Boreman reported fifteen hundred children in the Mormon Church schools, including, presumably, Brigham Young Academy at Provo.

[77] *Report of the Governor,* 1889, p. 16.

[78] *Report,* 1892, p. 16. "Denominational schools still exist in different parts of the Territory, though I have been informed that there is a steady decrease in the number of those attending them. I believe it is the intention of nearly all the denominational schools to gradually withdraw from competition with the public schools."

encies of that system, were matters of outstanding importance. McLeod had his train of followers. A lecture on Christian dogma could hardly hope to rank as news in the esteem of the Gentile press, but a rousing denunciation of polygamy, blood atonement, or "Mormon atheism" was certain to rate prominent headlines. The editor of the *Daily Tribune* indicated the desirable policy:

> Especially must the Christian Church in Utah fairly meet the issue forced upon them [*sic*] by the dominant ecclesiastical party who now hold the reins of political power. . . . Hitherto it has largely banished from its pulpits a serious consideration of the errors and evils claimed by the Mormons to be sanctioned and sanctified by the Old Testament. . . . It has relegated to the press its responsibility and duty in this respect, and lost its proper position in the forefront of the battle.
>
> The conflict is based upon moral grounds, upon the assumed right of the Mormon Church to ally itself with the State, as also . . . that polygamy is sanctioned by revelation. It falls within the province of the pulpit to disprove these assumptions, and more especially is it the bounden duty of the Christian Church to reach out and instruct the mistaken votaries of error.[79]

In the Methodist chapel in Salt Lake City, the congregation was inured to lectures such as "The Bible and the Book of Mormon Compared" wherein there was "so complete a demolition of an antagonist that there was not a vestige of him left," of "Brigham Young's Record of Blood," in which the Reverend C. P. Lyford acquainted his hearers with the sad necessity of being equipped with revolver as well as Bible in the perilous work of preaching the gospel in Utah.[80] The Reverend Theophilus Hilton, head of the Methodist Seminary, expounded the striking similarities between Mormonism and Mohammedanism, winning editorial commendation: "Utah cannot be overburdened by these public lectures which tend to keep the evils of Mohammedanism in America and the blighting effects of Priestcraft before the people." [81] The Methodist Episcopal Conference, meeting in Ogden, July 9, 1881, noted that "the leaders of Mormonism, the great Apostles of lust," were

---

[79] *Daily Tribune*, January 8, 1878.
[80] *Ibid.*, September 7, 1875; January 22, 1876, and *passim*.
[81] *Ibid.*, March 25, 1881.

preaching polygamy with unabated forwardness. The conference thereupon resolved, "That Mormonism is a system that would disgrace any land, and is a foul blot on our national escutcheon." Toying with politics, it was declared to be the sense of the meeting that "the laws of the Territory should be made by a Council appointed by the President of the United States and confirmed by the Senate." [82]

Early in November of that same year the General Missionary Commission of the Methodist Episcopal Church met in New York City. Bishop I. W. Wiley of the Utah Conference presented his case, insisting that "something must be done soon with the great evil of polygamy, and there is nothing to hinder the Government from handling it if the politicians would not interfere." The Bishop's plan was simplicity itself: "There are in Utah 80,000 females, 40,000 of whom are marriageable and well married. The other 40,000 can be got into the mission schools and the power and influence of Mormonism over them be broken." [83]

The local conference, convening in Provo two years later, found much in the situation to deplore:

> 1. The thorough organization of Mormonism is the first difficulty met in prosecuting our work in Utah. We know of no system whose organization is more complete. . . . Mormonism is almost impregnable.
> 2. Much of the fruit of our work is not apparent because of the fluctuation of those we may be able to reach. Our missionaries labor faithfully for results. Souls are converted and added to the Church. But the population thus reached being so transitory incident upon the mining and railroad interests that no figures can give an estimate of the work accomplished. For example, in nearly all our charges the membership has almost wholly changed within the last three years.
> 3. Another most serious embarrassment to our Utah

---

[82] *Ibid.*, July 10, 1881; July 14, 1881. It is interesting to note that the famous preacher of the Brooklyn Tabernacle, DeWitt Talmadge, a violent anti-Mormon, in a sermon delivered October 2, 1881, accused Guiteau, assassin of President Garfield, of Mormonism. Representative Haskell, of Kansas, repeated the charge in Congress, January 9, 1882. *Congressional Record,* January 10, 1882, p. 326.

[83] *Ibid.*, November 13, 1881.

work has been the paralyzing effect of the Church debts. Very little money can be raised in Mormon towns for Church building, and as we cannot expect aid from the Board of Church Extension except in small sums, and that only on condition that a larger sum be raised in the community . . . we are unable to meet the demand.[84]

The ensuing decade, however, saw Utah Methodism relieved of its pressing financial worries, for approximately twenty thousand dollars were allotted annually by the national organization.

Presbyterianism in Utah had its share of difficulties and problems. Writing from the meeting of the Presbytery of Utah in Springville, a few miles south of Provo, March, 1880, Robert McNiece quoted the minutes:

Resolved, that as a Presbytery we hereby call the attention of the Mormon authorities to the fact that, in towns under their control, our meetings are frequently disturbed by hootings through the windows, cursings against the teachers, and by boisterous singing and shouting around the doors. Our buildings have also been defiled in unmentionable ways, our property injured by stoning and our books cut in pieces and scattered under the seats by those attending our services. These things are a disgrace to the Nineteenth Century, and would be tolerated in no part of the United States outside of Utah. We hold the Mormon priesthood responsible for these things, since they have exclusive control of the municipal government in all these towns.[85]

The complaint thus voiced was frequently repeated. Mormon vandalism, inspired by the priesthood or not, was evidenced too often for the missionaries to feel any great degree of security, although there is no indication of personal molestation.[86] The Presbyterians agreed with their Methodist brethren that the state of affairs in Utah demanded drastic exercise of federal power. In April, 1886, the Presbytery gathered at Nephi and adopted the following resolutions:

---

[84] *Ibid.*, August 8, 1883. The conference closed on the preceding day.

[85] *Daily Tribune*, March 22, 1880. This letter was undoubtedly written by McNiece, who handled most of the Presbyterian publicity.

[86] *Ibid.*, July 10, 1883; November 3, 1885; December 22, 1885, and *passim*.

In regard to the statement recently telegraphed over the country from Washington that no further Congressional legislation is needed for Utah because of the work which churches and schools are accomplishing there, it is recommended

First—that this statement be declared unwarranted by the facts, and calculated to do great mischief.

Second—That while the Christian churches and schools are doing most salutary work which is increasing in power every year, there is still great need for radical legislation by Congress.

Third—That if our Government had done its duty as faithfully as the great Christian churches have done theirs, Utah would have been Americanized years ago, as is shown by the fact that since the Government has begun to assert its authority . . . the freedom of the people to attend the churches and schools has been greatly augmented.[87]

Fearlessly Presbyterianism strode into the political arena, proclaiming at the session held in Manti, August 27, 1887:

Affairs have reached a crisis in Utah. After years of defiance and determined evasion of the laws, a very plausible policy has been adopted by the Mormon leaders. A Constitutional Convention has been called, a constitution has been framed and submitted to the Mormon people and adopted by them. In this constitution is a clause making polygamy a crime, to be punished by fine and imprisonment.

This is the pretext by which they hope to deceive Congress and to gain admission as a State.

The Presbyterian elders then proceeded to review the real facts:

1. The so-called revelation of polygamy stands yet unrepealed by any authority from the church; it is, therefore, as binding as ever upon the whole Mormon people.

2. Up to the very meeting of this Constitutional Convention men brought before the courts refused to promise to obey the laws against polygamy, and are yet being arrested for the same crime. . . .

3. Up to the present day any Mormon who promises to obey the laws against polygamy is considered a traitor to his religion, and is treated as such.

[87] *Ibid.,* April 2, 1886.

4. This movement for Statehood is altogether a Mormon movement. The Gentiles take no part in it, and are now a unit against it.

5. The Mormon people are as firm believers in polygamy today as they ever have been; they have no disposition to give it up; but through a strange policy recently adopted, they have made this sacred tenet of their religion a crime, whilst yet believing in its divine origin.

In view of these facts, we, in common with the other loyal citizens of Utah, do most earnestly protest against this whole movement for the following reasons:

1. Because there is no sincerity in it. It is a fact well known to us who are here, and admitted to be such by many Mormons, that the real intention is not to abolish polygamy, but to obtain Statehood, get entire control of affairs in Utah, and thus defeat the execution of the laws. For with Mormon Judges, officers and jurors, no law against polygamy would be enforced. Hence, this constitutional clause . . . is only a blind.

2. Because it would leave the power of the priesthood untouched. The twenty-five thousand men to whom obedience is pledged . . . would only be entrenched in their present stronghold.

3. Because it would be a death-blow aimed at our American homes; it would check our Christian work, and give up forever this entire Territory to Mormon rule and policy.

4. Because the whole scheme means treason against the Government and its laws.

We therefore call upon the ministers and members of the Presbyterian Church, North and South, to raise their voices in protest against this religio-political chicanery.[88]

With the defeat of Cleveland, rumored to be well-disposed toward Mormon aspirations for statehood, local Presbyterians breathed a sigh of relief. Their Salt Lake Pastor, McNiece, rose to the occasion:

There has been fear here that if the present administration was re-elected, it would put back the progress of Utah many years. Why, in the Southern part of the Territory, the President has been referred to as "Brother Cleveland" (sensation) and the Mormons in Salt Lake have regretted his defeat as "he was preparing to do so

[88] *Ibid.,* September 4, 1887.

much for our people." Many easterners have been afraid to migrate to Utah, and have gone to Montana's severe climate, because of the hostility here to American institutions. . . . Now a man has been called to the presidential chair who understands the Utah situation, and will sustain us in the struggle.[89]

In a letter to H. H. Bancroft, then preparing his volume on the history of Utah, he wrote, September 18, 1884:

My experience of seven years has led me to look upon the history of Utah as mainly the history of the Mormon priesthood in its attempt to subordinate the State to the Church, and make the authority of the priesthood superior to that of the United States Government. In my judgment this attempt is the main cause of all the political trouble in Utah for more than thirty years. I am aware that those at the head of the Mormon priesthood profess, with a great deal of smiling and bowing, to be zealous friends of the Constitution and the Federal Government. But what could be more preposterous than such profession, coming as it does from those who are continually performing a war dance on the one, and teaching their people to hate the other?[90]

To the gathering of the Saints in Zion had come thousands of Scandinavian converts, the fruit of the missionary zeal of the Mormon elders who combined the argument of a new dispensation with financial aid to the immigrant and assistance to the farmer who would till the soil as a faithful son of the Church. As Lutheranism, the baptismal creed of most of these newcomers, was not as yet organized in Utah to embark on a program of re-conversion, this labor was taken up enthusiastically by Presbyterians and Methodists.

---

[89] *Ibid.*, November 13, 1888.

[90] McNiece to Bancroft, Bancroft Library, Utah Correspondence. On April 3–5, 1888, a "Christian Convention" of the Protestant churches was held in Salt Lake City. The topics were: "The Mormon Priest one of the Chief Obstacles to American and Christian Progress in Utah"; "The Anti-American Influences in Utah"; "Mormon Perversion of the Bible and True Religion"; "Mormon Theory of Life, Society and Morals"; "The Christian Home, Its Perils and Opportunities in Utah"; "Lessons from Mormonism"; "Christianity, Only Hope for those Whose Faith in Revealed Religion has been Wrecked by Mormonism" (*Tribune,* April 5, 1888).

Two Swedish evangelists, under Presbyterian auspices, entered the field in 1879, and centered their activities around Mount Pleasant, in the heart of the region settled by their countrymen. After a year's labor, they could report only thirty souls snatched from the burning in Mount Pleasant and sixteen in the nearby village of Ephraim.[91]   Chapels were erected, but the work languished.   In 1882 the Methodists attacked the problem, making much of the fact that the missionary in charge, the Reverend A. H. Franklin, was himself a convert from Mormonism.[92]   Largely through his efforts, Methodism extended the work to no less than eighteen communities in the Territory, building, wherever possible, separate church edifices where the Scandinavians could enjoy the use of their native tongues in worship.[93]   Trained missionaries were lacking in sufficient numbers,[94] however, and while it would seem that a few of the immigrants, perhaps as a result of disappointment or disgust with the conditions which they had to face, both moral and agricultural, professed their rejection of Mormonism, still fewer remained fixed in that determination, and with the final settlement of the polygamy issue, Methodism was able to hold but a handful.   The Scandinavian missions declined, and by the end of the century, they were generally abandoned.

If the heralds of Protestant Christianity were too often forced to harangue empty benches in Utah, they found in the East abundant balm for their bruised spirits.   The appearance of a missionary from the land of the Mormons in an eastern pulpit was a welcome diversion from the normal course of foreign mission appeals. Here was living evidence of the reality of an American problem of vital interest to the national conscience.   The contribution of these men in the way of keeping the country aroused on the issue of polygamy, and their influence, direct and indirect, upon the enactment of legislation for the solution of that problem, can hardly be exaggerated.   The record of their multiple activities defies documentation, inasmuch as these propagandists circulated throughout the country carrying their message to innumerable congregations. Pulpit and press were thrown open to them, and the perennial fas-

---

[91] McVicker, *loc. cit.*, p. 237.

[92] Mabry, *loc. cit.*, p. 273.

[93] *Ibid.*, p. 274; *Daily Tribune*, July 3, 1885; July 5, 1888.

[94] *Report of the Governor of Utah*, 1885, p. 10.

cination exercised by their strictures upon the popular morality of Utah was a prominent feature of the journalism of the period.

As early as 1872, C. P. Lyford, Methodist missioner at Provo, took his sermon on "Revolver and Bible in Mormondom" to the eastern states, to edify the faithful and to collect funds for his chapel and school.[95] A review of a sermon by Bishop Tuttle, delivered in St. Louis that year, reached the office of the *Deseret News,* and prompted a savage expression of Mormon resentment:

> The Bishop said he had been crafty in his movements here, "pursuing a conservative course in order not to defeat his ends by arousing unnecessarily the prejudices of the people." The Bishop is a sly dog, but he has thus let out the thinness and hypocrisy of his conservatism. His *ruse de guerre,* he said, had been successful, the success being almost entirely with fledglings, the old birds being too wary to be caught with his chaff. In other words, his schools were a large success, though rather on the loaves and fishes order; "half the scholars being given their tuition free" for, says the Bishop, "it is through this source that the cause is daily gaining strength. . . ." [96]

At the general Methodist conference held in Cincinnati, May 24, 1880, the Reverend H. D. Fisher of the Salt Lake City congregation presented a report on conditions in Utah. Judge Jacob Boreman, zealous layman and pillar of the chapel in Beaver, seat of his district court, offered a resolution denouncing polygamy and demanding its extirpation by congressional action. This was unanimously adopted.[97]

The Salt Lake *Daily Tribune,* June 15, 1881, noted as "an encouraging sign of the times" that the churches throughout the country were taking up the Mormon question:

> If the local pastors of all these churches would individually and for his congregation, ask of each Representative his personal and active support of a bill, say, to have Utah governed by a Commission in place of a Legislature, such a bill would pass like a whirlwind.

---

[95] *Daily Tribune,* January 22, 1872.
[96] *Deseret News,* March 13, 1872; *Daily Tribune,* March 14, 1872.
[97] *Daily Tribune,* May 30, 1880.

The *Tribune's* enthusiasm was prompted by the "thorough discussion" of the Mormon question by the Congregational Home Missionary Society, which met in convention at Chicago earlier in the month. The Reverend Walter Barrows of Salt Lake City there described Utah as "our Turkey at home." Dudley C. Haskell, congressman from the second Kansas district, took the devious history of Mormonism as his theme, dipping into the possible solution for the existing evil. "He is clearly of the opinion that the remedy is with Congress, and it will evidently take no pressure to induce him to support any reasonable bill which the Gentile people here will agree upon." Haskell considered his views worth publishing:

> The same methods by which Christianity has been carried into the jungles of India and the wilds of Africa will be required to carry and hold it in Utah. The citadel of polygamous Mormonism must be invested by a Christian army. . . . This is a battle to be won with the Bible and the school book.
> There is no free public school in Utah, but an Academy in the charge of a hard-working Christian minister has been established in Salt Lake. Sustain it—that it may be made to furnish the needed teachers. A little band of devoted women have begun there the anti-polygamy crusade, and have started a paper, the *Anti-Polygamy Standard*. Aid them. Circulate their paper. If the wives and mothers of America are made fully aware of the extent and character of this degradation of their sex . . . the onrushing tide of public sentiment they will set in motion will sweep away polygamy in a year.[98]

The Utah Review, a magazine edited by the Reverend Theophilus Hilton, reported a meeting of the Union Home Missionary Society (Presbyterian) held at Buffalo, May 27, 1881. Mrs. Dr. Horace Eaton, of Palmyra, New York, cradle of Mormonism, read a paper on the origins of the sect, in which she enlarged on the favorite theme:

---

[98] *Mormonism, an Address by the Hon. D. C. Haskell, M.C., of Kansas at the National Anniversary of the American Home Society, in Chicago, June 8, 1881* (New York, 1881), pp. 25–26 (Copy in the Bancroft Library).

The women of the Synods of Western New York are doing much for Utah. Aware that the poisonous virus went out from us, we feel that there is a relevancy, a fitness, in our following it with the counteracting, neutralizing, healing antidote, the gospel of our Lord Jesus Christ.

. . . This is of a kind, dear sisters, that goeth not out, but by prayers and fasting. Professor Coyner, our missionary at Salt Lake City, thus analyzes it:

"Mormonism is made up of twenty parts. Take eight parts diabolism, three parts of animalism, from the Mohammedan system, one part bigotry from old Judaism, four parts cunning and treachery from Jesuitism, two parts Thugism from India, and two parts Arnoldism, and then shake the mixture over the fires of animal passion and throw in the forms and ceremonies of the Christian religion, and you will have the system in its true component elements." [99]

Three years later, Coyner betook himself to Madison, Wisconsin, to deliver an address before the National Educational Association, July 15, 1884. Declaring that his years in Utah had engendered within him a "love for the home of my adoption," he expounded his attitude:

I would not do what I am now doing if I did not believe that in thus exposing that fearful system I am the true friend of those now influenced by it. . . . And although the Mormon priesthood see fit to personally malign those who oppose them, I shall ever let them fight the battle on the line of their own mode of warfare, and leave the world to judge the purity of motive by the daily walk and conversation.

. . . For many years I have listened to their speakers, and I have never yet heard a discourse that has not in it the elements of treason, those things calculated to array both head and heart against our country, and it is high time that we regard the Utah problem not as connected with a system of religious belief worthy the respect of the thinking world, but a political organization that has one settled purpose which it is pursuing with all the energy that characterizes its founder, and that is the overthrow of our government.

---

[99] *The Utah Review,* I, No. VIII, February, 1882, 238–242 (Partial file in Bancroft Library).

Coyner felt that he lived under the baleful glare of Mormonism's "All-Seeing Eye":

> I have weighed well not only every statement made, but the expression of that statement, and hold myself responsible, let the "consequences be what they may." I admit I have hesitated to do what I have now done, not because of personal interests connected either with myself or the work with which I am connected in Salt Lake City, and which is as dear to me as life itself, but from the fact that I well know that every time the Mormon Tiger is excited, the furious lashings of his tail are felt by the unprotected missionaries scattered over Utah Territory.[100]

During the summer and autumn months of 1887, McNiece toured the Middle West and East, enlightening the Presbyterian laity on the difficulties faced by the Christian mission in Utah. In Kansas City, he lectured on "The Redemption of Utah," pointing out that "In ten years' residence . . . I have discovered but one moral principle, viz., whatever helps to maintain the Priesthood's power and overthrow the United States is right." [101] Upon his return to Salt Lake City, December 3, 1887, the *Daily Tribune* interviewed him:

> While there [New York City] I had a chance to talk with the editors of the *Times,* the *World,* and the *Herald,* and had correspondence with the editor of the *Tribune,* and they are all wide awake on the situation of affairs in Utah, are all strongly anti-Mormon, and take a deep interest in the matter. I went to the house of the editor of the *Herald* and after giving him some documentary evidence, he assured me that he would do everything he could to keep Utah from coming in as a State.
> "How did you find the people in the East on this subject?"
> "They have thought but little about it, and I assure you there is danger if we do not use our influence and labor against Statehood. While some of the papers are on the Mormon side, I notice they are of the inferior

---

[100] John M. Coyner, Ph.D., *The Utah Problem, An Address Delivered before the National Educational Association, July 15, 1884, at Madison, Wis.* (n. p., n. d.) (Bancroft Library).

[101] *Daily Tribune,* August 14, 1887.

class, but the Mormons are busy to secure every paper
and influence they can. . . . One leading editor of one
of the great New York papers said to me: 'You would
be surprised if you knew how many Mormons come into
my office. . . . It was only a day or two ago that John
W. Young and the editor of the *Deseret News,* Penrose,
were here urging us to favor Statehood for Utah.'"

"After being East so long, what do you think can be
done about it?"

"It is my judgment we can't be too active in dis-
seminating information through the East. That is the
idea of many people I have met, and out of it has grown
good work among the Christian women of the Presbyterian Church, who have begun the general circulation
of petitions to Congress, to be signed by voters, protesting against the admission of Utah. . . . I think this
will be taken up by other denominations and become general."

A Congregationalist missionary, M. W. Montgomery, spent
the winter of 1887–88 touring the eastern seaboard with a series
of lectures featuring these tempting topics: "Sixty Years of
Mormonism"; "The Present Situation in Utah"; "Is Mormonism
Gaining Strength"; "Interviews with Leading Mormons, Men
and Women." [102] In 1890 he published *The Mormon Delusion:
Its History, Doctrines, and Outlook in Utah.* Therein, he laid
stress on the need for muscular Christianity in Utah, rehearsing
the bitterness of the 1870's:

Under the intolerant rule of Brigham Young the
pioneer missionaries took their lives in their hands. The
Sunday-school Superintendent of the Congregational
mission was assassinated upon the streets of Salt Lake
City; a Presbyterian missionary was repeatedly threatened with the loss of his life, while the Methodist and
Episcopalian, and all the other early missionaries were
necessarily the stuff of which martyrs are made. At
first the Mormons could best be reached through the
free schools for their children. These schools were
followed with religious services, and later with preaching. So much progress has thus been made by the teacher
and missionary that for several years past the whole
Territory has been open to the preaching of the gospel.

---

[102] *Ibid.,* December 16, 1887.

There are heroes and heroines in these latter days among the Christian missionary workers in Utah. No foreign missionary service requires a more self-sacrificing spirit. The laborer in Utah has particular burdens which are not found in any other field. . . . A moral miasma exists in the whole social atmosphere. . . .[103]

The most indefatigable propagandist in the evangelical cause was the Methodist minister, Thomas Corwin Iliff. Veteran of the War between the States, he regarded the struggle in Utah in the light of a Glorious Revolution, an assault upon the enemies of Christian morality, and he lost no opportunity of acquainting the outside world with the "paganism" of the Mormons. He arrived in Utah in 1882, served as pastor of the Salt Lake congregation, and later as the superintendent of the missions of the conference.[104]

Concerning his activities, in 1884, the *Daily Tribune* carried the following:

Dr. Iliff has returned from an extended visit to sixteen Eastern Methodist Conferences, where he met with such pleasing success and made so favorable an impression that six bishops with many ministers and laymen, have requested him to take another eastern trip to explain more in detail the condition of affairs and prospects in Utah. . . . The Doctor found a remarkable interest in Utah's religious condition. . . . They were all eager to see the Asiatic Church crushed, wiped off the face of the earth, and the cause of the American home and the Christian Church made triumphant in this Territory. . . . The doctor confidently hopes that the appropriations for Utah in 1889 . . . will be $100,000, and that the next five years will see $500,000 poured in here to push Methodist evangelical work.[105]

Though Iliff was to be disappointed in his roseate dreams, he continued his crusade to awaken America to the problem which absorbed his interest. On his return from one of his many sub-

---

[103] Rev. R. W. Montgomery, *The Mormon Delusion: Its History, Doctrine and Outlook in Utah* (Boston, 1890), pp. 328–329.

[104] James David Gillilan, *Thomas Corwin Iliff* (New York, 1919), *passim;* Merkel, *op. cit.,* pp. 62–74.

[105] *Daily Tribune,* December 14, 1884.

sequent trips to the East, the *Tribune* again gleaned from his findings:

> Until a year ago, public interest has been largely confined to the Mormon antiquities and the Mountain Meadow Massacre, but now these are all cast aside and people are asking about the political and social situation with regard to future progress and development. . . . The signs of victory are already detected in the air by the Eastern Christian Churches, so that they are more ready now than ever to . . . help along the glorious mission work here among Utah's Asiatics. The cry from the Utah Christians of Come over into Macedonia and help us! is being recognized as never before.
>
> Dr. Iliff found people greatly amused by such paradoxical expressions as "The Saints are at war with the Utah Christians; the Methodist Philistines are come to capture Zion; the Christian missionaries are come up to Aphek to fight against Israel . . ."; and when he told that the L. D. S. regarded the Methodists, Baptists and Congregationalists, as Israel of old regarded the sons of Anak, the Perrizite, the Hittite, the Hivite, the Girgashite . . . his audiences just lay back and roared.[106]

Whatever the quality of his humor, Iliff was at least a fighter. In later years, he took a prominent part in fostering local agitation against the seating of Brigham H. Roberts, an avowed polygamist, in the House of Representatives, the success of which movement was his greatest victory.[107]

The evangelical crusade, in the light of its master ambition to conquer Mormonism as a religious faith and as a political power must be written down as a failure. The gains in denominational membership as noted in the census reports indicate merely a growth proportionate to the general increase of the population of the Territory.[108] Conversions from Mormonism to the sects played very little part in the religious history of Utah during the period. By the time of the Manifesto on polygamy (1890), the mission school system had already entered upon its decline. It

---

[106] *Ibid.*, June 9, 1889.

[107] Merkel, *op. cit.*, p. 73; Gillilan, *op. cit.*, pp. 88–90.

[108] Utah Historical Records Survey, *Inventory of Church Archives of Utah* (Salt Lake City, 1940), pp. 49–51.

was only in the national field that militant Protestantism, urged on largely by the Utah missionaries, was able to bring pressure to bear upon Congress to legislate for the eradication of Utah's peculiar morality. Alone among the non-Mormon groups, the Catholic Church, through immigration and the concentration of Irish workers at the mines, registered a significant increase. Bishop Scanlan's pre-occupation with the spiritual welfare of his own people afforded pleasant relief in a story of religious antagonism as bitter as any which mars the pages of American history.

CHAPTER VII

THE GENTILE LADIES HOIST THEIR
STANDARD

"LET EVERY Man have his own Wife, and Let every Woman have her own Husband." [1]   St. Paul's injunction to the unstable Christians of Corinth seemed to have been penned by design to serve as a text whereon to pin a sermon on the abomination of polygamy.   Undaunted by the battle scars of the vanished years, Harriet Beecher Stowe mounted the pulpit stairs to preach one more homily to her devoted audience:

> To the Women of America:
>   Let every happy wife and mother who reads these lines give her sympathy, prayers and efforts to free her sisters from this degrading bondage.   Let all the women of the country stand united for them.   There is a power in combined enlightened sentiment, before which every form of injustice and cruelty must finally go down. [2]

Here indeed was a challenge to the Christian womanhood of America.   The victims of the paynim Mormons were their own unhappy plural wives, bond-slaves to a dogma which stank in the nostrils of the determined monogamists of the land.   And the paladins, arrayed in the shining armor of domestic virtue, were the ladies who constituted the backbone of militant American Protestantism.

In thousands of church parlors throughout the nation, these ladies gathered to discuss the salvation of their Mormon sisters. Sober, dignified and purposeful, they sat on horse-hair sofas around tables covered with worn green baize and passed resolutions. But they did more.   With them it was a matter of national con-

---

[1] I Cor. 7:2. The text was conspicuously printed beneath the mast-head of the *Anti-Polygamy Standard.*

[2] *Anti-Polygamy Standard,* I, No. 1, April, 1880, 1.   (Hereafter A. P. S.)

science, for upon their shoulders rested the care of all the churches. From their capacious reticules came the dollars that made possible the maintenance of the sectarian missions and mission schools in far-off Utah. They it was who sent out teachers and paid their salaries. And it was to them, as to a rock of refuge and strength that the Gentile women of Utah confidently turned for encouragement and support as they launched their campaign to strike the shackles of polygamy from the women of Mormondom. Here was a woman's problem, to be handled only by her own sex. The politicians, mere men, might debate the expediency of the Poland bill or the Edmunds bill to force submission upon the recalcitrant, stiff-necked Mormon hierarchy; they might ponder the wisdom of denying the right of suffrage to polygamists or the legal justification for supplanting Utah's legislature by an appointive commission. Basically, these were surface measures. Christian womanhood conceived it to be her healing mission to open the eyes of her deluded Mormon sisters to the folly and indignity of their way of life. Hers it was to see that the unfortunate relicts of an outlawed system should experience the tender care of practical Christianity.

What the Mormon women themselves thought of all this was hardly the question. The Christian women were prepared to realize that votaries of error have a way of clinging to their fleshpots. And if the plural wives insisted upon signing petitions to Congress asking, in intention, if not in so many words, that they be permitted to continue their immoral way of life, it could be ascribed to the nefarious influence of the Mormon priesthood rather than to the inner corruption of their souls. The windows needed to be flung open and the evils of polygamy exposed. So thought the embattled ladies of the Anti-Polygamy Society, and behind them stood the serried ranks of the women of America, "in combined enlightened sentiment and sympathy."

It was under such auspicious circumstances that the *Anti-Polygamy Standard,* organ of the Society, made its bow in April, 1880, bravely flaunting St. Paul and Mrs Stowe.[3] The editor "dipped her pen in her heart's blood" for her impassioned salutatory:

---

[3] *Cf.* J. Cecil Alter, *Early Utah Journalism* (Salt Lake City, 1938), pp. 330–331. This was a monthly magazine which ran for three years, the final issue appearing in April, 1883. A file is preserved in the Salt Lake Library.

It took long years of agitation before the Anti-Slavery party of the United States succeeded in abolishing that system which was a shame and a disgrace to our country, but they did succeed at last! And the women who inaugurated the Anti-Polygamy Society are determined to persevere and keep this subject agitated until it, like the other twin relic of barbarism shall no longer be a foul blot on our escutcheon as a nation, but shall also be a thing of the past. How this little band of noble, earnest, disinterested women came to form themselves into a permanent organization, their manner of work, and what they have already accomplished, will be told in the columns of the *Anti-Polygamy Standard*.

In an early number . . . we intend to commence the publication of a series of articles upon the effects of polygamy, showing the physical, mental and moral results of the system, as exemplified in some of the leading polygamous families of the Territory. The writer has made a thorough study of the subject at the request of a leading medical journal.

What the Gentile women of Utah lacked in numbers they compensated for in zeal. During the sixties, of course, they were but a handful. Bishop Tuttle found but three of his communion when he arrived in 1867.[4] As the following decade advanced, they began to gather strength, although it may be reasonably doubted whether all the "Gentile ladies" who appeared on the streets of the mining camps were exactly social acquisitions. Mormon critics certainly felt no hesitancy in calling spades by their proper names, bewailing the moral deterioration of their cities with the influx of sirens who plied their ancient trade by night.[5] But the government officers, the Gentile tradesmen and mine-owners gradually brought with them their families, and a nucleus of feminine social life emerged. The Godbeite schism incorporated into the Gentile fold the wives of dissenting Mormons, although it may have been something of a problem of protocol as to which Mrs. Godbe, Mrs. Lawrence, or Mrs. Kelsey was to be

---

[4] Tuttle, *Reminiscences*, p. 104.

[5] *Cf.* Franklin D. Richards, "Crime in Utah" (MS, Bancroft Library, 1884).

accepted as the legitimate bearer of her name.[6] As early as 1871 a group of Gentile ladies are recorded as organizing a "society for mental culture" under the inspiration of a certain evanescent Congregational minister, T. L. Spear, of California.[7]

In the following issue the *Anti-Polygamy Standard* vouchsafed to sketch the history of the society. It appears that during the autumn of 1878 a young English woman, brought to Utah as a convert to Mormonism, found herself entangled in a polygamous union. To several of the Gentile women of Salt Lake City she brought her tale of woe and her problem. They at once exalted the sordid business into a *cause celebre:*

> By the intervention of these Gentile acquaintances the matter became of public notoriety, was brought into court and created such an intense excitement in Salt Lake City that the ladies thought the time opportune for action. Consequently a mass meeting of women opposed to polygamy was called for November 7th and at the appointed hour the meeting convened at Independence Hall.[8]

The case in question was that of Miss Carrie Owen, who had contracted marriage with John Miles on the same day that he had taken to himself another wife. It was later disclosed that Miss Owen was aware of the arrangement at the time of her nuptials. She immediately repented her action, however, and reported her bigamous situation to the United States marshal.[9]

---

[6] Several of the Godbeites, having contracted polygamous unions prior to their defection from the Church, continued the maintenance of plural households for some years. Henry Lawrence, later mayor of Salt Lake City, applied for amnesty in 1882. (Department of Justice, Amnesty Cases, Utah. Special Docket A.)

[7] *Daily Tribune,* June 22, 1871.

[8] *A. P. S.,* May, 1880.

[9] Whitney, *Utah,* III, 56–75. The account of the affair given by the Gentile press differs considerably from that given by Whitney. Subsequently, Miss Owen accepted a minor post in the government service in Washington, D. C., and appeared as an anti-Mormon witness in the hearings in regard to the sequestration of the property of the Church, 1887 (III, 560) ; P. H. Van Zile to Attorney General Devens, June 3, 1879 (D. J. MSS) : "I consider her a lady in every way though she was induced to marry the miserable cur John Miles."

The "mass meeting" of the Gentile women—two hundred in number—drew up a statement addressed to "Mrs. Rutherford B. Hayes and the Women of the United States":

> It is more than thirty years ago since polygamy was planted on the shores of Great Salt Lake. During these years, Congress has entirely failed to enact efficient or enforce existing laws for the abolition of this great crime, and we believe that more of these unlawful and unhallowed alliances have consummated the past year than ever before in the history of the Mormon Church. The Endowment Houses, under the name of Temples, are being erected in different parts of the Territory, costing millions. It is impossible to ascertain the exact number of polygamous marriages, for they are consecrated in these Endowment Houses, an institution no Gentile is permitted to enter, and the brotherhood and sisterhood are sealed and bound by oaths so strong that even apostates will not reveal them, and to maintain which, witnesses on the witness stand unblushingly perjure themselves and on the jury violate all considerations of oath and duty. Considering all our surroundings, polygamy has never taken such a degrading and debasing form, in any nation or among any people, above the condition of barbarians, as in Utah. . . . That it should be practised in the name and under the cloak of religion, that an apostle, a polygamist, with four acknowledged wives, is permitted to sit in Congress, only adds to the enormity of the crime, and makes it more revolting to our common Christian principles.
>
> Our legislature is composed almost entirely of polygamists and members of the Mormon priesthood, and they have thrown around polygamy every possible legislative safeguard in their power, and the right of dower has been abolished to break down the distinction between the lawful wife and concubine.

Infiltration of the Mormons into neighboring territories was cited as further proof of the danger inherent in the system thus allowed to flourish unchecked:

> We call upon the Christian women of the United States to join us in urging Congress to empower its courts to arrest the further progress of this evil and to delay the admittance of Utah into Statehood until this

is accomplished. We ask you to circulate and publish our appeal in order to arouse public sentiment, which should be against an abomination that peculiarly stigmatizes woman. It it our purpose to ask names to a petition designed for Congress, and we hope, also, that every minister of the gospel will commend it to the women of his congregation and that all Christian associations will do all they can to obtain signatures.

With the cordial co-operation and concentrated action of the Christian women of the land, we may confidently hope that the great sin of polygamy will be abolished.[10]

There can be little doubt but that the society, through the years to come, was a power to reckon with, and one of the most potent forces in the crusade against polygamy.[11] Lucy Hayes was but one of countless ardent supporters of the movement, and it would be interesting to know how far her influence weighed the balance of her husband's attitude on Mormonism as displayed in his messages to Congress.[12]

With the foundation of the society, prompt re-action was registered by the Mormon women. On November 16, 1878, they united in protest, declaring that, "We, the women of the Church of Jesus Christ of Latter-day Saints have been misjudged and

---

[10] A. P. S., June 1880; Whitney, op. cit., III, 61–62.

[11] Whitney, op. cit., III, 60–61. "It was that case which brought the Anti-Polygamy Society into being, and it was that Society which gave birth to the wide-spread political and religious agitation that led to the enactment of the Edmunds law." The Springfield Republican, January 7, 1880, carried an article descriptive of the work of the Society, and indicative of the close interest with which the movement was being followed.

[12] During early September 1880, President Hayes and his lady visited Salt Lake City. The Daily Tribune, September 7, described the event: "After the banquet the party retired to attend divine service at the Methodist Church of which . . . Mrs. Hayes has been a member ever since her school days. . . . The church was filled in anticipation of their coming. . . . Dr. Fisher occupied the pulpit and preached on the text: 'Seven women shall take hold of one man saying We will eat our own bread and wear our own apparel, only let us be called by thy name to take away our reproach.' His theme was, as a matter of course, polygamy. . . ."

September 8: "While in Salt Lake, Mrs. Hayes assured the Gentile ladies that they should have her cordial cooperation in the Anti-Polygamy movement inaugurated by them."

misrepresented to the nation by those in our midst of our own
sex. . . ." They affirmed their constitutional right to worship
God according to the dictates of conscience and resolved:

> That we solemnly avow our belief in the doctrine of
> the Patriarchal Order of Marriage . . . revealed and
> practiced by God's people in past ages, and now re-
> established upon the earth . . . , a doctrine which, if
> lived up to and carried out under the direction of the
> precepts pertaining to it, and of the higher principles of
> our nature, would conduce to the long life, strength and
> glory of the people practicing it, and we therefore en-
> dorse it as one of the most important principles of our
> holy religion. . . .[13]

Truly, these Mormon women were more than disappointing;
they were patently ungrateful. It remained for the Anti-Polygamy
Society to wage open war upon their morbid illusions. But first,
it was necessary to enlist the active support of all the Gentile
women of Utah. "Why do you not join the Anti-Polygamy
Society?" queried Mrs. B. A. M. Froiseth, wielding the editorial
pen:

> Is it because you have business dealings with the Mor-
> mons? Because you think the Government should as-
> sume the responsibility? Because you regard the whole
> business of polygamy as too vile for delicate women to
> handle? We agree with you that the subject is not a
> very agreeable one to deal with . . . but what evil in
> the world is there that Christianity sets out to combat,
> to which the same analogy is not applicable?

The heroic shades of Elizabeth Fry, Helen Chalmers and Lady
Burdett Coutts were summoned to lend their inspiration to the
cause. A note was addressed to the pastors of the Christian
churches:

> If this paper should fall into the hands of any Min-
> ister of the Gospel, will he kindly give it to some ener-
> getic lady of his congregation, and ask her to get up a
> club for it. . . . Let this subject be kept in agita-
> tion. . . .[14]

---

[13] Whitney, *op. cit.*, III, 63.
[14] *A. P. S.*, May 1880.

The promised series of articles exposing the dire effects of polygamy hardly lived up to the expectations aroused. In the issue of September, 1880, appeared a gloomy story of the black-guard scion of a polygamous family, who had wound up his infamous career by being lynched. A "Church authority" came to console the afflicted mother, only to be met with bitter reproaches:

> You are responsible for the fate of my poor boy, you and the infernal doctrine of polygamy. . . . Polygamy made our home the abode of satan. For months before the birth of that boy, I felt as if I wanted to kill his father's second wife.

A note to this modern instance informed "eastern papers" that they could copy with confidence, the facts being guaranteed.

A typical meeting of the society in Independence Hall, September 12, 1880, was duly chronicled:

> Mrs. Hunt, a member of the Society, and one who has drunk the bitter cup of polygamy to the very dregs . . . drew a ghastly, but accurate picture of the foul demon that desolates happy homes; . . . the pathos and infinite sadness of Mrs. Hunt's impassioned word painting could only have emanated from the depths of a woman's heart, whose noblest instincts and most sacred feelings had been immolated upon the altar of a false God.
>
> The next speaker was Mrs. A. G. Paddock, who discoursed upon the impossibility of being neutral. . . . Witty, scornful and sarcastic by turns, Mrs. P. held the audience by an almost magnetic power. She aimed some telling shafts at those whose policy is to remain neutral. . . .[15]

Acknowledged leader of the society, Mrs. Paddock was indeed a lady of considerable versatility. Not only could she play upon the heartstrings of her companions or point the finger of well-deserved scorn at the slacker, but she was a novelist as well. *In the Toils—America's Valley of Death* (1879), was advertised as a historical tale embodying the principal facts in the history of Utah. It may seem incredible, but this screed, written in exag-

---

[15] *Ibid.*, October, 1880.

gerated vein and a masterpiece of bathos, drew from the aged Whittier words of praise:

> I had read it in the *Almanac* with deep and painful interest. It seems scarce possible that such a state of society as is there depicted so graphically and forcibly can exist in our country. Yet all history tells us that there are no limits to atrocities and cruelties which even those who are naturally good and gentle may commit under the influence of religious fanaticism.
>
> How to deal with this great evil I confess is to me a difficult problem. While it exists, I trust that Congress, however demoralized by party politics, will not admit Utah as a State into the Union.[16]

Her crowning literary achievement, however, was *The Fate of Madame La Tour, a Tale of Great Salt Lake,* published in 1881. Commendatory letters from Governor Eli H. Murray, Justice Boreman, former Secretary Black, and Mrs. S. A. Cook, president of the Anti-Polygamy Society, prefaced the volume, and the author added a foreword:

> The present tale, while following chiefly the misfortunes of a single family (the main incidents of which are only too truthfully related) traces the development of the Mormon system in these distant "valleys of the mountains". . . I do not pretend to tell the worst of the doings of the Saints, for no decent pen could describe and no decent reader peruse the shocking facts. On the other hand, I have carefully avoided all such elements as would tend to have a corrupting influence or to offend the sensitive and pure-minded.[17]

In the opinion of the admiring *Salt Lake Tribune,* the name of Mrs. Paddock deserved to be written "in shining letters." Her blows were telling, her pen "incisive as though it had diamond points."[18] The second edition of *Madame La Tour* ran to one hundred thousand copies, indicating, if not the refinement of

---

[16] This letter is found printed, without pagination, in *The Fate of Madame La Tour* (New York, 1881), and is dated "Danvers, Mass., 8 mo., 18, 1879."

[17] Mrs. A. G. Paddock, *op. cit.,* p. ix.

[18] *Daily Tribune,* March 2, 1882.

American literary taste of the period, at least the prevailing interest in Mormonism.[19]

In the following year Mrs. Ḅ. A. M. Froiseth, a companion-at-arms of Mrs. Paddock, brought out *The Women of Mormonism,* which purported to relate the "inside facts" about polygamy as they came from the mouths of its victims. Her dedication read:

> To the happy wives and mothers of America whose homes are protected from invasion by the majestic arm of the law; to those to whom the wail of their first-born is sweeter than the music of the spheres, because that babe is the pledge of the united affection of *one man and one woman,* to those whose children do not bring to them a birthright of sorrow, and whose motherhood is not a badge of shame, this book is appealingly dedicated by some of the women of Mormonism.[20]

Miss Frances Willard contributed a prefatory chapter:

> I have read its pages with thoughts too deep for tears. Some sulphur-shrouded planet may have a vocabulary fiendish enough to fitly characterize what they reveal, but mere English is only the vocabulary of a prating parrot in the presence of such pathos and such woe.
> There is something chivalric as the knights of old in the Author's defence of Mormon womanhood from the harsh criticism made by the uninformed upon their course. . . . Surely it is time that the Christian women of this nation arouse themselves to *organized action* against this sum of all curses.[21]

The *Tribune,* reviewing the book in terms of unmeasured praise, artfully suggested that "Miss Willard is by some people esteemed the most intellectual woman in America." Her preface, it informed its public,

> . . . was mantled with all the delicate taste and studied diction which invariably distinguish a pure and cultured woman's production; and yet, from the first line to the last, it is one unbroken anathema against the

---

[19] *Loc. cit.*
[20] Mrs. B. A. M. Froiseth, *The Women of Mormonism.*
[21] *A. P. S.,* April 1882.

rule which, in Utah, under the guise of religion, makes
of women slaves. . . .[22]

In the nature of things, the Gentile ladies could not devote
their time exclusively to the arena. The narrow things of home
made their demands. But even in the bosom of Gentile domesticity
the effects of polygamy were felt. The problem of the Mormon
servant-girl was prominently to the fore:

> Since the President vetoed the anti-Chinese bill, the
> people of San Francisco are talking of organizing a
> society to import girls directly from Europe to take the
> place of the Chinese who are now employed. . . . It
> would not be a bad idea for the ladies of Salt Lake to
> organize also, and bring on a carload of either white or
> colored servants to this city. . . . The Mormon leaders
> are counselling the girls not to live in Gentile families any
> longer, and in many instances they obey the counsel.
> . . . We recommend that a meeting of the ladies of
> the city be called . . . and initiatory steps be taken for
> liberating the Gentile housekeeper from the tyranny of
> the Mormon servant girls.[23]

Throughout the decade the Gentile press echoed the theme:

> The orders of the holy priesthood of the Mormon
> Church that all servant girls employed by Gentiles should
> leave their employers and go into polygamy has been
> [sic] implicitly obeyed. The polygs are now patiently
> waiting for more victims in the cargoes to arrive from
> Europe in April.[24]

Polygamy could be attacked as un-Christian and un-American
with few save the Mormons themselves to gainsay the charge.
It was more difficult for the Gentile ladies to enlist support for
their attack upon the privilege of franchise granted to the women
of Utah by the territorial legislature in 1869. It was, indeed, a
peculiar reversal of roles. The Mormon women, although it
would seem that relatively few of them availed themselves of the
ballot, could and did protest that the Gentile opposition to female

---

[22] *Daily Tribune*, March 12, 1882.
[23] *A. P. S.*, May 1882.
[24] *Daily Tribune*, February 9, 1883; May 17, 1888.

suffrage was essentially illiberal. Nor were they without unexpected allies in their defence. A number of the ardent advocates of suffrage in the East, impressed by the advantage gained for their sex in Utah Territory, were willing to ignore polygamy, or partially to condone it, while extending the right hand of fellowship to the pioneer suffragettes of Mormondom. Rumors of this new peril were investigated by the *Daily Tribune* as early as 1874:

> The suffrage ladies who so ably conduct the *Woman's Journal* are doing serious detriment to their cause by perversely sustaining the corrupt Woman Suffrage Law of Utah. They have been informed from intelligent and trustworthy sources that this law, while it ostensibly invests the women of Utah with a priceless political privilege, is really used by the designing and profligate knaves who procured its passage to hold the women of this Territory in the foul embraces of polygamy.

Let the women of Utah be made free, the editor demanded, before investing them with the franchise.[25]

Pressure politics engineered by the gentler sex found pointed illustration during the ensuing decade. Impelled by the Anti-Polygamy Society, thousands of signatures were obtained from all parts of the country to memorialize Congress to deprive the women of Utah of their voting privilege. Thus, the Woman's Home Missionary Society of the Methodist Episcopal Church, meeting in Cleveland, Ohio, October, 1884, heard a report of the committee entrusted with the work of securing such signatures. Two hundred and fifty thousand names were stated to have been forwarded to Senator George Frisbie Hoar. The temper of the meeting was further demonstrated by its reflections upon Mormon missionary enterprise:

> Think of it, O ye Christian women of the churches! From this Christian Republic to the nations of the world are sent these hordes of men and women to back what? A blasphemy of the Divine Father. . . . A heaven whose

---

[25] *Ibid.,* March 4, 1874. *Cf. The Woman's Journal* (Boston, Mass.) October 9, 1880. Lucy Stone, the editor, wrote: "It is hardly possible that so bold an attempt to disfranchise citizens who have exercized the right to vote for ten years can be accomplished. It would certainly never have been attempted if these citizens had not been Mormons. . . ."

jasper walls are reared for the defense of lust through
the long cycles of eternity. . . .[26]

These efforts were brought to fruition when, on March 15,
1887, the Edmunds-Tucker bill became a law without presidential
signature. Section 20 provided:

> That it shall not be lawful for any female to vote at
> any election hereafter held in the Territory of Utah for
> any public purpose whatever, and no such vote shall be
> received or counted or given effect in any manner what-
> ever; and any and every act of the legislative assembly
> . . . providing for or allowing the registration or voting
> by females is hereby annulled.[27]

Such drastic legislation was not received by the suffrage leaders
with unqualified approval. In the face of uneasy murmurings, both
at home and abroad, the Gentile ladies of Utah were obliged to lay
emphasis on their own spirit of self-sacrifice. They had deprived
themselves of a precious privilege—so ran their apology—in order
to cure an intolerable disorder.

> ˌ Mrs. Lily Devereux-Blake stated last evening . . .
> that the National Woman's Suffrage Association, for
> which she is the Vice-President for New York, now
> fairly understands the situation in Utah, and is reconciled
> to seeing women disfranchised here because of the anom-
> alous condition of local affairs. She was not surprised,
> now, that Gentile Utah women, who believed in woman's
> enfranchisement generally, should sacrifice adherence to
> extending that principle here in Utah, where Mormon
> rule prevailed and would be made more permanent by al-
> lowing women to vote.[28]

All suffragettes, however, were not as amenable to sweet rea-
sonableness as was Mrs. Devereux-Blake. Several, visiting Salt
Lake City, had the audacity to interview Mormon women.[29] Off

---

[26] *Ibid.*, May 16, 1885.

[27] *Public Document, No. 183,* State Department, March 15, 1887, p. 5.

[28] *Daily Tribune,* August 11, 1888.

[29] *Ibid.*, October 11, 1888: "Mrs. Colby . . . was so content with their
manners and customs that she had no desire to investigate any but the rosy
side of Mormon institutions, and rumor has it that she was, before leaving,

to Detroit hurried Mrs. Froiseth, to capture the ear of Julia Ward
Howe and the attention of the Association for the Advancement of
Woman, before the enemy should sow the field with cockle.

> Her trip was attended with such signal success that
> she has completely checkmated all that Mrs. Colby and
> Mrs. Saxon hoped to do, and has besides not only left ex-
> cellent impressions as to the fight out here, but has turned
> the faces of many worthy people this way. . . . The
> ladies of the Association recognized the importance of the
> Utah work by according Mrs. Froiseth all possible cour-
> tesies . . . and placed her with Frances Willard among
> the speakers of the first evening's session. The Gentile
> missionary was introduced by Mrs. Howe herself with
> very complimentary remarks and spoke on "Nine Reasons
> Why Utah Should Not be Admitted as a State. . . ."
> Mrs. F. could not attend the convention at Cincinnati
> of the Woman's Suffrage Association, . . . but as she
> fully posted Mrs. Howe and left abundant material with
> her, there is no doubt but that the distinguished lady will
> be able to lay Mrs. Colby out cold, and Mrs. Saxon too,
> if she shows up.[30]

Home again, Mrs. Froiseth confronted Mormon insurgency.
Two of their leading women, Mrs. Franklin Richards and Mrs.
Emmeline B. Wells, called upon her as vice-president of the
Woman's Suffrage Association for Utah to organize a branch in
the Territory.

> . . . Mrs. Froiseth replied that while she herself was
> a believer in woman suffrage, on general principles, she
> did not believe in it for Utah, because of the anomalous
> condition of affairs here, and . . . when tried before, it
> resulted so deplorably. She further informed her callers
> that another motive that influenced her was the impossi-
> bility of co-operating in any cause with women who be-
> lieved in the rightfulness and propriety of polygamy.
> Then Mrs. Richards asked if Mrs. F. had any objection

---

prevailed upon to accept a heavy retainer, in the way of merely an evidence
of the esteem of the Mormon ladies." It was fortunate for the *Tribune* that
laws against libel were hardly in force in the Territory.

[30] *Daily Tribune*, November 23, 1888. One of Mrs. Froiseth's "Nine
Reasons" was that the Mormons took little interest in the matter of sewage
disposal. The Detroit *Free Press* thought ". . . that the fair lecturer appeared masculine."

to her—Mrs. R.—as Second Vice-President, calling such a meeting. Of course she could have no objection and no power in the matter. So she expects that the call will be made and largely responded to, and she desires the Association in the East to understand why, as an officer, . . . she can take no part in establishing a branch here.[31]

Victory, thus, was fleeting. With statehood came restoration of woman suffrage, and the sceptre of leadership passed from the grasp of the Gentile ladies. Polygamy, of course, had to go, but one may ponder whether the tactics of some of these "Christian" women of Utah in hastening its departure were inspired by enlightened wisdom or by something akin to petty spite.

A forgotten lecturer of the period, Kate Field, figured persistently in the activities of the Gentile group. Shuttling back and forth between Salt Lake City and Washington, D. C., she multiplied her efforts to break the power of the Mormon hierarchy. "Polygamy, she thinks, is merely a side issue," commented the editor of the Leadville (Colorado) *Herald:*

> Her idea is that the Mormons are more bent upon having a controlling voice in politics than upon having a plurality of wives. . . . She urges the establishment of a Commission to administer the government of Utah. When she has told the nation's legislators all she wants to tell them, she will commence work on a book on Mormonism, which will be the most complete treatise on the subject that has been written so far. . . .[32]

Her lecture on "The Mormon Monster," delivered in many cities throughout the country during the closing years of the eighties, served as an obbligato to the philippics of the evangelical missionaries which were being broadcasted at the same time.[33] Her appearance before the Woman's Relief Corps of the Grand Army of the Republic, in Salt Lake City, was prefaced by the indomitable Mrs. Froiseth:

---

[31] *Ibid.,* January 11, 1889.

[32] Quoted by the Salt Lake *Tribune,* February 17, 1885.

[33] *Ibid.,* May 13, 1887. Miss Field proudly displayed the following note from Mr. P. T. Barnum (Waldemus, Bridgeport, Conn., Feb. 12, 1887): "If every voter in America could hear you talk on the enormities and treason of Mormonism, it would be justly killed in a short time."

On a previous occasion, when we opened our doors to
our friends, our esteemed comrade, Miss Monroe, said
. . . that Utah was the only place in the country where a
woman felt it a disgrace and a reproach to be a woman.
. . . It would be absurd to deny this assertion. . . .
But, mark you,—the spirit of prophecy is upon me this
afternoon—the day shall come when the shame and the
reproach shall be taken away, and it will be a glorious
thing to be a woman in Utah. And why, do you ask?
Because I believe that it will be largely through the efforts
of the women of America, spurred on and incited by the
loyal women of Utah, that the country will be forced to
deal with the Mormon monster as it deserved.
. . . The 40,000 members of the Relief Corps are
pledged never to cease their efforts until the institution is
doomed and the Cross planted over its grave.[34]

It was during the summer of 1880 that Mrs. Angie F. Newman,
of Lincoln, Nebraska, visited in Salt Lake City. This lady, filled
with enthusiasm for the advancement of Methodism and the
abolition of polygamy, conceived a project to the fulfillment of
which she bent her considerable and restless energies, as well as
her flair for political action, during the entire decade. This was
the establishment in the Territory of a house of refuge for abandoned or repentant plural wives. As the plan was first outlined,
at the Utah conference of the Methodist Church, in 1881, it was
to be a purely sectarian venture in the shape of a home to be
built near the Methodist chapel in Salt Lake City. The conference
immediately raised $660.00 to further the venture, and the
Woman's Home Missionary Society earmarked three thousand
dollars of its annual allotment for Utah for this purpose.[35] At that
point, however, Mrs. Newman was temporarily forced to suspend
her activities. The idea, nevertheless, had taken root. A Presbyterian missioner, C. M. Parks, of Logan, Utah, took it with him
to the General Assembly of his Church in 1883, and developed it
in the pulpits offered to him during his sojourn in the East.[36]
In November, 1883, Mrs. Newman resumed the gage of battle.

[34] *Ibid.*, April 30, 1887.
[35] *Ibid.*, March 16, 1886.
[36] Jeanette H. Ferry, *Industrial Christian Home of Utah* (Salt Lake City,
1893), p. 3.

At the Cincinnati meeting of the Woman's Home Missionary Society, she led a vigorous denunciation of federal laxity in regard to Utah.

> Mrs. Newman then offered a resolution in favor of building in Utah an "industrial home" for women and an "asylum for orphans," and read letters from Governor Thomas of Utah and Rev. Mr. Iliff, resident missionary, indorsing the project.
>
> The resolution and letters acted like a new inspiration upon the company, and many contributions began to flow into the treasury forthwith, and life memberships were taken in rapid succession, the sum involved in each case being $20. The whole amount thus secured in less than an hour . . . was $6,500. Great joy was manifested. Mrs. Newman exclaimed, "Surely the Lord has honored our venture." [37]

Mrs. Rutherford B. Hayes beamed approval, as did Mrs. Joseph B. Foraker of Ohio and a long list of the wives of Methodist bishops. An inter-denominational committee was formed to confer with Mrs. Newman and the evangelical leaders of Utah.[38] It developed, however, that the financial assistance of the mission societies could not be reckoned on in sufficient amounts. Federal aid was recognized as the ultimate answer. With this in mind, Mrs. Newman inspired the formation of "The Industrial Home Association of Utah," on "a Christian but undenominational basis," the incorporators being a group of the Gentile civic and religious leaders of Salt Lake City. The incorporation was effected March 15, 1886, under the laws of Utah, Article VI declaring:

> The objects, pursuits and business of this corporation, as near as may be stated generally, are as follows: to found, build, equip, provide for, maintain and regulate . . . industrial homes, boarding houses, schools, hospitals and places for instruction, aid, betterment, and general benevolent and charitable purposes at Salt Lake City and other places in Utah Territory, and elsewhere, and in which to promote and accomplish the fitting of persons for industrial and all other pursuits.[39]

---

[37] *Daily Tribune,* December 2, 1883.

[38] Ferry, *op. cit.,* p. 3.

[39] *Ibid.,* p. 4. The incorporators were George A. Lowe, Henry W.

This was non-committal enough, but the actual purpose was hidden from none, least of all the Mormons themselves, who vociferously expressed their resentment of the implied reflection upon the practical workings of patriarchal marriage.[40]

It was shortly before this, on March 6, that a mass meeting of the Mormon women had been called at the Salt Lake Theatre to protest to Congress against what they considered the harshness and partisan bias of the federal courts in their attempts to enforce the Edmunds law:

> We learn that measures are in contemplation before your honorable bodies to still further harass and distress us. . . .
> We ask for justice. We appeal to you not to tighten the bonds which are now so tense that we can scarcely endure them. We ask that the laws may be fairly and impartially executed. We see good and noble men dragged to jail to linger among felons, while debauched and polluted men, some of them Federal officers who have been detected in the vilest kinds of depravity, protected by the same court and officers that turn all their energies and engines of power towards the ruin of our homes and the destruction of our dearest associations. We see pure women forced to disclose their conjugal relations or go to prison, while the wretched creatures who pander to men's basest passions are left free to ply their horrible trade. . . . And now we are threatened with entire deprivation of every right and privilege of citizenship, to gratify a prejudice that is fed on ignorance and vitalized by bigotry.[41]

Lawrence, Margaret D. Zane, Fanny Stenhouse, Eli H. Murray, Edward P. Ferry, Melvin B. Sowles, Mrs. W. S. McCornick, and Mrs. Jacob S. Boreman.

[40] *Deseret News,* June 11, 1886. "Here is a proposition before Congress to give a little knot of schemers in Utah $100,000 to establish a home for 'escaped' polygamous wives. It will not be surprising if it is given to the plotters to spend as they please. . . . The committee, of which Senator Blair is the chairman . . . were led away by the fantastic stories told by an experienced religious subscription circulator. Her name is Angie F. Newman. Her home is in Nebraska; she is an adept in gathering in dollars and dimes for sectarian purposes, and she claims to speak on this subject as a resident of Utah."

[41] Quoted by Whitney, *op. cit.,* III, 495.

In the audience, though presumably not by special invitation, was Mrs. Newman. Bristling with indignation she hurried home to pen the following diatribe:

> Am I in America?
> I have travelled all over this fair land . . . and I have today heard for the first time treasonable utterances from the lips of my own sex; for the first time a defiance of the laws which shelter womanhood. . . . Any woman in the States who should so insult the representatives of this great republic would invite a fate more speedy and none the less terrible than that of J. Wilkes Booth.
>
> As a Christian wife and mother, I, on behalf of the Christian homes of this republic, repudiate the oft-repeated charge of the speakers in the theatre, that the lasciviousness of the age is due to monogamous or Christian marriage. . . .
>
> And let it be known to the women of the Territory that nowhere in the States did woman ever sink to such depths of dishonor as to stand before a public audience and vindicate their illicit alliances, much less declare they were entered into and perpetuated by direct command of God. . . . It may yet appear that the women of this Territory are "building the gallows to hang themselves. . . ." [42]

All the more determined was Mrs. Newman that something must be done. With the cordial approbation of Governor Murray and other territorial officers, the movement gained headway.[43] To W. S. Holman, chairman of the Appropriations Committee of the House of Representatives, the Utah Commissioners wrote, March 12, 1886:

> An organization under the general incorporation laws of this Territory, has been perfected by Christian women of Utah for the establishment of an industrial home for the helpless and dependent of their own sex and their children at or near the city of Salt Lake.
>
> The Trustees of the Association are prominent business men of known ability, integrity and good financial standing. . . . The Executive officers are representative Christian women. . . .

[42] Ferry, *op. cit.,* p. 12, and *Daily Tribune,* March 10, 1886.
[43] *Ibid.,* p. 6.

It is proposed to establish an institution upon a basis broad enough to meet the exigencies that may arise from the exceptional conditions of this Territory.

We believe that such a beneficence, supplemental to the enforcement of the laws for the suppression of polygamy in Utah, will effectively aid in accomplishing the result sought through congressional legislation. It may be reasonably hoped that this provision for the maintenance and industrial education of polygamous wives and children will induce the withdrawal of many who are now held through fear of the distress and suffering that would inevitably result to them from such a separation.[44]

In the wake of the letter, Mrs. Newman betook herself to Washington, carrying with her a memorial endorsed by the Woman's Christian Temperance Union, the Woman's Home Missionary Society, and the Presbyterian Missionary Society, alleged to represent a total membership of three hundred thousand. Stressing "the anomalous social condition of Utah Territory under the Mormon regime," the document declared "it is hopeless to expect a Mormon legislature to appropriate funds to meet a condition of things which the Mormon leaders declare does not exist." The proposed industrial home, it suggested, would temper the law with mercy. And with means for rehabilitation offered, "it is a well-known fact that there are many who would voluntarily abandon polygamic relations. . . . Pupils from the domestic department will find immediate employment in the Gentile homes of Utah." [45]

The Senate Committee of Education and Labor, headed by Henry W. Blair, of Missouri, heard Mrs. Newman's presentation of her case, "an argument remarkable for its eloquence and power," on May 7, 1886. Impressed, the committee recommended that an amendment be made to the Sundry Civil bill, providing an appropriation of $40,000 for the purpose.[46] By August 4 of that year the bill was law:

---

[44] *Ibid.*, p. 7.

[45] *Ibid.*, pp. 9–10. The memorial was presented by Senator Blair, April 30, 1886.

[46] *Report of the Education and Labor Committee on an Amendment intended to be proposed to the Sundry Civil Bill providing for an appropriation to aid in the establishment of a School in Utah . . . with a view to the suppression of polygamy therein.* U. S. 49th Congress, 1st Session, Senate Report 1279. A group of Mormon women appeared before the committee,

To aid in the establishment of an industrial home in the Territory of Utah, to provide employment and means of self-support for the dependent women who renounce polygamy, and the children of such women of tender age . . . said sum to be expended upon requisition of and under the management of a board of control to consist of the Governor and Justices of the Supreme Court, and the District Attorney of said Territory. . . .[47]

Tirelessly had Mrs. Newman pursued her career as a lobbyist. On her return to Salt Lake City, October 13, 1886, she was accorded a triumphal reception by her admirers, headed by the obliging Governor Caleb West, who had succeeded Eli H. Murray in office.[48]   Soon a temporary building was rented and a matron installed.   Confident that the popular response would effectually silence Mormon criticism, she prepared a circular:

---

protesting the measure.   "As we are the representatives of the Mormon women, we do, in their name, most emphatically protest against any such pretext being used for obtaining a share of the public funds.   No Mormon woman, old or young, is compelled to marry at all; still less to enter into polygamy. . . .   Mormon girls have homes as happy, as pure and as desirable as any of their Eastern sisters, and far more independent.

"Mrs. Newman has no right to insult the noble band of Mormon matrons and maidens by asking public alms for their benefit, while she is industriously circulating the malignant falsehoods by which bitter prejudice has already been created against them and their religion.

"We most positively assert that there is not a Mormon wife, whether plural or otherwise, who would accept charity at the hands of those who have procured . . . laws whose enforcement has brought sorrow and desolation into their once happy homes."

[47] *Ibid.*, p. 12.

[48] The Reverend S. J. Carroll, pastor of the Methodist Church, gave the principal address: "Our sister has enshrined herself by her faith, courage and genius, and has inaugurated a grand philanthropic movement for the disenthrallment of the women of Utah.   From these vales, so beautiful, so fruitful and so magnificent, there has for thirty years been a great cry going up to the throne of God and to humanity for help. . . .   She stood alone, in the midst of men whose brains were filled with great thoughts of business . . . but with unflinching faith she has overcome the obstacles that were presented." *Tribune,* Oct. 14, 1886.   Later, Governor West proved less obliging, insisting, as presiding officer of the association, on a strict interpretation of the act, and even going so far as to authorize a former Mormon lady to discover if there were actually any women who would apply to the Home.   This called forth a protest from Mrs. Newman to President Cleveland. (Department of the Interior, Utah File, November 13, 1886.)

A permanently established Industrial Home is now prepared to receive such occupants as conform to the provisions of the act, and who may have been left destitute by abandonment or by neglect or by the results of the enforcement of the United States Law against criminal practices peculiar to this Territory.

It is the sceptre of justice in one hand and the olive branch of mercy in the other, extended in sympathy and tenderness to the suffering, to the erring and to the repentant.

The prayers and supplications of forsaken women for themselves and their children are now abundantly answered. . . .

Encouragement, hope, sympathy, instruction and love extend their arms to welcome you and provide for you. . . .[49]

In spite of these honeyed words, few Mormon women sought release from the "chains of polygamy" within the sheltering walls of the Industrial Home. The official report, written by Mrs. Jeanette H. Ferry in 1893, states that by September, 1887, there were thirty-three inmates—eleven women and twenty-two children.[50] It is not altogether clear, however, whether all of these were actually victims of the operations of the anti-polygamy legislation, according to the sense of the law. On the other hand, the claim frequently asserted by Mormon apologists that the home never received any former polygamous wives, does not seem to have real basis.

Initial lack of success, however, merely spurred on the zeal of Mrs. Newman. In order to secure a freer hand in the administration of the funds, she prevailed upon Senator Edmunds to sponsor a bill to transfer the actual management of the home to the original association, with the members of the Utah Commission acting in the capacity of a board of control.[51] A site for the building was purchased on Fifth East Street in Salt Lake City, and construction was begun on a relatively elaborate scale, which speedily exhausted the available funds. Through the good services of Senator Eugene Hale, of Maine, and of Representative Isaac S. Struble, of

---

[49] Ferry, *op. cit.*, p. 17.

[50] *Ibid.*, p. 17.

[51] *Ibid.*, p. 18.

Iowa, a further appropriation was made by Congress, October 19, 1888, to complete and furnish the structure.[52]   Seemingly, the anticipation was that the federal government would continue to set aside annual sums sufficient for the maintenance of the home.

By 1889 the Industrial Home was in full operation, save for the dearth of inmates.   Rather than an increase, the records disclosed a sharp decline.[53]   Wrote Mrs. Ferry as president of the association:

> The acceptance or rejection of this beneficence by the few or the many, is merely an incident in its history, revealing its environment.   Opposition has been systematic and relentless; when objections were met, and answered in the permanent building, enlarged scope of the law, and opportunities for industrial pursuits opened, then the animus of the "church" was apparent, not only in forbidding women to apply, but repeatedly, after they have made application and have been accepted, they were influenced not to enter.[54]

The *Tribune,* surveying the situation from a staunchly Republican viewpoint, found a partial answer in political chicanery, naturally of Democratic origin:

> The Democrats in Congress oppose the Industrial Home in Utah.   This is due no doubt to Mr. Caine's efforts and his assurances that no such home is desirable.   But it adds a straw to the cumulative evidence that there is a good deal going on, of which Statehood would be the final outcome.
> As to the Industrial Home, could the idea on which it was originated be carried out, it would from the first week overflow with inmates.   There are thousands of first wives and destitute polygamous children who would

---

[52] *Ibid.,* p. 18.   "When the building shall have been completed and furnished, it shall be placed in the custody of the Industrial Christian Home Association of Utah Territory, to be used and occupied by it for the purpose of aiding in the suppression of polygamy."   The Utah commissioners were instructed to return an annual report to Congress.

[53] *Annual Reports of the President of the Industrial Christian Home* (printed in Ferry, *op. cit.,* pp. 64–73).   September, 1887—33 inmates, 11 women, 22 children; October, 1888—19 inmates, 5 women, 12 children; August, 1889—9 inmates, 6 females, 3 males.

[54] Ferry, *op. cit.,* p. 27.

gratefully accept a retreat of that kind. . . . Why Democrats should oppose a measure of mercy like the one proposed is incomprehensible except on the theory that an alliance offensive and defensive has been formed.[55]

But not even Republicanism, triumphant in the person of President Harrison, could bolster up the moribund institution. The Utah Commissioners, reporting to Congress in regard to its management, December 19, 1889, tacitly admitted that the project was a failure:

> These ladies and gentlemen (of the Association) are courageously working to break down the prejudices of the Mormon Church against the institution, and . . . to win the confidence of those for whom this shelter is erected. They are working to accomplish a great reform among a people who cling . . . to this relic of Asiatic barbarism.
> As to the ultimate success of the Home, the Commission express no opinion. It is an experiment which only time can solve. Whether the deluded women of polygamous marriages will, after a while, as the coils of the law slowly circle them about, avail themselves of the munificence which the Government offers them . . . remains to be seen. As yet, but few have done so, and . . . the number seems to be lessening.
> The occupants at this time are three women and six children. . . .[56]

With the publication of the Woodruff Manifesto, September 24, 1890, announcing the abrogation of the doctrine of plurality of wives, national interest in the Industrial Home rapidly waned. Senator Edmunds reserved a spark of his old fire:

> No, don't close it up, but keep its doors open, and thus show to the people of Utah and the rest of the world that the General Government has provided the means for caring for this portion of the unfortunate subjects of polygamy, and if it fails of success, let the blame be on others and not on the General Government.[57]

---

[55] *Tribune,* October 4, 1888.

[56] *Report of the Utah Commission as to the Management of the Industrial Christian Home* (Washington, G. P. O., 1890), p. 1.

[57] Quoted in Ferry, *op. cit.,* p. 62.

Fighting to the bitter end, Mrs. Newman haunted the lobbies of Washington, seeking to insure the annual appropriation.[58]   By 1893, however, in spite of all her efforts, none was forthcoming, and the association was constrained to notify the Utah Commission that the home would close its doors on June 15 of that year.[59]   Ingloriously, the building was transformed into headquarters for the Commission during the few remaining years of that body's existence.[60]

That there was Mormon pressure brought to bear against the home goes without saying.   Whether the pride of the Mormon women would have rendered its services nugatory in any case may well be suspected.   The Industrial Home of Utah takes its inconspicuous—though certainly unusual—place in history principally as the expression of the determination of a group of the Gentile ladies to leave no stone unturned in their campaign to destroy what they considered the paramount evil of their day.

---

[58] *Tribune,* March 2, 1890: "The affairs of the Industrial Home, it seems to us, should be readjusted. The debt should be paid Mrs. Newman. It is a shame for an association to keep a lady in Washington and not pay her current expenses."

[59] *Report of the Utah Commission* (Washington, G. P. O., 1893), p. 4.   As her final effort, Mrs. Ferry suggested turning over the remaining occupants, along with the building.   This met with a decided refusal from A .B. Williams, chairman of the commission.

[60] *Ibid.,* p. 5.

CHAPTER VIII

THE GENTILE VICTORY

ON MARCH 22, 1882, President Arthur appended his signature to the Edmunds act. Phrased impersonally to amend Section 5352 of the Revised Statutes of the United States, the new law attempted a more exact definition of polygamy:

> Every person who has a husband or wife living who, in a Territory or other place over which the United States have exclusive jurisdiction, hereafter marries another whether married or single, and any man who hereafter simultaneously, or on the same day, marries more than one woman, in a Territory or other place . . . , is guilty of polygamy, and shall be punished by a fine of not more than five hundred dollars and by imprisonment for a term of not more than five years. . . .

Enoch Arden marriages and contracts entered into by those legally divorced were excluded from the provisions of the law. The second section safeguarded the prosecution of offenses arising out of the original Act of 1862. The third defined cohabitation with more than one woman as a misdemeanor to be punished by a maximum fine of three hundred dollars or six months imprisonment, or both, and the fourth added that actions against polygamy and cohabitation might be joined in the same indictment.

More specifically germane to the intention of the law was the fifth section, providing for the challenge as jurors in trials rising under the act not only of those guilty of polygamy or cohabitation, but also of those who believed in the lawfulness of such action. Those testifying to such belief or practice were protected from suit based on self-incrimination, but their rejection as incompetent for jury service was fixed. The courts were empowered to question jurors under oath. Presidential amnesty for those who had contracted polygamous unions before the passage of the act, when its conditions should have been fulfilled, was approved in the sixth section; the seventh legitimatized the issue of polygamous unions "known as Mormon marriages," born in the territories before January 1, 1883.

The eight section touched the main point. Practicing polygamists of both sexes were disfranchised and declared ineligible for public office. It was for the enforcement of this provision that the ninth section declared vacant all election and registration offices in the Territory of Utah, and established an appointive board to supervise the elections until such time as the legislative assembly, properly elected, should make due provision for the filling of the vacated offices. For the direction of the commissioners it was specified that individual opinion as to the legality of polygamy could not be made a test for the exercise of franchise or for the right to hold office.[1]

The Utah Gentiles received the Edmunds act with mingled feelings of exultation and disappointment. The ladies of the First Methodist Church of Ogden set to work on "a beautiful silk quilt . . . with the name and full official title of Senator Edmunds embroidered in the center," designed as their gift to the wife of the champion of Christian morality,[2] but the judgment of the Liberal party leaders was less enthusiastic. The editor of the *Park Mining Record* penned the sentiment of the radicals when he wrote, "When the Edmund's bill was passed into a law, there was an outside pressure . . . but the law is a farce; it is a homeopathic dose weakened to the one-hundredth attenuation of nothing. . . ."[3] The Mormons were sternly warned that the passage of the act meant no cessation in the fight against "Church slavery."

The selection of the commissioners was eagerly awaited:

> It has been proposed in some quarters to treat the Mormons in this matter as Indians are treated on their reservations; to give the handling of them to the different religious denominations of the country and make up the Commission of the ministers . . . sending here men of such distinguished character that no slanders on their work would be believed.[4]

[1] *U. S. Statutes at Large,* XXII, 30–32 (47th Congress, 1st Session, Chapter 47).

[2] *Daily Tribune,* March 16, 1882.

[3] *Park Mining Record,* November 24, 1883.

[4] *Daily Tribune,* April 2, 1882.

The dawning of the realization that the board would include no local anti-Mormons called forth disgusted protest:

> If there is any one thing which the soul of the average Western man recoils against, it is the condescending air of familiarity which very wise men of the East often adopt. . . . If these Eastern Commissioners make the mistake to think that inasmuch as they are going among semi-civilized tribes they must adopt an unnatural style either to win or bully them, it will be just like the Utah Gentiles to drop them like hot potatoes, and let them work out their own salvation.[5]

On June 17 came the news that the Utah commission had been named with ex-Senator Alexander Ramsey of Minnesota as chairman, George L. Godfrey of Iowa, Algernon S. Paddock of Nebraska, Ambrose B. Carlton of Indiana and James R. Pettigrew of Arkansas as members.[6] The *Tribune's* conviction that the nomination was a "slight and a reproach to Utah" was strengthened by a Washington dispatch indicating that Pettigrew, a Democrat, had been indiscreet enough to interview ex-Delegate Cannon, who reportedly told him that "all the people wanted out there was that we should carry out the letter of the law."[7]

Local elections for all offices save that of the congressional delegate were scheduled for early August. It was realized that the commissioners would not reach Salt Lake City in time to make proper provision for the balloting. It was in view of this contingency that Senator George F. Hoar of Massachusetts, on August 2, moved to introduce an amendment to the civil appropriations bill empowering the governor of Utah Territory to fill vacancies arising as a result of the suspension of the regular elections. Stressing the necessity of such action in view of the fact that many of the incumbents were polygamists, Hoar carried his motion, and on August 5 the House gave its sanction.[8] Governor Murray

---

[5] *Ibid.,* April 15, 1882.

[6] Paddock was a cousin of Mrs. A. G. Paddock, Salt Lake City's literary lady.

[7] *Daily Tribune,* July 7, 1882.

[8] *Congressional Record,* August 2, 1882, p. 6778; August 5, 1882, pp. 6979, 6982, 6987.

hastened to exercise this power by providing a number of Gentiles with temporary offices. The Gentile press felt partially mollified:

> A great many Mormons will be displaced, but . . . we do not believe the Governor is so bitterly opposed to the Mormons as to put in office incompetent Gentiles. . . . If polygamists are removed from office, whose term has expired, he does nothing more than any loyal officer would do who has any regard for the obligation he assumes when he enters upon the duties of his office. . . . Governor Murray has no prejudices against the Mormons as a religious sect any more than he has against any other denomination. Polygamy irritates him, and he feels it his duty to suppress it. . . . Our National lawmakers say that polygamy must be crushed out, and Governor Murray is sent here by the Government to see that the laws are obeyed.[9]

Acting as attorney for the interests of the Mormon Church, Jeremiah S. Black wrote to Secretary of the Interior, Henry H. Teller, of Colorado, that the surrender of such extensive powers to so unprincipled a man as he considered Murray to be was inviting chaos in Utah:

> I am instructed by my clients there that the Governor within a few days past has by proclamation made one hundred and four appointments to various offices which the present incumbents chosen by the people will not yield up without a contest. I presume he intends to carry his point by force unless you forbid him. If he succeeds, he and the small anti-popular faction that backs him will possess themselves of unlimited authority which they will use for the foulest purposes. They will seize all offices as their lawful prey, put the people under their feet and trample the life out of society. Owning every assessor and collector of taxes, every custodian of public money, and being at the same time masters of the whole police— the County Magistrates, Sheriffs and Constables—they will revel in plunder. It will not cost their ingenuity an effort, nor their conscience a pang, to burden the Territory with debt, sell the bonds, put the proceeds in their own pockets, and tax labor to death for their payment. . . . Peculiar circumstances not found in any other territory may be, and are already, set up as excuses for

---

[9] *Park Mining Record*, August 12, 1882.

robbing the churches. To justify these acts of oppression the privacy of families, in their most sacred relations, their kitchens and their bed-chambers, will be exposed and mis-represented by eavesdroppers and lying delators.[10]

Black's perturbation, simulated or real, was unnecessary. There seems to have been little if any local complaint as to abuse of office on the part of the Gentile appointees. Indeed, litigation over the post of territorial treasurer resulted in a technical decision adverse to a Gentile claimant.[11]

The commissioners arrived in Salt Lake City on August 18, 1882, and made it their first object to study the situation. The problem which immediately arose was that of the pending election of a congressional delegate. Here, apparently, they met with strong opposition on the part of the Liberal leaders, who took the position that since it would be impossible to elect one of their own choice to that office, it would be just as well to leave it vacant.[12] However, the decision to proceed with the election as scheduled thwarted Liberal anticipations in this respect, and the commissioners, after due consultation with "leading citizens here," appointed the registration officers for the several counties. They informed Secretary Teller that they were in no way apprehensive of trouble at the polls:

From present indications it appears that that class of persons who are deprived of the right of suffrage by the act of Congress, will not attempt to register or to vote. These will number, male and female, probably 10,000

---

[10] Black to Secretary of the Interior (n. d., but from internal evidence c. October 15, 1882, N. A., Department of the Interior Files, Utah). The rather wild statements made by the distinguished Pennsylvania lawyer may be in part ascribed to his advanced age. He died during the following summer (August 19, 1883).

[11] For a detailed treatment, see Whitney, op cit., III, 213–220. In a decision rendered January 6, 1890, the United States Supreme Court upheld the power of the territorial governor to fill non-elective posts by appointment. (U. S. Reports, X, 190–194.)

[12] Report of the Utah Commission, August 31, 1882 (Salt Lake City, 1883), pp. 6–7. (Copy in the archives of the Utah State Historical Society.) "A strong disposition with some of the non-Mormon citizens against preparing for the election of a Delegate in Congress manifested itself before the work of preparation therefor was commenced."

voters. Many of the non-Mormons have hitherto refrained from voting, but it is believed that at the November election they will cast a much larger vote than at any
time heretofore. . . .

A later embarrassment came in the form of a demand
on the part of certain non-Mormon citizens of high
character that the Commission should assume jurisdiction
and decide the local statute authorizing women to vote
to be illegal and void. We concluded that it was not
competent for the Commission to repeal or modify that
statute in the manner suggested.[13]

Commissioner Carlton communicated his impressions of Utah
to his Indiana friends. Mormons, he reported "are not all fools
or knaves"; rather, "Many of them are intelligent and well-edu-
cated men and women." He solved the puzzle with the pronouncement that: "The common herd among them are honest and stupid
fanatics. It is evident that many of the Saints especially those
who come from the States, are cranks." [14]

Nevertheless, the commission, in general, tried to work out an
honest policy. With John T. Caine triumphantly elected to Congress by the People's party, a second report was sent to Secretary
Teller, outlining the more mature impressions of the members.
From the returns of the registrars, they judged that "above twelve
thousand" had been disbarred by reason of polygamy. In the absence of an exact commentary on the Edmunds act, they concluded
"that it was the intention of Congress to leave it largely to the
discretion of the commission to determine the means of discriminat-
ing between the legal and illegal voters." This brought up the
question of the form of oath to be taken by the voters, a matter
which was to be the subject of considerable discussion between the
Department of Justice and interested parties. The commissioners
recommended a rigid law governing the celebration and registration of marriages, with the contracting parties forced to sign af-
fidavits disavowing polygamy. The woman suffrage act they
thought should be annulled.

We have been engaged in the discharge of our trust
only a few months, not long enough to fully test the opera-

---

[13] *Ibid.*, pp. 7–8.
[14] *Daily Tribune,* October 7, 1882, quoting *Terre Haute Gazette.*

tion of the law as to its ultimate results. But, so far, it has been a decided success in excluding polygamists from the exercise of suffrage; and we are of the opinion that the steady and continued enforcement of the law will place polygamy in a condition of gradual extinction and that the domination that is complained of by non-Mormons in Utah . . . will be much ameliorated.

   . . . It is an encouraging sign that many of the "Liberal" meetings have been largely attended by Mormons, and in many instances they have composed the chief part of the audiences. It is proper to add that so far as we have learned, these meetings have been characterized by exceptional good order, good humor and decorum. . . .

The population is about 150,000, about 40,000 being non-Mormon, many of whom are so-called apostates from the Mormon Church.[15]

The oath administered by the election registrars, drawn up by the commissioners, contained the following significant passage:

   . . . And I do further solemnly swear (or affirm) that I am not a bigamist nor a polygamist; that I am not a violator of the laws of the United States prohibiting bigamy or polygamy; that I do not live or cohabit with more than one woman in the marriage relation. . . .[16]

In the opinion of United States Attorney Van Zile this was hardly inclusive enough. To Attorney General Benjamin H. Brewster he wrote suggesting a revision: "That I am not a member of, nor do I believe in the doctrines, or covenants, or revelations of the Church of Jesus Christ of Latter Day Saints. . . ."[17] Brewster replied that the proposed clause was patently unconstitutional: "I can see no end to be gained by inserting such a clause; in fact, it might incite hostile criticism . . . even by those who are most hostile to the Mormon Church and most Catholic and orthodox in their convictions."[18] Ultimately, the decision of the United States Supreme Court which upheld the constitutionality of the

---

[15] *Report of the Utah Commission, November 17, 1882* (Salt Lake City, 1883), pp. 11–12.

[16] Copy of the oath in full in N. A., D. J. File, Utah; Whitney, *op. cit.,* III, 228.

[17] Van Zile to Brewster, December 19, 1882 (N. A., D. J. MSS, Utah).

[18] Brewster to Van Zile, June 29, 1883 (N. A., D. J. Instruction Book N).

Edmunds act, March 3, 1885, pronounced it beyond the competence of the Utah commission to formulate the oath.[19]

If the commissioners were sanguine of the good results of their work in Utah, their sentiment was hardly shared by the Gentile press. Godfrey, one of the group, was severely criticized for his abounding optimism:

> He seems still determined to advertise his determination not to learn anything about the way or spirit of the Mormons. He asserts that there are . . . not to exceed 15,000 polygs. Of course, that leaves the impression that less than one-ninth of the population are polygamous. In point of fact nearly or quite one-third of the people of marriageable age . . . are in polygamy. That is not all. Those in polygamy are the ones that control the whole system, and that means the temporal as well as spiritual affairs of this Kingdom.
>
> Mr. Godfrey believes the Gentiles will pour in here and speedily outnumber the Mormons, and wrest the offices from them. Will he explain what these Gentiles are going to do when they pour in here? The agricultural land is already in the hands of Mormons. How are these thousands of Gentiles . . . going to sustain themselves from one election day to another?

The *Tribune* editor was willing to agree that polygamy was falling into disrepute among "the more refined classes," but he reminded his readers that the process would be painfully slow.[20]

The *Reports of the Utah Commission* (1882–1895), contain a vast amount of pertinent material bearing on the vexed relations between Mormons and Gentiles during this period when Mormonism was on trial, so to speak, before the nation on the score of polygamy. As late as 1884, these reports insisted that the Edmunds law would prove effectual. If the "elderly men who already have a plurality of wives and several families of children" could not be persuaded to amend their ways, it was felt that "the

---

[19] *Murphy, et al. v. Ramsey.* 114 U. S., 15.

[20] *Daily Tribune,* July 11, 1883. Commissioner Paddock was considered "safe" by the radicals. He apparently took credit for inspiring President Arthur's pronouncement in his annual message, December 7, 1883, that the Utah problem could be solved only by the exercise of absolute federal force in Utah (*Tribune,* December 11, 1883).

young men of the Territory, many of whom are ambitious and aspiring . . . would not like voluntarily to embrace political ostracism." The Church must learn its lesson:

> The leading Mormons, who are generally in polygamy, evidently perceive this tendency; and therefore, ever since the passage of this act, they have assiduously taught their people that this measure is transient, and that it will soon be set aside by the Federal courts or by the action or non-action of Congress. . . .
>
> That a doctrine and practice so odious throughout Christendom should have been upheld so many years against the laws of Congress and the sentiments of the civilized world, is one of the marvels of the nineteenth century, and can scarcely be appreciated even by those who are familiar with the world's history in relation to the difficulties of governmental control . . . of religious fanaticism.[21]

But in November, 1884, following another contest for the congressional seat in which the Liberal candidate, Ransford Smith, trailed John T. Caine by 19,915 votes, the commission admitted that its hopes had proved delusive. The Mormon Church, though its leaders were in hiding, continued to preach the doctrine and practice of patriarchal marriage. Indeed, "during the present year there appears to have been a polygamic revival." Baffled, the members recommended an increase in the number of territorial offices to be filled by presidential appointment, the empaneling of all juries by open venire when cases involved federal laws, and the enactment of a specific provision excluding polygamous trials from the benefit of the statute of limitations.[22] Unwilling to go the full length of the way with the Utah Liberals, they refrained from recommending a legislative commission, the favorite panacea, as an immediate necessity. Rather, they drew the attention of the secretary to what they professed to recognize as the first signs of revolt on the part of the younger Mormon element:

> Every step forward by the Government will give more strength and courage to the man whose desire is to respect

---

[21] *Report of the Utah Commission, 1883* (Washington, D. C., 1884), pp. 113–114.

[22] *Report, 1884* (Washington, D. C., 1885), pp. 5–6.

and obey the law. A single step backward in legislation or the administration of the present law, if nothing more shall be given in the way of legislation, will help the church to crush out this growing spirit of opposition and perhaps lose to the movement against polygamy all that has been gained by the passage of the Edmunds act.[23]

Cleveland's election held the threat that a slackening in the anti-polygamy drive might follow. Closeted with the new executive, shortly after his inauguration, the commissioners were agreeably relieved to discover that he was thoroughly conversant with their work and heartily in sympathy therewith.[24] Unofficially, as the decade advanced the group appears to have come to regard itself as a bureau of information relative to conditions in Utah. Its point of view more and more closely harmonized with the prevailing Liberal opinion as to the proper measures demanded for the suppression of the "twin relic" and as to the necessity of the postponement of statehood until the Mormon Church had definitively repudiated the practice. While acknowledging that the Mormons as a class were "kindly and hospitable," possessing traits of character and qualities of religious devotion which "under wise leadership would make them a useful and prosperous people," the commissioners insisted that, "there has always been something in their methods which have [sic] excited the opposition and mistrust of every people among whom they have lived."[25]

On the other hand, "The non-Mormon element has brought to Utah enterprise and capital, the school-book and the Bible." The majority of the Gentiles were described as "enterprising and public-spirited citizens, who are warmly attached to their country and its laws." Yet, in Utah, they were regarded as "intruders" and "outsiders." *The Report of 1887* recalled the Mormon feeling against the Gentiles by quoting an alleged Tabernacle address: "We ought never to have let them secure a foothold here." It was against the Gentiles rather than against the nation as a whole, the commissioners wrote, that Mormon resentment was kindled at the passage

---

[23] *Report, 1885* (Washington, 1885), pp. 4–5, 8.

[24] *Daily Tribune,* April 14, 1885, enlarging on an interview with A. B. Carlton.

[25] *Report, 1887* (Washington, D. C., 1887), p. 8.

of the laws which weighed so heavily upon them.[26]   As for statehood, the same *Report* cited with evident approval the reaction of
the Gentiles to the call for a constitutional convention issued June
30, 1887:

> The non-Mormons were distrustful of the move, and
> unitedly declined to join the convention or to recognize
> it. They gave as reasons for declining that in view of the
> past history of Utah it was a proper case for Congress,
> in accordance with the general rule, to say when the time
> for such a move had arrived, and by an enabling act give
> it authority when, how, and by whom the convention
> should be called . . . ; they did not understand this
> sudden, and to them, unannounced call ; that the entire pro-
> ceeding was carried out by the dominant party, and dele-
> gates chosen without regard to forms of election or dis-
> qualification of voters ; and above all they did not think
> the attitude of the great majority of the people of Utah
> towards the laws and authority of the General Government
> had been such as to invite the full confidence of Congress
> in their fidelity to the laws . . . and to justify that body
> in granting sovereign statehood.[27]

On March 3, 1887, in default of Cleveland's signature, the
Edmunds-Tucker bill became law by the ten-day rule.[28]   Basically,
this measure was an attempt to implement the Act of 1882, and as
such had long been agitated both in the House and in the Senate.
Several of its provisions are of interest.   For polygamous trials,
the testimony of the lawful wife or husband, given with the consent of the other party, was to be admitted.   A writ of attachment
might substitute for the regular subpoena, whenever, in such trials,
it was reasonably believed that the witness would seek to escape.
Commissioners of the territorial supreme and district courts were
given concurrent powers with the justices of the peace and the
commissioners of the circuit courts of the United States.   Il-

---

[26] *Ibid.*, p. 117.

[27] *Ibid.*, pp. 19–20.

[28] *Cf. Daily Tribune*, March 5, 1887: "The failure of the President to
sign the Edmunds-Tucker bill was a grievous disappointment to those of the
loyal men of Utah who are of his political faith. . . .   It revealed an apparent dissimulation on the part of the President that had been supposed altogether foreign to his character."

legitimate children born later than one year after the passage of the act were to derive no benefit from inheritance laws, and territorial statutes to the contrary were annulled. The provision of the Law of 1862 which prohibited religious corporations in the territories from holding properties in excess of a valuation of fifty thousand dollars, was to be enforced, and property, escheated under the law, other than churches, parsonages and cemeteries, was to be disposed of by the Secretary of the Interior for the benefit of the common schools. The corporation of the Church of Jesus Christ of Latter Day Saints was declared dissolved. County probate judges of Utah were henceforth to be appointed by the President. Woman suffrage was abolished; and the voters' registration oath was extended to include a statement denying any intention of aiding, counselling or advising others to defy the anti-polygamy laws.[29]

The stringency of this statute impelled action on the part of the Mormons who still enjoyed the franchise. Thus it was that on June 30, 1887, when the constitutional convention met in Salt Lake City, the Mormon delegates, taking the reins into their own hands, incorporated into the instrument a provision (Article XV, Section 12) declaring bigamy and polygamy misdemeanors punishable by fine and imprisonment.[30]

In view of this apparent change of front, the Utah commission, while refusing to lend official sanction to the constitutional referendum, made it known to the judges of election that they might act in their normal capacity:

> Whereas, the prohibition of polygamy is the paramount object of the special legislation of Congress as applicable to Utah, we are of the opinion that when the great body of the legal voters of the Territory manifest a disposition to place themselves on record against polygamy, in howsoever an informal manner, they ought to be encouraged therein, the object of the Government being not

---

[29] "An Act to amend an act entitled 'An Act to amend section 5352 of the Revised Statutes of the United States,' in reference to bigamy, and for other purposes." U. S. 49th Congress, First Session, Senate Document 10. (Washington, 1886, 32 pp.) Public Document 183, March 15, 1887; *U. S. Statutes at Large*, XXIV, 635–641.

[30] *Constitution of the State of Utah and Memorial to Congress* (n. p., 1887), p. 14.

to destroy, but to reform the Mormon people; therefore we recommend to the favorable consideration of the Judges of Election a compliance with the terms set forth in the following communication:

Resolved: the Utah Commission having considered the proposition of the Committee from the Convention of delegates to frame a Constitution, now sitting in Salt Lake City, making a proposition that this Commission shall take charge of the election for the adoption or rejection of the proposed Constitution . . . are of the opinion that the Commission has no express authority to take any official action . . . , but considering the fact represented . . . that the proposed Constitution will contain a prohibition of the institution and practice of polygamy, . . . and a further prohibition of the union of Church and State, the Commission are willing to recommend to the Judges of the election . . . that they may receive all the ballots which may be cast. . . .[31]

Adopted by the convention July 7, the constitution was submitted to the electorate on August 1, 1887, and was approved by a vote of 13,195 to 504. Presumably, the bulk of the Gentiles did not consider it worth while to oppose it at the polls, relying on the probability (which proved to be the fact) that Congress would reject the measure. The Utah commission was divided on the matter. The majority reported as its opinion, "that Utah should not be admitted to the Union until such time as the Mormon people shall manifest by their future acts that they have abandoned polygamy in good faith," [32] and finally, it went so far as to suggest approval of the orthodox Liberal cry for a legislative commission.[33] The two Democratic members, however,[34] submitted a minority report, sharply disagreeing with their fellows:

Many of the Gentiles in Utah claim that this anti-polygamy movement among the Mormons is "all a sham." But we do not think so. After careful and impartial

---

[31] *Additional Recommendations to Judges of Election* (printed form, Salt Lake City, July 8, 1887), enclosed in letter from the commission to Secretary Garland, July 17, 1887 (N. A., D. J. File, Utah).

[32] *Report, 1887,* p. 26.

[33] *Ibid.,* p. 29.

[34] A. B. Carlton and General John A. McClernand, of Illinois, a recent appointee of the Cleveland administration.

investigation and consideration, our conclusion is that, whatever may be their motives, and whether they are influenced by choice or necessity, the generality of the monogamous Mormons (who are more than three-fourths of the Mormon population) have deliberately and wisely resolved that their highest earthly interests . . . and the avoidance of the odium which attaches to them throughout the civilized world, demand that polygamy should be abolished.

Since the Mormons seemed disposed to obey the law, the minority did not feel called upon to subscribe to "further legislation of a hostile and aggressive character, almost, if not entirely, destructive of local self-government. . . ." [35] The era of Brigham Young was gone, "nor . . . can the fading and dissolving spectre of the past be justly . . . invoked as an excitative to legislation proscriptive of religious opinion." Salt Lake City, once the mysterious capital of a sinister theocratic kingdom, they described as "one of the most cosmopolitan places on the continent, a resort for tourists, savants, statesmen and scholars from abroad." [36]

There would seem to be little doubt that in its estimate of the trend of events, the minority report was more accurate. As the decade of the eighties wore away, it became increasingly evident that neither radical Liberals nor stand-pat Mormons represented the majority opinion of the Territory or even that of their respective factions. Certainly, the bulk of the Mormon people were ready and anxious for the Manifesto of 1890 which relieved their consciences of the obligation of the divine injunction concerning patriarchal marriage. Sentiment, indeed, had been growing for some years that the revelation was "permissive" rather than obligatory, which, aside from the obvious economic and social factors involved, may have accounted for the relatively small number of the Saints who actually followed their peculiar ideal of life. [37] On the other hand, the more moderate Gentiles manifested more than

---

[35] *Minority Report of the Utah Commission, 1887* (Washington, D. C., 1887. Printed together with the majority report above cited), pp. 36–37.

[36] *Ibid.*, pp. 39–40.

[37] Few of the "young Mormons" who were rising to positions of trust in the Church during the eighties,—men like Caine and Frank Cannon, the son of the Apostle, who was later to be Utah's first Republican Senator—were practicing polygamists.

a theoretical desire for harmonious relations with their Mormon fellow-citizens. The organization of the Salt Lake City Chamber of Commerce, with a membership made up of both elements, followed closely upon the publication of the Edmunds-Tucker act (April, 1887).[38]

The following year witnessed the birth of a boom period in the Territory. The continued flow of wealth from the mines, and the exploitation of the region's natural resources, did much to increase the non-Mormon population. The local outlook was changing. While antagonisms burned as brightly as ever, it was evident that a new spirit was abroad. The minority report of the Utah commission for that year laid stress on these hopeful indications:

> This year, in the real estate excitement in Utah . . . the Mormons freely sold their city lots and other real estate to Gentiles as well as to others; and this notwithstanding the general understanding that the Mormon Church leaders have deprecated and remonstrated against their people selling their land to Gentiles. This is another strong evidence of the spirit of independence among the monogamous Mormons that is influencing young Utah, and of the general disposition to repudiate the authority of the Church leaders, in secular and civil affairs. "Business is business," and it has a wonderfully cosmopolitan effect upon all classes of men.[39]

President Cleveland's nominee for the governorship of Utah Territory was Caleb W. West, a Kentuckian who had fought with the Confederacy as an officer in Morgan's brigade.[40] Confirmed by the Senate, the new executive arrived in Salt Lake City early in May, 1886, and immediately ran foul of the Liberals by accepting the proffer of a reception given in his honor by the Mormon civic authorities.[41] Less inclined that his predecessor to foster extreme partisanship, West nevertheless was quick to define his position

---

[38] *Report, 1887*, p. 10; Whitney, *op. cit.*, III, 610–614.

[39] *Minority Report of the Utah Commission, 1888* (Washington, D. C., 1888), p. 22.

[40] Edward A. Anderson, "Territorial Governors—Caleb W. West," in *Improvement Era*, IV, No. 10, August 1901, 721–724. West was reappointed to his post in 1893, and served until 1896, when he was succeeded by Heber M. Wells, first governor of the new State.

[41] *Daily Tribune*, May 8, 1886.

with reference to the enforcement of the anti-polygamy legislation. One of his first acts was to publish a proclamation (July 14, 1886) warning all Mormons as well as all prospective converts to the sect that it would be his duty as the ranking representative of the federal government to administer such legislation without fear or favor.[42] Thwarted in his well-intentioned efforts to extend amnesty to the polygamists detained in the Utah penitentiary by their consistent refusal to promise obedience to the Edmunds law,[43] he gradually stiffened his attitude. During the following winter he lent his counsel to the formulation of the Edmunds-Tucker bill.[44]

Reviewing the effects of the operation of the latter act in his report to the Secretary of the Interior for the year 1888, West found reason to comment on the amelioration of local conditions:

> It is with much satisfaction that I am enabled to state that marked and decided changes for the benefit and advancement of the people and the prosperity of the Territory have taken place. To some extent there has been a bridging of the chasm that has separated the Mormon and non-Mormon people since the settlement of this Territory. . . . Without having the control, they [the Mormons] have united with non-Mormons in public organizations for the protection of an increase in trade. . . .
>
> They have . . . liberalized the municipal government of the city by giving representation therein to the non-Mormons. They have done likewise in the boards controlling the Asylum for the Insane, the Deseret University, the Reform School, the Agricultural College, and the Territorial fair. . . .[45]

Yet the governor was not willing to foster any impression that the problems of the Territory had found their solution. He was still convinced "that there is an irreconcilable political difference, fundamental in character, between the Mormon system and the

---

[42] *Ibid.*, July 15, 1886.

[43] Whitney, *op. cit.*, III, 507–515. Apostle Lorenzo Snow, of Brigham City, Utah, was the principal offender in the custory of the warden. Forty-seven others joined the Apostle in refusing West's offer.

[44] *Daily Tribune*, December 9, 1886.

[45] *Report of the Governor of Utah Territory for the Year 1888* (Washington, D. C., 1888), p. 19.

government established by the United States." Irrepressible conflict would necessarily rage until it be settled. Mormon exclusionism, though weakened, was yet the dominant note:

> It is generally true . . . that only the faithful to the church or those not of the faith who are willing to serve the interests of the church, are given place and employment in all the various enterprises and business of the community conducted and controlled by the Mormons. No matter what the capability and merit of a non-Mormon . . . no door of employment or advancement is opened to him. . . . To an extent truly surprising their dealing in business affairs is with and among themselves, emphasizing forcibly the truth of the designation that they have applied to those not of the faith that they are "outsiders." [46]

It was this same "irrepressible conflict" that was the keynote of West's message to the legislative assembly which met in January, 1888. In his review of the history of religious and social strife which had disfigured the territorial record, and which had resulted in "the defiance of law, . . . the disgrace of flight, the gloom and misery of the prison," and the consequent destruction of property and the suffering of women and children, he laid the cause at the door of the theocracy. He denied that the Gentiles had waged the conflict "upon the principle that minorities should control," but rather in defense of the lofty ideal, "that freedom should be established and prevail here as elsewhere in our land." He bespoke mutual accord:

> I would not have you or the people of the Territory misunderstand me. I am anxious to serve them well and do them good. With you and them I have no religious controversy. That the Mormon Church can by the sublimity and beauty of its teachings and the moral and religious conduct of its members, subdue and dominate the world, it is not . . . my province to question. . . .[47]

Honest, if pedestrian, West failed to placate the fire-eaters of either party. His report for 1888 was attacked by the Liberal and

---

[46] *Ibid.,* pp. 22–23.
[47] *Daily Tribune,* January 9, 1888.

Mormon press alike. Irritated, he addressed an open letter to the various local editors, suggesting that since no other means of compounding their differences had been found successful, they unite with him in recommending to the President the creation of an investigating committee to inquire into the conduct of the government officials of Utah during the past:

> It doth appear from the representations made as to the character of Federal officials, who have served in this Territory, that most, if not all, have been weak and corrupt, inspired by hope of gain, love of power, or animated with a spirit of malice or hate towards a portion of the people. The committee or commission I suggest is to be created by the highest sources of power in our land; no political advantage is to be given; it is to be constituted equally of the two great political parties. Having regard to the source of creation, it is fair to presume that strong, fair, capable men would be sent to us. . . .[48]

Unfortunately, this luminous idea failed to find favor either within the Territory or at Washington. It is possible that the mottled history of Utah might have been rendered far easier to write had it been acted upon. With the inauguration of President Harrison, West was promptly removed to give place to a Republican, Arthur H. Thomas, a native of Chicago who had come to Utah in 1879 as territorial secretary under Governor Murray. During West's administration, Thomas had been appointed as the first resident of the Territory to serve as a member of the Utah Commission.[49] A conscientious executive, but an active Liberal partisan, Thomas devoted his energies throughout his term to a strenuous effort to ward off the impending admission of Utah into the sisterhood of states.[50]

Concomitant with the political developments that occurred in the Territory following the passage of the Edmunds act and its sequel of 1887, the federal authorities, acting through the district courts, began a remarkable series of prosecutions which resulted in the conviction and imprisonment of hundreds of Mormons and

---

[48] *Ibid.*, November 3, 1888.

[49] Edward A. Anderson, "Territorial Governors—Arthur H. Thomas," in *Improvement Era*, IV, No. 11, September, 1901, 801–803.

[50] *Cf. Reports of the Governor of Utah Territory, 1890–1893* (Washington, D. C., 1890–1893).

forced the supreme authorities of the Church to "go on the underground." While this phase of the problem under consideration involved far more than the purely local antagonisms between Mormon and Gentile, it reflected the outgrowth of that feeling and provided the background against which the relations of the two groups were set during the period when their mutual recrimination was the most exasperated. Roughly, the period from 1884 to 1889 marked the climax of the long-drawn crusade against polygamy. At the outset Mormon leadership professed its absolute determination to resist the operation of laws which they deemed incompatible with their religious beliefs. Time wrought its changes, however, and under the continued pressure of federal prosecution, the sentiment of the monogamous Mormons that accommodation would have to be made, gradually gained ground.

By 1887, as has been noted, the dominantly Mormon constitutional convention was ready to incorporate into the fundamental law of the proposed state provisions abjuring polygamy and the idea of union of Church and State. On July 25 of that year, John Taylor, successor of Brigham Young in the First Presidency of the Church of Jesus Christ of Latter Day Saints, died in "exile" while avoiding apprehension. Three years later Wilford Woodruff, as the "prophet, seer and revelator" for the Saints, announced that it was indeed the will of God that the practice of patriarchal marriage should be suspended. The non-Mormon world, less orthodox in its viewpoint, tended to regard the pronouncement as the capitulation of the old guard, not only to the federal government and the American conscience, but to the more moderate elements within the sect itself.

On July 5, 1884, Charles Shuster Zane, judge of the circuit court of Springfield, Illinois, was commissioned chief justice of the supreme court of Utah Territory. A native of New Jersey, Zane had moved to Illinois, studied at McKendry College, and is said to have applied to read law in Abraham Lincoln's office. In 1861, he entered partnership with William Herndon, and maintained that relation until 1869, when he entered the legal firm of Shelby M. Cullom, who, as congressman and senator, was long identified with anti-Mormon legislation.[51] In Zane, the Utah judiciary received a

---

[51] Whitney, *op cit.*, III, 369.

chief justice gifted with wide legal knowledge, a man of severity tempered by salty humor, and inspired by the determination to apply the law relentlessly.   In the preceding February, an enterprising Nevada lawyer, W. H. Dickson, had been appointed district attorney, and had succeeded in having his partner, Charles S. Varian, named as his assistant.[52]   Stephen P. Twiss and Jacob S. Boreman were associate justices.   Undoubtedly, the stage was ready for the enactment of the final drama.

Preparing for the onslaught, Dickson wrote to Attorney General Brewster, August 26, 1884, soliciting permission and funds for a secret detective service in Utah:

> The impenetrable secrecy attending the practice of these offenses is such that I feel assured it will be found well-nigh impossible to accomplish any substantial results under this law by the employment of ordinary methods alone.   True, we may and doubtless will, at rare intervals, be able to convict some one of the masses, beyond this, however, nothing can well be anticipated.   At the same time I have every reason to believe . . . that these crimes are on the increase throughout the Territory.
> . . . It is well known that all the members of the First Presidency of the Mormon Church and very many of the bishops have plural wives; indeed no secret is made of this. . . .   The plural wives, of all who can afford it, have separate establishments, the husband ostensibly living with one only; it is correctly believed, however, and such doubtless is the fact, that he visits and cohabits with all of them in turn. . . .[53]

Brewster allotted six hundred dollars for the employment of a special detective.   Early in February, 1885, Dickson reported "highly satisfactory results."   Indictments had been found against a number of ranking Mormon officials, including Charles Penrose, editor of the *Deseret News,* George Teasdale of the Council of the Twelve Apostles, and Royal B. Young, step-son of the late President of the Church.   Others, the district attorney stated, had sought refuge in concealment.   With further funds available for

---

[52] N. A., D. J., Appointment Clerk's File, 1884.
[53] Dickson to Brewster (N. A., D. J. File, Utah).

more detectives, he was certain that "victory would be ours in another year." [54]

Delegate John T. Caine, in the interests of his harried constituents, appealed to the Attorney General to put an end to such extraordinary methods of procedure. He charged, moreover, that legal wives had been forced to bear witness against their husbands, children against their fathers. "Very rarely in the Administration of justice among the English speaking people have more lawless proceedings been resorted to by those clothed with judicial authority." [55] Attorney General A. H. Garland, Brewster's successor, referred the letter to Dickson, insisting upon explanation. To this the district attorney replied with a categorical denial that the federal officers in Utah had transgressed any due limits in their zeal:

> . . . I find it also stated in the honorable gentleman's communication, that "while his constituency looks upon the laws of the United States as subversive (!) of justice and morality, etc." It required much hardihood on the part of the honorable gentleman to venture such an assertion as this, in view of the fact that nine-tenths of that constituency, acting under the most perfect of organizations, have at all times not only refused submission to the law, but, acting under the advice of their leaders, have at all times met, by the most determined opposition, any attempt . . . to bring offenders . . . to justice.

Dickson was prepared to admit, however, that "in order to accomplish that we have . . . the office here has resorted to the most rigorous measures. . . ." [56]

Ten days later Garland was informed that indictments had been found against John Taylor and George Q. Cannon. "Both defendants are secreted and evading arrest, and the information of this office is, that they intend leaving the United States and going to Mexico." [57] Garland immediately gave orders to the district attor-

[54] To the same, February 8, 1885 (N. A., D. J. File, Utah).

[55] Caine to Brewster, March 3, 1885 (N. A., D. J. File, Utah).

[56] Dickson to Garland, March 19, 1885 (N. A., D. J. File, Utah).

[57] To the same, March 28, 1885 (N. A., D. J. File, Utah). It was at this time that the Mormon authorities began the planting of colonies in Sonora and Chihuahua, Mexico, their intention evidently being to establish a place of refuge for prosecuted polygamists (Whitney, *op. cit.,* III, 343). President

neys and marshals of the neighboring states to be on the alert for
the apprehension of the fugitives.[58]   The United States marshal for
Utah, Edwin Ireland, whose numerous arrests of violators of the
Edmunds act were filling the Utah penitentiary as well as the district court dockets, outlined his problems to the Attorney General
in a letter dated November 2, 1885:

> I beg leave to call the attention of the department to
> the fact that while we have made many arrests . . . of
> persons charged with the crime of Polygamy . . . they
> have been principally in and around the larger towns. . . .
> The people in the interior towns are very jubilant over
> this. . . .   It is thought by the Mormons that when the
> material about the larger towns has been all used, there
> the prosecutions must practically end. . . .
> The whole power of the church is used to throw ob-
> stacles in the way of U. S. officers, they control one of the
> Railroads running through the Territory, and the Tele-
> graph line of that road; people along the road are advised
> of the presence of a Deputy Marshal on board any train
> always in advance, the County Sheriffs and deputies, and

Taylor made his last public appearance in the Salt Lake Tabernacle on Sunday, February 1, 1885, counselling the Saints to exercise patience, but to resist and evade the law.

[58] Garland to United States Attorneys and Marshals of California, Colorado, and Nebraska, April 2, 1885 (N. A., D. J. Instruction Book N).   An
interesting communication from Post Master General Vilas to Garland, dated
June 18, 1885, is in the Utah File of the Department of Justice.   Vilas enclosed a letter found in the Dead Letter Office, as follows:

"Mt. Pleasant, Utah, Feb. 22, 1885.   Pat McGee, Schofield: I enclose two
officers stars which you will use as no doubt you will see fit.   You will call on
old man Williams representing yourself as a deputy U. S. Marshall at the
same time showing your star and stating that you are authorized by the laws
of the United States to arrest him on a charge of Polygamy, and that he will
board at the expense of the government for about three years before his trial
will come off.   Then you begin to express sympathy with him and offer to let
him off for $1000.00 provided he will hide himself or keep out of the way for
a certain time.   The $1000 of course will be to pay your expenses in case
you are found out that you have let him escape. . . . The old man will give
you the money easy.

"The people here in his condition are fleeing to the mountains and keeping
out of the country.   You can have some fun and get some money. . . . Yours,
James Bayley."

It need hardly be added that the letter seems a shade too transparent to be
genuine.

entire police of the towns are employed to watch the movements of officers and to secretly aid the criminal and witnesses to escape.

The lot of his deputies, the marshal continued, was unenviable. Dogged by spies, refused board and lodging in the Mormon villages, constrained to travel in pairs for fear of violence, they were made the pariahs of society. And again the plea was made for a "contingent fund" to finance successful operations.[59]

On February 13, 1886, Ireland received word from Winnemucca, Nevada, that George Q. Cannon had been seized while en route to Mexico, after a reward of five hundred dollars had been posted for information leading to his capture. At Promontory Point, Utah, on the return trip to Salt Lake City, the elderly Mormon leader eluded his guards and was only re-taken after a chase across the barren sands of the desert. Marshal Ireland described the event to the Attorney General:

> . . . We left Winnemucca at 2:30 p.m., February 15th, myself and one deputy with Cannon in charge. The following morning at daybreak the prisoner jumped the train near Promontory this Territory, he was quickly missed, the train stopped, and recaptured within an hour, in his pockets were found a loaded revolver, two loaves of bread, a bottle of water, no doubt passed to him on the train.
>
> We were compelled to remain at Promontory for the next regular train, or 24 hours. During the day telegrams were poured in upon me advising that the excitement in Salt Lake and Ogden was intense; great crowds of people gathering, and at Ogden arms and ammunition being sold, that there was great danger of a rescue on our arrival . . . which of course meant serious loss of life.
>
> Deputy Vandercook, who was left in charge of my office, appreciating the danger called for Troops to go to Promontory by Special Train and escort us in at an early hour in the morning, thereby avoiding the crowd and dan-

---

[59] Ireland to Garland, November 2, 1885 (N. A., D. J. File, Utah). Garland replied suggesting that it might be as effective not to scour the countryside, but to concentrate on the conviction of "large offenders." But he assured Ireland that all needed funds would be placed at his disposal. (N. A., D. J. Instruction Book T.)

ger of a collision. . . . My investigations since fully satisfy
me of the wisdom of Deputy Vandercook's action. . . .[60]

Placed under bond to the amount of $45,000, Cannon evidently
deemed his case sufficiently perilous to incur forfeiture and took
refuge in Arizona. Dickson wired the Attorney General, March
17, 1886, asking that a further reward of two thousand dollars be
posted for Cannon, but Garland curtly refused.[61]

Concealed by trusted friends, President John Taylor continued
to escape detection. "It is evident that he lacks the courage to meet
the consequences of his transgressions," thought the district attorney.[62] The noted New York lawyer, George Ticknor Curtis,
retained as counsel by the Mormon Church, complained to Garland
that the clerk of the Salt Lake district court, on application, had
refused to issue a copy of Taylor's indictment to the latter's agents
on the ground that the defendant was still at large. Curtis decried
this as a manifest violation of the spirit of the Sixth Amendment
of the Constitution.

> I am about to submit to the President a full and de-
> tailed statement of Mr. Taylor's conduct since the Ed-
> munds Act first went into operation. . . . I propose to
> do this for the purpose of asking that your Department
> take such steps as may be thought proper to verify the
> statement that I shall submit, in order that it may be con-
> sidered whether it is not best, alike for the interest of the
> Government and the defendant, that the pending prosecu-
> tion be discontinued, so that Mr. Taylor can return to his
> home, and use his influence in reconciling his fellow-be-
> lievers to that cheerful obedience to the laws which I sin-
> cerely believe he earnestly desires to promote.[63]

On July 25, 1887, however, President Taylor died after an
"exile" of two and one-half years. "He left his people harassed
and troubled and tossed about, even as a dismasted ship is tossed

---

[60] Ireland to Attorney General, March 22, 1886 (N. A., D. J. File, Utah) ;
Cf. Whitney, op. cit., III, 478–491, for a strongly-colored Mormon account of
the incident.

[61] Dickson to Garland, March 17, 1886 (N. A., D. J. File, Utah) ; Garland
to Dickson (N. A., D. J. Instruction Book T).

[62] To the same, May 27, 1886 (N. A., D. J. File, Utah).

[63] Curtis to Garland, New York, May 26, 1887 (N. A., D. J. File, Utah).

when left to the buffetings of pitiless storms and confused seas . . . ," wrote Judge C. C. Goodwin, editor of the *Tribune*.[64] Wilford Woodruff, senior member of the Council of the Twelve Apostles, was recognized as the heir-apparent, although he was not formally sustained as President until the April Conference of 1889.[65]

Chief Justice Zane, in full career as the relentless exponent of the law, was sacrificed, as a Republican, to the demands of unsatisfied Democratic office-seekers. Elliott Sandford, an elderly New Yorker, was appointed in his stead on July 20, 1888.[66] A year earlier District Attorney Dickson had yielded place to George S. Peters, of Ohio. The effect was a marked lessening in the rigor of the anti-polygamy prosecutions and in the number of those brought to trial. And at once the Gentiles of Utah, dominantly Republican in party loyalty, began to flood Washington with appeals for a reinstatement of the jurist and prosecutor who had waged so successful a campaign against the "ecclesiastical power." [67] Soliciting the aid of Senator William H. Stewart of Nevada, Baskin wrote:

> . . . In our fight here for the cause of good government we have reached a crisis where the need of tried and true men in each of those places is imperative. The Mormons have taken heart greatly since Zane was succeeded by Sanford [*sic*], Dickson by Peters. . . .
> It seemed to us that we could not afford to take chances on untried men, ignorant of our peculiar situation here, no matter how good they may be. Inexperience of Utah affairs alone, would make true Gentiles here feel that the man possessing such . . . was a danger, in official position.[68]

With the change of administration, March 4, 1889, W. H. H. Miller, as the new Attorney General, heard the Mormon rebuttal

[64] *Daily Tribune*, July 27, 1887.

[65] Whitney, *op. cit.*, III, 587.

[66] N. A., D. J. Appointment File, 1888.

[67] The Appointment Clerk's File of the Department of Justice contains bundles of these appeals, emanating not only from Utah, but from a number of the Woman's Home Missionary units, the New West Education Commission, etc., etc.

[68] Baskin to Stewart, April 13, 1889 (N. A., D. J. Appointment File, Utah).

furnished by Delegate Caine. "When it is demonstrable that his [Zane's] zeal and severity are confined to offenders who are known to be Mormons, I think his judicial qualifications may be justly called into question."[69] Miller, however, was not to be swayed. On May 10, 1889, he wrote to Sandford that it was the President's opinion that "public interest will be subserved by a change in the office of Chief Justice of Utah."[70] Two weeks later, Zane was restored to his post. The *Tribune* echoed the rejoicing of the Liberals in the "vindication" of "the Columbus who discovered the route by which the execution of the laws could be found in Utah."

During District Attorney Peters' term of office, on August 27, 1888, G. A. Jenks, acting Attorney General, requested a summary statement of the number of convictions secured in the territorial federal courts under the anti-polygamy statutes of 1862, 1882 and 1887. Peters' reply was not without interest. Convictions for polygamy, from 1875 to 1888, totaled only sixteen, of which fourteen had been secured since 1884. Apparently, the three year statute of limitations had effectively prevented federal prosecutors from pressing that particular charge.[71] Under the law against unlawful cohabitation (Section 3 of the Edmunds act) the bulk of Zane's convictions had been secured. Five hundred and fifty-seven persons had been found guilty under this statute, and $44,235.30 had been assessed in fines and costs. He added that the court dockets then listed two hundred and ninety-three cases to be considered at the approaching terms.[72]

---

[69] Caine to Miller, May 6, 1889 (N. A., D. J. Appointment File, Utah).

[70] Miller to Sandford, May 10, 1889 (N. A., D. J. Instruction Book, Judges and Clerks), IV, 7.

[71] John W. Judd, Associate Justice of Utah (2nd Dist.) to W. H. H. Miller, July 2, 1889: "The habit of the Mormons of late years since the laws have been so vigorously enforced is to marry their 'plural wives' which is done in great secret, and then to be sent off by the Church upon a 'mission' to stay 3 years, until the offense shall be barred by the 3 years limitation, and then return and defy the law. . . ."

[72] Peters to Garland, n. d. (probably October, 1888) (N. A., D. J. File, Utah). The occasion for the report was a resolution offered by Delegate Fred T. Dubois of Idaho, August 25, 1888, requesting the Attorney General to furnish the desired information. Dubois was a vigorous opponent of Mormonism, and sponsor of the Idaho test oath against the doctrines and practices of that religion. (Caine to Jenks, September 26, 1888, D. J. File, Utah.)

The Edmunds-Tucker act of 1887 provided, as has been noted, for the dissolution of the corporation of the Church of Jesus Christ of Latter Day Saints on the grounds of violation of the terms of the Act of July 1, 1862, limiting the property holdings of religious organizations in the territories to $50,000. Action in this matter was initiated on July 30, 1887 by District Attorney Peters. The assets of the corporation were estimated at $3,000,000, and the suit prayed for the appointment of a receiver to take charge thereof until proper disposition could be made in favor of the territorial common schools. The case was argued before the territorial supreme court from October 17 to October 21, and decision was rendered on November 5, in favor of the United States. The federal marshal, Frank Dyer, a Mississippian by birth who had settled in the mining community of Park City, was named receiver. A few days later Dyer filed bonds to the amount of $250,000, and moved to take possession of the various pieces of property, personal and real, other than actual church buildings and "parsonages" held by the late corporation in alleged violation of the law. Throughout this phase of the litigation District Attorney Peters was favored with the advice and encouragement of Attorney General Garland, with whom he kept in constant communication.[73] The lengthy judicial process which followed culminated in the arguing of the case before the Supreme Court of the United States, which, on May 19, 1890, finally rendered judgment sustaining the constitutionality of the Edmunds-Tucker act. The general argument submitted by the attorneys for the United States contended for the power of the Congress to annul all territorial enactments, the invalidity of the incorporating act in question, since it set up an organization part of whose purpose was to defy the Constitution, and the appropriateness of receivership and escheat, since such methods alone could secure the desired effect.[74]

---

[73] N. A., Instruction Books Y and Z, *passim.;* D. J. File, Utah, 1887–1888.

[74] U. S. Reports, X, 732–812, 884; also, *The United States v. the Late Corporation of the Church of Jesus Christ of Latter-Day Saints* (1893), 150 U. S., 145. By a joint resolution of both Houses of Congress, October 5–21, 1893, the escheated personal property, to the value of $438,174.39 was returned to the Mormon Church, and with the admission of Utah as a State, President Cleveland signed an act restoring the real property to the revived corporation. (March 28, 1896.)

Submitting his resignation to President Harrison, March 9, 1889, Marshal Dyer commented on the case:

> The hostility of the Mormon people to this law and the proceedings to enforce it are well known. It was believed that in anticipation of its passage large amounts of property really owned by the Church, but held in the names of private parties in trust in its favor, had been conveyed to evade the enforcement of the law. It seemed to the Supreme Court, that the means and powers which as Marshal I had at command, would greatly facilitate my acquisition of this property as Receiver. . . . I accepted this post with hesitation, though had I then known of its magnitude I would have declined it altogether. I gave a bond for the faithful performance of my trust in the sum of a quarter of a million dollars, and although there was voluntarily delivered to me by the Church authorities property to the amount of One Hundred and Forty-Five thousand dollars in value, in less than eight months I had with the aid of persons . . . in my employment unearthed of property held in secret trusts and reduced into my possession . . . a further amount . . . aggregating nearly Six Hundred thousand dollars.[75]

Dyer, like many another federal officer in Utah, had run foul of both extreme groups. Acting for his friends, the radical Liberals, Senator Edmunds laid their case against the marshal before Attorney General Miller, May 1, 1889. His enclosures included letters from William Goodwin, a Gentile leader of Logan, Utah, charging that the Church authorities in that locality were making plans to move huge herds of cattle to neighboring Nevada and to the Mormon settlements in Alberta, Canada, and from R. N. Baskin, stating that Dyer's action "has been of great detriment to the cause of progress here and is considered a scandal by all disinterested and loyal persons." Specifically, Baskin charged that the marshal, having obtained permission of the territorial supreme court to compromise the suits seeking to escheat certain of the real estate holdings of the late corporation, had proceeded to mislead the court, accepting in settlement amounts far short of the actual value, and failing to report the terms of his agreements with the Church authorities. Further, he accused Dyer of making no effort to

---

[75] Dyer to Harrison, March 9, 1889 (N. A., D. J. File, Utah).

attach personal property owned by the late corporation, estimated at a valuation of $268,000 (and this sum, Baskin added, was considered by "many informed citizens" not to exceed one-fourth the real total) but offering, instead, to compromise the whole for a cash payment of $7,500.[76]

The Gentile press, which shared Baskin's open disgust with the supine methods of Dyer, found consolation in the subsequent appointment of Henry W. Lawrence, one of the Godbeites of a score of years before, as receiver:

> There is poetic justice in the appointment. . . . On principle Mr. Lawrence found it necessary to oppose some of the pretensions of Brigham Young. His manhood made that necessary. As a result he was excommunicated under circumstances that tried his courage to the utmost. It would have required but a word to have caused the fierce fanatics around him to rend him limb from limb. . . . Now he, as an American, is given the place of Receiver to manage and dispose of the property which, under the law, has been seized from the church and is to be turned over to the school fund. No better appointment could have been made.[77]

Lawrence seems to have administered his trust with commendable justice and wisdom during the following years. The full story of the case, which lies outside the scope of this study, is in urgent need of re-telling in the light of available documents. It may be remarked that Dyer's action in effecting a compromise with the Church authorities in regard to personal property, whatever his motive may have been, was probably the course best suited to the circumstances of Utah's turmoil.

The provision of the Edmunds-Tucker act making the territorial probate judgeships appointive rather than elective immediately suggested to the Liberals the possibility of securing still more political plums and thus to extend their influence into the agricultural Mormon strongholds. It should be remembered that the probate courts had concurrent power with the marshal to select the

---

[76] Edmunds to Miller, May 1, 1889 (N. A., D. J. Appointment File, Utah); enclosing letter from Goodwin to Baskin, Logan, Utah, April 22, 1889, and from Baskin to Edmunds, Salt Lake City, April 25, 1889.

[77] *Salt Lake Tribune*, July 17, 1890.

jury panel. Governor West showed himself sympathetic with the plan, though with prudent reserve. On July 19, 1888, he wrote to President Cleveland, submitting a list of available appointees:

> Believing that the purpose of Congress in making these offices appointive by the President was to wrest from the Mormon people the power of filling them by election, and at least, to place in the hands of others those offices, in every instance where a capable non-Mormon could be found to fill the place he has received my recommendation. But while observing the above rule, I have carefully endeavored to select and recommend only fair and just men who cannot properly be found fault with by the Mormon people. . . . In counties where no non-Mormons of character and capability reside . . . suitable and proper Mormon names have been given.

Many of those on his list, West remarked, had once been Mormons, but had "heretofore severed their religious and political relations," in spite of the attendant risk. "I hold to the opinion that it is wise to uphold and encourage those who, seeing their error, have the courage and manliness to forsake it. . . ." [78]

Delegate Caine lost no time in controverting the governor's thesis. Congress, he wrote to the President, had had no intention of excluding all members of the Mormon Church from the offices in question. The Gentiles of Utah had complained that although they paid "quite a large share of the taxes, they had no voice in the disbursement of the monies." That was the mainspring of the congressional measure. He pointed out that in the case of Utah County, of which Provo was the seat, the "Delegate Election" of 1886 had scored 2,550 votes for the People's candidate, as against only 204 for his Liberal opponent. Yet West's list included the name of a man highly objectionable to the majority, "an improper person to select one-half of the jurors for the District Court which sits in that County." [79] However, with a few exceptions, Governor West's recommendations were acted upon.[80] The way was finally

---

[78] West to Cleveland, July 19, 1888 (N. A., D. J. Appointment File, Utah).

[79] Caine to Cleveland, August 3, 1888 (N. A., D. J. Appointment File, Utah).

[80] The list of oaths recorded in the Appointment Clerk's File, N. A., indicates as much.

open for the empaneling of Gentile juries in almost every county of the Territory.

Upon still another front was the attack against Mormon political control directed. As a result of the missionary activity of the Saints abroad, thousands of converts to the faith had come to Utah in the firm conviction that it was the land of Zion. The British Isles and the Scandinavian countries furnished the bulk of the immigrants, the majority of whom were sturdy, pious folk eminently suited to the difficult and often unrewarding task of tilling Utah's soil. Once naturalized, it was to be expected that these immigrants would largely submit in entire confidence to the political suggestions or instructions of the Church party. Insistently, but ineffectually, the Gentile press had stressed the charge of "foreign domination," and had cried out against granting the privilege of American citizenship to those who accepted as part of their creed the doctrine of plural marriage.

In the fall of 1889, anticipating the forthcoming elections, a number of foreign-born submitted their applications for naturalization at the court of Associate Justice T. J. Anderson, in Salt Lake City. Encouraged by their recent success, the Liberals, acting through their attorneys, made strenuous objection to the process. On November 9, while the court was examining the qualifications of John Moore, a Liberal publicist, Joseph Lippman, declared his readiness to prove to the satisfaction of the court that the Mormon endowment ceremony included oaths of blood vengeance against the United States government for its "acquiescence" in the death of the Prophet Joseph Smith. Justice Anderson, recognizing a test case, deferred the hearing until November 14. On the appointed day, Lippman was only able to produce testimony of a vague and general character, and the sessions for the succeeding days were given over to an embittered rehearsal of all the alleged Mormon atrocities of past years.[81]

The *Salt Lake Tribune* endorsed the charges with admirable assurance:

> The exposures now going on in the Third District Court of the awful nature and treasonable forms of the Endowment House Oaths are having a deep effect upon this community. Especially is this effect marked upon

[81] Whitney, *op. cit.*, III, 693–698.

> newcomers and upon young men raised in the country
> . . . who have never taken much interest in the alleged
> "religion." . . . The nature of these oaths is told by wit-
> ness after witness with such cumulative effect that the
> force of the evidence cannot be evaded.
>
> The truth is that all of these matters . . . have been
> notorious for years; only just now they are put with
> a coherency . . . and practical force never before at-
> tempted.[82]

The case, of course, aroused excited interest throughout the
country, the news value of Mormon history receiving full play.[83]
Mormon refusal to reveal the full ceremonial of celestial marriage
constituted undoubtedly the strongest argument in support of the
mysterious oaths, the positive evidence bearing thereon being of a
highly dubious nature.   Nevertheless, Justice Anderson found in
the testimony sufficient force to enable him to reach a decision,
which he pronounced on November 30:

> The evidence in this case establishes unquestionably
> that the teachings, practices and aims of the Mormon
> Church are antagonistic to the Government of the United
> States, utterly subversive of good morals and the well-
> being of society, and that its members are animated by
> a feeling of hostility towards the Government and its
> laws, and therefore, an alien who is a member of said
> church is not a fit person to become a citizen of the United
> States.[84]

"Everybody shook hands with everybody else, and every Gentile
countenance wore a smile of satisfaction," wrote the triumphant
editor of the *Tribune*.   "This decision, broadly viewed, fixes the
status of the Mormon Church as a disloyal conspiracy."   The next
question was inevitable: "Are the native born members any
better?" [85]

In high spirits the Liberals turned to the Salt Lake City elec-

---

[82] *Salt Lake Tribune*, November 14, 1889.

[83] *Cf. New York World*, November 18, *Chicago Inter-Ocean*, November 21, *Montreal Star*, November 16.

[84] *Ibid.*, December 1, 1889.

[85] *Ibid.*, December 1, 1889. As early as November, 1885, Justice O. W.
Powers, sitting in Provo, had denied citizenship to one Niels Hanson on
similar grounds. (*Provo Territorial Enquirer*, November 10, 1885.)

tions slated for February, 1890, which were to deliver the municipal government into their keeping. Their elation over the happy outcome of the contest knew no bounds. Orlando W. Powers, former associate justice of the Territory, who had devoted his marked oratorical and managerial abilities to the cause, gave expression to their feeling at a banquet held in the Walker House to celebrate the downfall of the Mormon regime: "Our victory was the triumph of civilization. It was the turning point in the history of our city. It was a victory for pure homes, free schools, an extended commerce and American institutions." [86]

But to the critical eye of a correspondent for the *Chicago Herald,* surveying the local situation, there were other aspects to be accounted for:

> It is greatly to be regretted that the Gentile population of Utah, on which the country is relying for the eradication of the polygamy cancer, is no better in many respects than the Mormons themselves. The whole population, without respect to religion or politics, is a stranger to sober reason, and is madly given over to everything that is radical and proscriptive. Fierce accusation, foul vituperation, unscrupulous plots and an insane violence and intensity mark everything that they do. This is extremely offensive to the people of the United States. They would like to have a Gentile population in Utah which would reform the Mormon Church and not plunder it, and which would set an example of dignified and sensible citizenship.
>
> The Utah character is a moral phenomenon. It has the appearance, to a visitor from the East, of epidemic insanity. How such a type of humanity was developed, with nothing like it in the surrounding States and Territories, is at first sight something of a puzzle. The probable explanation of the character of the Gentiles is that they have caught the spirit of the Mormons, and probably the Mormon character is the result of religious fanaticism embittered by persecution.[87]

From 1882 to 1890, the Saints had fought a good fight. In the face of increasing disabilities and political disfranchisement, they had displayed courage and remarkable spiritual cohesion.

---

[86] *Ibid.,* February 16, 1890.

[87] *Chicago Herald,* February 11, 1890.

Frowned upon by the nation, annoyed by the turbulent minority within their own borders, they had nevertheless sustained their leaders in their effort to maintain the teaching and practice of polygamy.   Inasmuch as the practice was never popular among the masses, it is the more noteworthy that the teaching should have inspired such loyalty.   Ultimately, however, the decision had to be faced: the choice lay between adherence to the dogma and the gradual extinction of their civic privileges.   The frontier had closed in upon them; the attempts to revive mass migration to Mexico had proved abortive.   The era of Mormon wanderings, from Ohio to Missouri, from Illinois to Utah, was over long since. Statehood, they were coming to realize, could never be theirs so long as plural marriage was supported by them as a doctrine applicable to life in nineteenth century America.   Territorial status held too many threats—many of them already revealed—of congressional dictatorship.

The point was that the Gentile, with all his failings, his arrogance and self-assurance, had come to Utah as the representative of American political and social morality.   The Mormon aspiration to "build a wall around Zion" has proved no more than wishful thinking.   Instead of a mountain fastness of ideal isolation, as it had seemed in the summer of 1847, Utah by 1890 had become an integral part of the American nation.   Polygamy was the last irreconcilable element of its separatism.   The Gentile in Utah, though he might ardently desire to do so, could not destroy the Mormon Church, but it was his firm conviction that his duty as a Christian and as an American was to destroy the peculiar institution of "this people."

It was on September 24, 1890, that President Wilford Woodruff published the document known as the "Manifesto," substantially a denial of allegations that plural marriages had been performed during the preceding year with the sanction of authority, and a profession of his intention to submit to the laws of the United States in regard to the practice.   His advice to the Latter Day Saints was that they "refrain from contracting any marriage forbidden by the law of the land." [88]   At the semi-annual Church Conference, held in Salt Lake City early in October, the President's

---

[88] Whitney, *op. cit.*, III, 744–748.

message was read to the assembled Saints, and solemnly ratified by them. God, according to the Mormon theologians, had seen fit to suspend the dispensation revealed to the Prophet Joseph Smith.[89]

Thenceforward, the quarrel between Utah and the nation, between Mormon and Gentile, was on a different footing. It died slowly; if indeed it may be said to be wholly appeased even today, after the lapse of more than fifty years. It was reduced to the more readily comprehensible terms of disagreement between a numerically dominant religious majority and an economically wealthy minority eager to gain or to hold political leadership. To that extent, at least, the Gentiles of Utah had achieved their victory.

---

[89] Frank J. Cannon, *Under the Prophet in Utah* (Boston, 1911), p. 97, describes an interview with President Woodruff shortly before the publication of the Manifesto: "Brother Frank, I have been making it a matter of prayer. I have wrestled mightily with the Lord. And I think I see some light." *Cf.* George B. Arbaugh, *Revelation in Mormonism* (Chicago, 1932), pp. 181–182.

ESSAY ON THE SOURCES

THE REPUTED qualifications of Mitford as a historiographer—violent partiality and extreme wrath—have been shared in ample measure by the bulk of those who have written on Utah history. An essay on the sources in this particular field runs the danger of turning into an indictment of most of the publications that have appeared. There are few who have shown themselves inclined to turn a dispassionate eye upon the story of Mormonism. Diatribes and apologies abound; of unbiased history there is little. This is the more regrettable, since it has seriously retarded the study of a most interesting phase of the religious and social history of the West.

Inevitably, the present study of the relations between the Mormon and non-Mormon groups in Utah has involved much of the general history of the territory. It is not the purpose of this essay to attempt what would be in substance a bibliography covering the whole ground. Such bibliographies exist, and may be consulted. Moreover, the mere enumeration of books, pamphlets, and magazine articles dealing with Utah and the factors of her history would seem to serve no useful purpose. The American travel literature of the late nineteenth century is replete with judgments on the "Utah Question" propounded by those who had spent anywhere from one day to a week "among the Mormons." Most of these items may be dismissed as valueless. A brief critical estimate of the sources which the writer has found helpful may be suggestive.

I. BIBLIOGRAPHICAL AIDS

Henry P. Beers, *Bibliography in American History* (New York, 1938) and Channing, Hart, and Turner, *Guide to the Study and Reading of American History* (New York, 1912) contain summary notices on Utah. More pertinent for research are a handful of special works. The first, in order of time, is Hubert Howe Bancroft, *History of Utah* (San Francisco, 1889, Vol. XXVI of his *Works*). Twenty-seven pages are devoted to a list of "Authorities Consulted," and at the end of the several chapters of the book, the sources alleged to have been used in the composition are noted. Those who know Bancroft's methods will not quarrel with the implication. A good many of the published works and manuscripts cited are preserved in the Bancroft Library, University of California. Some of the manuscript material, however, has disappeared.

In December, 1899, Helen Miller Gould presented to the New York Public Library the collection of Mormoniana assembled by the late William Berrian. *The Bulletin of the New York Public Library,* Vol. XIII (March, 1909), pp. 183–239, contains a checklist of the items, together with other books on Utah history to be found in the Library. Berrian's interest, seemingly, was not confined to purely Mormon history, and many of the titles are useful for reference in regard to the group conflict. A considerable number of books, pamphlets, and sermons, written by Utah Gentiles, are enumerated. With the possible exception of the library of Mormon and anti-Mormon literature in the office of the Church Historian, Salt Lake City, the New York Public Library is the outstanding depository of Utahana in the country.

More recently, Leland Hargrave Creer, in his book *Utah and the Nation* (Seattle, Washington, 1929. *University of Washington Publications in the Social Sciences, Vol. 7*) has published a bibliography (pp. 255–266) which is useful not only for the period of territorial history reviewed (1847–1861), but for the later period as well. Creer has also edited and annotated the posthumous work of Andrew Love Neff, *History of Utah, 1847–1869* (Salt Lake City, 1940), and has assumed responsibility for the bibliography appended to that volume (pp. 911–924). Neither of these guides lists more than a few of the strictly Gentile sources, printed or manuscript. It may be noted that the Archives of the Church of Jesus Christ of Latter Day Saints and the Bancroft Library are the only depositories of manuscript material referred to.

Under the somewhat inaccurate title, *Inventory of the Church Archives of Utah* (Salt Lake City, 1940) the Utah Historical Records Survey (Division of Professional and Service Projects, Works Projects Administration) has published what is actually a fairly comprehensive bibliography of printed sources for general Utah history.

II. General Histories

The first comprehensive treatment of the history of Utah is Edward W. Tullidge, *History of Salt Lake City* (Salt Lake City, 1886). This was followed by his *History of Utah* (2 vols., Salt Lake City, 1889; the second volume is referred to as *History of Northern Utah and Southern Idaho*). Tullidge, a Mormon publicist, was for a time attracted by the early promise of the Godbeite schism, but later returned to the parent fold and wrote from a zealously orthodox viewpoint. His reliance of earlier journalistic accounts lends interest to his work, but his frequent errors of fact and his obvious bias diminish its value. Nevertheless, Tullidge is the quarry from which most of the subsequent writers have extracted their basic material.

Bancroft's volume, cited above, is perhaps the least satisfactory of his imposing output. A glance at the extensive correspondence between Bancroft and his field agents furnishes an interesting footnote to his historical method. Bancroft wrote with an eye on the market, and the favorite talking-point of his advance salesmen to prospective buyers in Utah was that their names should appear in the forthcoming book. Apparently with the same purpose in mind, the editor—for Bancroft was no more than that—sedulously flattered the Mormon interpretation. Whatever Gentile sources he had at his disposal, he used them sparingly and almost invariably in an adverse sense. It is quite possible to agree with certain of his strictures on the federal policy in regard to Utah, but at the same time difficult to discover what the writer considered the proper procedure should have been.

Between 1892 and 1898, Orson F. Whitney, who died as an Apostle of the Mormon Church, brought out the three unwieldly volumes of his *History of Utah* (Salt Lake City).[1] With all its faults and inaccuracies—and they are legion—the work has not yet been superseded. Not a scientific historian, Whitney almost invariably failed to indicate his sources with any degree of precision. His straight chronological treatment makes for extreme diffuseness, and the work is padded with rhetorical passages of

---

[1] Volume IV (Salt Lake City, 1899), contains biographical notices of Utah notables, written for subscribers.

amazing ineptness.   The lack of a complete index is annoying.
Consistently, the Mormon record is purged of everything question-
able, if not by facts, then by verbosity.   Nevertheless, Whitney
presents a mass of detail, and where he is content to let the story
stand, his work is not without real value.   He wrote largely from
documents, though he used them uncritically, and his failure to
cite them is the more unfortunate since many of them have disappeared from view.

Professor Andrew Love Neff, of the University of Utah, died
before his *History of Utah, 1847 to 1869* was finished.   Neff was
a conscientious student, and his work displays a sincere, if pon-
derous, effort to achieve a balanced view.   It is difficult to understand why a man of his training and caution should have failed to
take into account the possibility that the government archives might
contain, as they do, rich stores of material that would modify, in
important respects, his conclusions.   It is understandable that the
preoccupation of the work is with the Mormon aspect of the story.
Why the author and editor should have wished to issue the book
with citations almost wholly omitted is hardly answered in the
prefatory note.

Less important are J. Cecil Alter, *Utah, the Storied Domain*
(Chicago, 1932, 3 Vols.) an attempt at documentary history with
editorial comment, John Henry Evans, *The Story of Utah* (New
York, 1933), a popular Mormon text, and Levi Edgar Young,
The Founding of Utah (New York, 1923), which lays emphasis
on social history, yet fails to discuss with sufficient detail the story
of the conflict.

It need scarcely be remarked that the need for a comprehensive
history of Utah, critical and unbiased, remains unfulfilled.

III. Special Works

Ecclesiastical History: The prominence of religion in Utah
is borne out in the number of published works dealing with the
Mormon Church and the other sectarian bodies.   Four hundred
and fifty-eight items are listed in the *Inventory of the Church
Archives of Utah,* referred to above.   However, the editors have
included a great deal of miscellaneous material from other fields.
Books and articles on Mormonism, naturally, are the most numer-

ous. Brigham H. Roberts, who was refused a seat in the National
House of Representatives in 1898 because of his avowed polygamy, has written *A Comprehensive History of the Church of Jesus
Christ of Latter-day Saints, Century One* (Salt Lake City, 1930,
6 vols.). For the period from 1860 to 1890, Roberts has added
little to the account given by Whitney, save certain information
regarding the internal workings of the Church. The author's
patent anxiety to exonerate his fellow-believers at every step
renders his book interesting apologetics but bad history. The
citations are careless and somewhat random. Anti-Mormonism
disfigures T. H. B. Stenhouse, *Rocky Mountain Saints* (New
York, 1873) and William Alexander Linn, *The Story of Mormonism* (New York, 1902), though Stenhouse, an apostate, reports
many facts from personal observation, and Linn's volume is still
a standard treatment of Mormon origins. Both deal sketchily
with the period under consideration, and are guilty of errors of
fact and interpretation.

Catholic history is poorly represented by William R. Harris,
The Catholic Church in Utah (Salt Lake City, 1909), and by
Louis J. Fries, *One Hundred and Fifty Years of Catholicity in
Utah* (Salt Lake City, 1926), who repeats the mistakes of
Harris almost verbatim. An accurate diocesan history is badly
needed. Daniel Sylvester Tuttle, *Reminiscences of a Missionary
Bishop* (New York, 1906), is still the only work of any importance covering Protestant Episcopal activities in Utah. Henry
Martin Merkel, *History of Methodism in Utah,* (Colorado Springs,
1938), is confused, inexact, and incomplete. John D. Thornley
has sketched *The Baptist Church in Utah* (MS, Salt Lake City,
1940) for the Utah Historical Records Survey. The same writer
has contributed an essay, "Religion in Utah," to serve as an introduction to the *Inventory of the Church Archives of Utah.*
Though based entirely on secondary accounts, this is the best short
summary available, and definitely supersedes *World's Fair Ecclesiastical History of Utah* (Salt Lake City, 1896), a compiled
work.

The military phase of territorial history is dealt with in Fred
B. Rogers, *Soldiers of the Overland* (San Francisco, 1938),
which substantially is a biographical sketch of General Patrick
Edward Connor. Secondary sources have been used; indeed, it

is doubtful whether the material in the National Archives from the War Department records are in a sufficiently well organized condition to permit their extensive use at the present time. Mining history has been investigated extensively by Edgar M. Ledyard in the volumes of *Ax-I-Dent-Ax* (Salt Lake City, 1925–1932, a monthly magazine published in the interests of the American Smelting and Refining Company. Robert S. Lewis and Thomas Varley, *The Mineral Industry of Utah* (*Bulletin of the University of Utah,* X, 11, Salt Lake City, 1919), have prepared (pp. 41–42) a useful bibliography of the available publications. George Thomas, *Civil Government in Utah* (Boston, 1912) lays stress on the earlier formative period. Katherine E. Coman, *Economic Beginnings of the Far West* (New York, 1912), II, 167–203, describes the genesis of the Mormon agricultural policy.

Education has been dealt with comprehensively by Laverne Bane, "A History of Education in Utah, 1870–1895" (MS, doctoral dissertation, Leland Stanford University, Palo Alto, California, 1939). Sister M. des Victoires, C. S. C., has written "A History of Catholic Education in Utah" (MS, Master's thesis, University of Notre Dame, 1929). The interesting story of the Congregationalist venture has been partially told by E. Lyman Hood, *The New West Education Commission,* 1881–1893 (Jacksonville, Florida, 1905), an account based on the annual reports of the commission.

The legal history of Utah is hastily and imperfectly outlined in an anonymous commemorative volume, *History of the Bench and Bar of Utah* (Salt Lake City, 1913). For decisions of the territorial supreme court, *Kinney's Index-Digest* (Salt Lake City, 1903), may be consulted. This is a calendar of cases decided from 1855 to the date of publication, drawn from the *Pacific Reports. Reports of Cases Decided in the Supreme Court of the State of Utah* (Salt Lake City, 1876, 12 vols.; 1876–1900, 24 vols.) is the ultimate source.

IV. CONTEMPORARY WORKS

The following list of contemporary works makes no claim to be exhaustive. It merely enumerates a certain number of titles which have been found useful in this study. So large did the questions of polygamy and Mormonism loom in the national consciousness of the period that hardly a single travel book describing Western America, from 1860 to 1890, fails to include a chapter on Utah. Emphasis has been placed on those items written by Gentiles who claimed Utah as their home long enough to have acquired some insight into the matters they discussed.

Barnes, Demas. *From the Atlantic to the Pacific, Overland: A Series of Letters.* New York, 1866.

Beadle, John Hanson. *Life in Utah; or, The Mysteries and Crimes of Mormonism.* Philadelphia, 1870.

———. *The Undeveloped West; or, Five Years in the Territories.* Philadelphia, 1873.

———. *Western Wilds, and the Men Who Redeem Them.* Cincinnati, 1878.

Beadle, J. H., assisted by Hollister, O. J. *Polygamy; or the Mysteries and Crimes of Mormonism.* Philadelphia, 1884.

Beers, Robert W. *The Mormon Puzzle and How to Solve It.* New York, 1887.

Bennett, Fred E. *A Detective's Experience among the Mormons; or, Polygamist Mormons, How They Live and the Land They Live In.* Chicago, 1887.

Blake, Mary E. *On the Wing; Rambling Notes of a Trip to the Pacific.* Boston, 1883.

Bonwick, James. *The Mormons and the Silver Mines.* London, 1872.

Bowles, Samuel. *Across the Continent.* Springfield, Mass., 1865.

Buel, J. W. *Mysteries and Crimes of America's Great Cities.* St. Louis, 1883.

Burton, Richard F. *The City of the Saints and Across the Rocky Mountains to California.* London, 1861.

Cannon, Frank J., and O'Higgins, Harvey J. *Under the Prophet in Utah.* Boston, 1911.

Cannon, Frank J. *Brigham Young and His Mormon Empire.* New York, 1913.

Cannon, George Q. *A Review of the Decision of the Supreme Court of the United States in the Case of George Reynolds vs. the United States.* Salt Lake City, 1879.

Carlton, Ambrose B. *The Wonderlands of the Wild West, with Sketches of the Mormons.* N. P., 1891.

Codman, John. *The Mormon Country, a Summer with the Latter-Day Saints.* New York, 1874.

Cook, Joseph. *Six Questions on the Mormon Question, with Replies by the Rev. Dr. McNiece, Judge Boreman, Judge Rosborough, Colonel Nelson, Attorney Royle, and Professor Coyner, of Salt Lake City.* Salt Lake City, 1884.

Coyner, John M. *The Utah Problem.* Salt Lake City, 1884.

———. *Letters on Mormonism.* Salt Lake City, 1879.

————. *Handbook on Mormonism.* Salt Lake City, 1882.

Dallin, William. *True Mormonism; or, The Horrors of Polygamy, from the Pen of an Ex-Mormon Elder, Who . . . Handles the Question without Gloves.* Chicago, 1885.

De Rupert, A. E. D. *California and Mormons.* New York, 1881.

Dickinson, Ellen E. *New Light on Mormonism.* New York, 1885.

Dunn, J. P., Jr. *Massacres of the Mountains, a History of the Indian Wars of the Far West.* New York, 1886.

Ellis, Charles. *Utah, 1847 to 1870.* Salt Lake City, 1891.

Forgeron, Kenelm D. *Treason in Utah; a True Account of the Insults Perpetrated by Rebellious Mormons against the Government on July 4, 1885.* Brattleboro, Vt., 1885.

Franklin, John Benjamin. *One Year at the Great Salt Lake City; or, a Voice from the Utah Pandemonium.* Manchester, England, n. d.

"Gentile." *Social Problems of Today; or, The Mormon Question in its Economic Aspects, by a Gentile.* Port Jervis, New York, 1886.

Greenwood, Grace (Mrs. Sara Jane Lippincott). *New Life in New Lands.* New York, 1873.

Hardy, Lady Duffus. *In the City of the Saints.* London, 1884.

Kane, Elizabeth D. W. *Twelve Mormon Homes, Visited in Succession on a Journey through Utah to Arizona.* Philadelphia, 1874.

Lamb, M. T. *The Book of Mormon, Is It of God?* Salt Lake City, 1886.

Lyford, C. P. *Brigham Young's Record of Blood! or, the Necessity for that Famous "Bible and Revolver."* Salt Lake City, 1876.

————. *The Mormon Problem, An Appeal to the American People.* New York, 1886.

McClure, Alexander K. *Three Thousand Miles through the Rocky Mountains.* Philadelphia, 1869.

McNiece, R. G. *The Christian Reconstruction of Utah: Two Sermons Preached in the Presbyterian Church, Salt Lake City, March 23–30, 1879.* Salt Lake City, 1879.

Marshall, Walter Gore. *Through America.* London, 1882.

Martin, Stewart. *The Mystery of Mormonism.* London, 1920.

Montgomery, M. W. *The Mormon Delusion, Its History, Doctrines and Outlook in Utah.* Boston, 1890.

Noble, Frederick A. *The Mormon Iniquity, A Discourse . . . before the New West Education Commission, November 2, 1884.* Chicago, 1884.

————. *The Need and Value of Christian Schools in the Present Exigency of the New West, a Discourse in the Old South Church, Boston, Mass., May 24, 1885.* Chicago, 1885.

Perkins, Nathan E. *Events and Travels of Nathan E. Perkins.* Camden, N. J., 1887.

Phillips, George W. *The Mormon Menace. A Discourse before the New West Education Commission, Chicago, November 5, 1885.* Worcester, 1885.

Pine, George W. *Beyond the West.* Utica, New York, 1870.

Richardson, A. D. *Beyond the Mississippi.* Hartford, 1867.

Robinson, Phillip S. *Sinners and Saints, A Tour Across the States . . . with Three Months among the Mormons.* Boston, 1883.

Stenhouse, Fanny. *Expose of Polygamy in Utah; A Lady's Life among the Mormons.* New York, 1872.

——. *Tell It All: The Story of a Life's Experience in Mormonism.* Hartford, 1874.

Stillman, James W. *The Constitutional and Legal Aspects of the Mormon Question.* Boston, 1882.

——. *The Mormon Question.* Boston, 1884.

Waite, Catherine V. *The Mormon Prophet and His Harem.* Cambridge, Mass., 1866.

——. *Adventures in the Far West, and Life among the Mormons.* Chicago, 1882.

Ward, Artemus (Charles Farrar Browne). *Artemus Ward's Lecture on the Mormons,* Edward P. Hingston, ed. London, 1882.

Wyl, W. *"Post Tenebras Lux," Mormon Portraits; or, the Truth about the Mormon Leaders from 1830 to 1886.* Salt Lake City, 1886.

Young, Ann Eliza Webb. *Wife No. 19; or, the Story of a Life in Bondage.* Hartford, 1875.

V. Newspapers and Journals

"A half century of forensic warfare, waged by the West's most militant Press," is the sub-title of J. Cecil Alter's *Early Utah Journalism* (Salt Lake City, 1938). The importance of the files of the Gentile or anti-Mormon newspapers for a reconstruction of the inner life of the minority group in Utah can hardly be over-estimated. Obviously, the material must be handled with care, and proper discount made for editorializing. Casual news items, however, are usually revealing and trustworthy. The files of a number of the Gentile newspapers have disappeared; others are incomplete. Those listed below are available for consultation at the depositories named.

The first Gentile publication in Utah was *Kirk Anderson's Valley Tan* (Camp Floyd and Salt Lake City), a weekly which ran from November 6, 1858 to February 22, 1860. Rabidly anti-Mormon, it was the organ of the soldiers of Camp Floyd, and with the closing of that post, publication was suspended. Files are preserved in the Bancroft Library, the Library of Congress, and the Salt Lake Public Library. Sponsored by Colonel P. E. Connor, the *Union Vedette* appeared on November 20, 1863, in Salt Lake

City. On January 5, 1864, it was issued as the first daily paper in the Territory, and continued until October 18, 1867. A complete file is in the Salt Lake Public Library. From that date until April 9, 1869, when the *Utah Reporter* began publication at Corinne, during that city's brief ascendency, there was no Gentile paper on the market. The *Reporter* became a daily on June 2, 1870, and continued until the beginning of 1874. The file in the Bancroft Library begins October 16, 1869, and ends July 19, 1873.

The Mormon Tribune made its appearance in Salt Lake City on January 1, 1870, as the organ of the Godbeite dissidents. By mid-summer of that year it had dropped all pretense of orthodoxy, and had become the *Salt Lake Tribune* under Gentile management. On April 15, 1871, the *Salt Lake Daily Tribune* began publication, and for years thereafter assumed the leading place in Gentile journalism. Complete files are preserved in the offices of the Tribune Publishing Company, Salt Lake City. The Library of Congress has files from 1874. The *Corinne Daily Journal,* launched in May 1871, terminated in July of that year. A file is in the Bancroft Library. Almost as brief was the career of the *Salt Lake Review,* (August, 1871-February, 1872), a weekly also filed in the Bancroft Library. The same depository has a few numbers of the *Daily Utah Mining Journal* (Salt Lake City), May to August, 1873. *The Salt Lake Mining Gazette,* 1873–1874, is in the Salt Lake Public Library.

The *Salt Lake Daily Press* ran for about a year, August, 1873 to August, 1874. A file is in the Salt Lake Public Library. The *Corinne Daily Mail,* another of the journalistic ventures of that hopeful community, ran from September 7, 1874 to October 15, 1875, according to the Bancroft Library file. The *Utah Evening Mail* (Salt Lake City) was a tabloid monthly edited by John M. Coyner from 1875 to 1876. Only a few copies are preserved in the Bancroft Library and the Salt Lake Public Library.

Volume I, Number 1, of the *Park Mining Record* (Park City, Utah) was dated February 8, 1880. The file, kept in the offices of the publishing company in Park City, begins with June 5, 1880. The *Western Mining Gazetteer* (Salt Lake City), a weekly, has a few issues in the Salt Lake Public Library to show for its existence from 1880 to 1881. Brief also were the careers of two religious journals, the *Rocky Mountain Christian Advocate* (Salt

Lake City), and the *Utah Review* (Salt Lake City), issued under Protestant auspices in 1881. The Bancroft Library has a few scattered copies. The *Salt Lake Evening Chronicle* ran from November 2, 1882 to May 16, 1885, and is on file in the offices of the Utah State Historical Society.

Much further information, contradictory or counterbalancing, is to be gleaned from the Mormon Church papers. Those consulted were the *Deseret News* (Salt Lake City, June 15, 1850 to date), and the *Salt Lake Daily Herald* (June 5, 1870-January 1, 1920), both substantially complete in the Salt Lake Public Library.

VI. Federal Documents

The Congressional Globe and the *Congressional Record* with their appendices, are invaluable for the study of the debates in Congress relating to the Mormon question. Much material also may be gleaned from the published and unpublished hearings of the Senate and House Committees on the Territories. Actually, there is need of a thorough study of the legislation in regard to Utah based on these documents.

Among the United States Public Documents the following are of special interest:

> *Letter from the Secretary of the Interior transmitting the report of the investigation of the acts of Governor Young, ex-officio superintendent of Indian Affairs in Utah Territory, January 15, 1862.* Washington, 1862, 124 pp. (U. S. 37th Congress, 2nd Session, House Executive Document 29).
> *Utah Territory: Resolution of Hon. John Bidwell, relative to affairs in Utah Territory, February 25, 1867 (With . . . report by Major General M. B. Hazen).* Washington, 1867, 5 pp. (U. S. 39th Congress, 2nd Session, House Miscellaneous Document 75).
> *Report of the Judiciary Committee on the memorial of the Legislative Assembly of the Territory of Utah, praying for a repeal of "An act to prevent and punish the practice of polygamy in the Territories of the United States," February 28, 1867.* Washington, 1867, 4 pp. (U. S. 39th Congress, 2nd Session, House Report 27).
> *A bill to provide for the execution of the law against the crime of polygamy in the Territory of Utah, and for*

other purposes, as reported by Mr. Cragin, December 21, 1869. Washington, 1869, 20 pp. (U. S. 41st Congress, 2nd Session, Senate Document 286).

Report of the Elections Committee on charges made against George Q. Cannon, delegate from Utah, January 21, 1875. Washington, 1875. (U. S. 43rd Congress, 2nd Session, House Report 106).

A bill to prevent persons living in bigamy or polygamy from holding any civil office of trust or profit in any of the Territories of the United States, and from being delegates in Congress, February 14, 1882. Washington, 1882. (U. S. 47th Congress, 1st Session, House Report 386).

Report of the Territories Committee relating to the government of Utah by a commission for the purpose of preventing the crime of polygamy, April 14, 1884. Washington, 1884. (U. S. 48th Congress, 1st Session, House Report 1351). *Minority Report, April 26, 1884,* printed as Part II.

An Act to amend an act entitled "An act to amend section 5352 of the Revised Statutes of the United States, in reference to bigamy, and for other purposes, June 10, 1886." (U. S. 49th Congress, 1st Session, Senate Document 10).

Report (favorable) of the Judiciary Committee on resolutions . . . for the amendment of the Constitution of the United States relating to polygamy, May 24, 1886. Washington, 1886. (U. S. 49th Congress, 1st Session, House Report 2568).

Report of the Education and Labor Committee on an amendment intended to be proposed to the sundry civil bill providing for an appropriation to aid in the establishment of a school in Utah to be under the direction of the Christian Home Association of Utah, and to provide employment and self-support for the dependent classes in that Territory, with a view to the suppression of polygamy therein, June 5, 1886. Washington, 1886. (U. S. 49th Congress, 1st Session, Senate Report 1279). This includes the committee hearings, and the constitution of the society.

United States Judiciary Committee: Suppression of polygamy in Utah, with an account of the "State of Deseret," June 10, 1886. Washington, 1886. (U. S. 49th Congress, 1st Session, House Report 2735).

Admission of Utah: Arguments . . . made before the Committee on Territories of the United States Senate, February 15, 1885. Washington, 1888, 44 pp.

(U. S. 50th Congress, 1st Session, Senate Document 93.)

Amendment to section 5352 Revised Statutes, proposed April 29, 1890 Cullom-Struble bill. Washington, 1890. (U. S. 51st Congress, 1st Session, House Report 1811.)

Annual Reports of the Utah Commission to the Secretary of the Interior, Washington, 1882–1896.

Annual Reports of the Utah Commission as Board of management of the Industrial Christian Home Association, Washington, 1888–1892, as follows:
1888—U. S. 50th Congress, 1st Session, Senate Executive Document 57.
1889—U. S. 51st Congress, 1st Session, Senate Miscellaneous Document 34.
1891—U. S. 52nd Congress, 1st Session, House Miscellaneous Document 104.
1892—U. S. 52nd Congress, 2nd Session, House Miscellaneous Document 6.

Reports of the Governors of Utah Territory to the Secretary of the Interior, Washington, 1878–1896.

VII. Manuscript Sources

In contrast to the Mormons, who seem to have sensed the importance of keeping diaries and journals, numbers of which have been collected and preserved by the Utah Historical Records Survey, the Utah Gentiles have left few personal memoirs that are available in manuscript form.

The Bancroft Collection, University of California, is in possession of a few unpublished sources written by members of the group or reflecting upon the mutual antagonism which existed between themselves and the Mormons. Those of importance have been cited in the text. The Huntington Library, San Marino, California, has the Boreman papers, including scattered correspondence of Justice Jacob S. Boreman, his *Recollections of Life in Utah, on and off the bench* (189–), and his shorthand record of the Lee trial which as yet has not been deciphered. The Manuscripts Division of the Library of Congress has a collection of forty letters and lecture drafts of Schuyler Colfax, some of which throw light on his anti-Mormon activities, as well as the papers of Jeremiah S. Black, which contain several of his briefs as attorney for the Church of Jesus Christ of Latter-day Saints.

The National Archives, Washington, D. C., is undoubtedly the richest repository of unpublished material bearing on Utah history. The documents are to be found in the various divisions. The State Department Archives have their Utah material bound in two volumes, the first covering the period up to the Utah War (1857), the second carrying the record up to 1872, when the Department of the Interior assumed the direction of territorial matters. It is worth remarking that the complete story of the Utah War must be written in the light of these documents. The Department of the Interior Archives are contained in two filing cases, and contain little of importance, save the complete series of the reports of the territorial governors and of the Utah Commission. The War Department Archives, at the present time, are not in a sufficiently coordinated state to permit of satisfactory research, though valuable material was discovered in the files containing the records of the military posts established in the Territory. The most extensive materials are in the Justice Department Archives. The documents here are grouped as follows: Attorney General's MSS, 1847–1870; Department of Justice MSS, 1870–1884; Department of Justice File, 1884 to the present; Solicitor of the Treasury, Letters Received, Utah; Department of Justice, Appointment Clerk file, Utah; Department of Justice, Pardon Attorney, Amnesty Cases, Utah. The correspondence of the officials of the various departments themselves may be found in the respective letter-books, although the task of research is made difficult by the fact that many of the earlier volumes are not indexed, and that when indices exist, the systems vary.

It is customary to list as manuscript sources the collections on file at the Office of the Church Historian, Salt Lake City, *The History of Brigham Young,* and *Journal History of the Church of Jesus Christ of Latter-day Saints.* However, the lack of an adequate index or catalogue practically nullifies their usefulness for anything more than spot reference.

INDEX

Akerman, Attorney General, 77.
Alemany, Joseph S., 156.
All Hallows' College, 157, 158.
Alta, 20, 59, 60.
Anderson, John, 1, 30.
Anderson, Mother Augusta, 157.
Anderson, T. J., 245.
Anti-Polygamy Act, 1862, 43, 143.
Anti-Polygamy Society, 191, 192, 194.
Anti-Polygamy Standard, 183, 191, 193.
Arthur, Chester A., 215.
Auerbach, F. H., 54.
Augur, C. C., 72.
Axtell, S. B., 94, 95, 130.

Banks, John, 107, 108.
Baptist Church, 165.
Barbee, W. T., 60.
Barrows, Walter, 183.
Baskin, Robert N., 46, 112, 119, 123, 127, 129, 135, 239, 242.
Bates, Edward, 14.
Bates, George C., 80, 82, 84.
Beadle, J. H., 81.
Beaver City, 98.
Beaver County, 128.
Bee-Hive House, 15.
Benner, O. H., 172.
Bidwell, John, 50.
Bingham Canyon, 19, 60.
Black, George, 134.
Black, Jeremiah S., 5, 218.
Blair, Henry W., 209.
Board of Missions, 153.
Bonanza City, 61.
Boreman, Jacob, 92, 99, 101, 102, 104, 173, 234.
Bourion, Father, 37.
Boutwell, J. M., 18, 19.
Bowles, Samuel, 29.
Brassfield, Newton, 47.

Brewster, B. H., 221, 234.
Brigham City, 62, 167.
Bristow, Benjamin, 82.
Bross, William, 29.
Browning, O. H., 10.
Buchanan, James, 1, 4.
Burton, Richard, 6.
Burton, Robert T., 107, 109, 110, 111.

Caine, John T., 146, 148, 220, 223, 235, 244.
California Volunteers, 1, 2, 12, 15, 48.
Camp Cameron, 99.
Camp Conness, 108.
Camp Douglas, 4.
Camp Floyd, 2.
Camp Rawlins, 72.
Campbell, Allen G., 139, 141.
Cannon, Frank, 228.
Cannon, George Q., 107, 127, 135, 140, 142, 235, 237.
Carey, William, 87.
Carlton, A. B., 217, 220.
Carrington, Albert, 11.
Carroll, S. J., 210.
Catholic Church, 34, 35, 36, 37, 38, 189.
Christiancy, Isaac P., 111, 119, 131, 132.
Church Association, 39.
Cleveland, Grover, 146, 179, 224.
Clinton, Jeter, 75, 109.
Clinton v. Englebrecht, 76, 85, 86.
Colfax, Schuyler, 29, 115.
Collin, Henry, 146.
Committee on Elections, 129.
Congregationalist Church, 32, 163, 164.
Connor, Patrick Edward, 1, 15, 17, 19, 21, 28, 34, 37, 48, 50, 70, 138.
Constitutional Convention, 1887, 226, 227.

265